Real Estate Marketing
& Sales Essentials:
Steps for Success

Dan Hamilton

THOMSON
SOUTH-WESTERN

Australia · Canada · Mexico · Singapore · Spain · United Kingdom · United States

Real Estate Marketing & Sales Essentials: Steps for Success, First Edition

Dan Hamilton

VP/Editorial Director: *Jack W. Calhoun*
VP/Editor-in-Chief: *Dave Shaut*
Publisher: *Scott Person*
Associate Acquisitions Editor: *Sara Glassmeyer*
Marketing Manager: *Mark Linton*
Production Editor: *Chris Sears*
Web Coordinator: *Karen Schaffer*

Manufacturing Coordinator: *Charlene Taylor*
Production House: *Interactive Composition Corporation*
Printer: *WestGroup, Eagan, MN*
Art Director: *Chris A. Miller*
Cover and Internal Designer: *Trish Knapke*
Cover Images: © Getty Images, Inc.

Library of Congress Control Number: 2005923684

For more information about our products, contact us at:

Thomson Learning Academic Resource Center

1-800-423-0563

Thomson Higher Education
5191 Natorp Boulevard
Mason, OH 45040
USA

Dedication

This book is dedicated to
Judge B. Fite and his lovely wife, Dene Fite,
for their life-long dedication to real estate
and the business of serving others.

Contents

Contents

Real Estate Marketing

Overview of Book

Real estate marketing is the avenue to making money in the real estate business. Marketing permeates all businesses including the real estate industry. It allows customers to know the real estate salesperson and how to reach them. It allows real estate salespersons to go out and bring customers to them. Marketing can cost a fortune or can cost very little and each can be effective. It can be extremely time consuming or it can take very little direct time. The best marketing is derived from the mind and the more the mind thinks about marketing, the reality of successful marketing becomes clear. This book is designed to open the reader's mind to the vast array of marketing for the real estate profession.

Objectives of Book

The first objective of this marketing book is to give the reader numerous avenues to make a great deal of money selling real estate. Readers should evaluate their inner strengths and weaknesses, determine what will work for them, and then do it. Most authors and trainers know less than one of one hundred people will do what is needed to become wealthy. This book is a guide to doing just that.

The book's second objective is to help the reader meet the requirements of the Real Estate Commission for Salesman's Annual Education (SAE) credit. It is designed for use in conjunction with 60 classroom hours of core related instruction by a certified trainer using this book.

This book concentrates on residential real estate, as most real estate licensed salespeople are residential. If you specialize in commercial, farm

and ranch, or other special types of real estate you can still benefit from
this book if you convert the thinking just a bit.

Dan Hamilton is an advocate for real estate education and is certified by the
Texas Real Estate Commission to train in 12 topics including real estate marketing, principles, finance, practices, and agency. Hamilton is the lead trainer
for Licensure and Renewal at the Real Estate Training Institute. He has been
an owner and a broker owner of successful real estate offices in Texas. In
5 consecutive years, he was awarded the honor of the National Who's Who
for business and has received other honors such as Top Office Producer,
Multi-Million Dollar Club, and Top Ten on the Board of REALTORS.
Currently, Hamilton is the Director of Training for Century 21, Judge Fite
and the Operations Manager for Real Estate Career Training School.

Where to write for Questions for the author

Dan Hamilton
1140 Empire Central, STE 520
Dallas, TX. 75247

888-782-2300
E-mail: MAINBROKER@AOL.COM

Chapter 1

Real Estate Professionalism and Ethics

Chapter Objectives

This chapter covers the aspects of ethics, including the National Association of REALTORS® code of ethics and a personal code of ethics. There will be questions and you must provide the answers. You will be more informed on the concepts of ethics and how they apply to your personal life as well as your business life.

In this chapter you should be able to recognize professionalism and act in accordance with being professional. You will also understand the power that a positive mental attitude has in relation with professionalism. Finally, you will be aware of the designations the real estate profession offers interested salespersons.

Key Terms

Affirmation: The act of affirming or the state of being affirmed, assertion. Something declared to be true, a positive statement or judgment. Self-talk. These are beliefs about you.

Attitude: A position of the body or manner of carrying oneself. This is how you act.

Award: To grant as merited or due. Awards are given for real estate production.

Contingency: An event that may occur but that is not likely or intended; a possibility.

Designations: Nomination or appointment. A distinguishing name or title.

Ethickos: Moral.

Ethics: A set of principles of right conduct.

Ethos: Character.

Features: The overall appearance of the face or its parts. Refers to an aspect of a quality real estate salesperson.

Memory: The mental faculty of retaining and recalling past experience. The act or an instance of remembering; recollection.

Performance: The way in which someone or something functions. Refers to an aspect of a quality real estate salesperson.

Quality: Degree or grade of excellence. Having a high degree of excellence.

REALTORS®: A service mark used for a real estate agent affiliated with the National Association of REALTORS®.

Reliability: Capable of being relied on, dependable. Refers to an aspect of a quality real estate salesperson.

Safety: The condition of being safe, freedom from danger, risk, or injury. Always keep yourself safe in real estate.

Serviceability: Ability to give long service, durable. Refers to an aspect of a quality real estate salesperson.

Subconscious: The part of the mind below the level of conscious perception.

Timeliness: Occurring at a suitable or opportune time; well timed. Refers to an aspect of a quality real estate salesperson.

Real Estate Professionalism

Introduction

The words "Real Estate Profession" are interesting. Real estate salespeople enjoy saying them, but few act on them. Being professional is important for self-worth and for top income. A real estate salesperson should strive to maintain professionalism at all costs. When some people enter the real estate business they are afraid to tell their friends because they feel that they do not have a "real job." This "job" is "real" because the person in the real estate field feels and acts professional, not because of what others think. The question a professional real estate salesperson should ask is: "Why should someone choose to do real estate business with me?"

Mike Ferry, a national real estate sales trainer, believes there are three main problems with the real estate industry. Number one is that it is too easy to get into. To become a licensed real estate salesperson you need only pay a couple of hundred dollars, take a class or two, and pass a state test, and congratulations you can sell real estate. What does it take to become a medical doctor? A LOT more! The second problem with real estate is that it is too easy to get out of. I have had my license for more than fifteen years. What would it take to quit? Nothing, I'd just quit. Try quitting the military after signing up for a six-year stint. The last problem with real estate is that you do not have to do anything while you are in the business. No one will tell you what to do. No one will be sure you are making money. You can sit home all day watching your favorite soap operas and no one will call. You won't make any money, either. Real estate offers no upper limit on what you can make and offers no lower limit on how little you can make. It is strictly up to you.

My dad was sold a bad bill of goods. He was told that to be a good father and husband he should work with one company until he retired and that company would take care of him and his family. That is a lie. My dad was fired twice in his life, both times because the company he was working for was sold. The new companies brought in new management staffs and each time my dad was let go. The last time he was in his fifties and could not find another job. I asked him to work with me as my real estate company maintenance man because it broke my heart to know he couldn't find work to make ends meet. For a man with my dad's education and will to work, he should have done much better.

When asked why I got in the real estate business my response surprises most people. Most people who join the real estate business do so for money and/or flexibility. I began my real estate career for job security. You see, I watched my dad. He was lied to. I wanted a career that could not be taken from me. I wanted to have a career that was limited only by me. If my current broker let me go today, how long would it take me to find a place of employment? I would be back on line within an hour. Once you know how to sell, that cannot be taken from you. You now have the confidence and peace that comes from job security.

Some people new to the real estate industry ask me how many hours per week I usually work. My response is: "How do you define work?" I define it as, "doing something when you would rather be doing something else." With that definition, I do very little work. When I am in front of sellers or students, or at a closing with buyers of their first home, there is no other place I would rather be while making money. Have you ever heard of someone winning millions in the lottery and their first remark is, "I can't wait to get back to work because I love it so much!" I would. That is where you need to strive to be. I had a garden once and I would go out and enjoy the earth. If that garden ever became "work" it was gone. That is what I am talking about—when labor is not work.

One last point, have fun in the real estate business! I had forgotten how depressed real estate salespeople seem to be until I did an office meeting for a manager friend of mine. In the meeting the real estate salespeople were complaining about this or that and no one said one positive thing. Too many real estate salespeople begin their careers so serious that they can't possibly have any fun. Don't be so serious that you lose your edge. Learn to laugh at yourself and your situation. I have taught MCE classes to experienced salespeople who want to renew their licenses. In these classes I have seen some of the worst faces. They are the faces of people who no longer have fun in real estate. Their positive attitudes are gone.

Attitude

Attitude is what we carry with us. It is always there, whether it is good or bad. It should consist of genuine concern. You should convey an attitude of trust and always give others your undivided attention. The good news is that we control our attitudes and we have the power to change our attitudes. Have you ever been in a good mood when someone comes by and mouths off a couple of negatives? Bam, where did our good mood go? On the other hand, have you ever been down when a friend comes by and with just a smile brightens your day? Notice the words I used, a "friend" and "someone." Who do you want to be, the "friend" or the "someone"? Watch people, notice which one everyone likes to be around. Who is always being asked to lunch? Who never speaks up at a meeting and yet is always asked his or her opinion? What is his or her mood? I'll bet it is not the sourpuss. Look for the opposite; who is outside of the group? Who is avoided? Who is talked about negatively? Is this person the real downer? I'll bet so.

The following is true about attitude:

REMEMBER:

God made the day; we have the choice to make it good or bad.

Attitude is just an outside sign of what is going on inside. If you change your belief on the inside your attitude will also change.

And what you think = what you bank.

A positive mental attitude is as important an aspect of real estate as the best education, but no one is immune from an occasional attack of downers. Unfortunately, being in a bad mood is a luxury not available to salespeople trying to make a connection with a client.

> **"Your attitude, not your aptitude, will determine your altitude."**   —*Zig Ziglar*

Here is a list of possible remedies for the "downers":

- Don't look "down" when you feel down. Do hold your head up and act and talk as though you feel great . . . always. As Mary Kay Ash, founder of Mary Kay, Inc., famously said: "Fake it until you can make it!" Stay out of the office when you can't be positive. No need to infect other productive real estate salespeople with your negative attitude; come back when things look brighter.

- Don't think and talk about unpleasant things, as they appear to be at the moment. Do something to make those things better. Change you and the unpleasant things will change.

- Don't dwell on the negative. Do you know a person that is constantly negative? Negativity is like a downward spiral. My mom tends to think negatively. One negative thing leads to another. It is sad to realize I cannot help her because once you begin to think negatively you continue to think negatively, until you see everything with a negative twist. Only you can change this. The opposite is also true. Positive thinking is an upward spiral.

- Don't be one of those people who experience a minor bad event and embellish it all day long, consuming an entire working day. Do think about, talk about, and envision things the way you'd like them to be. Accept the truth of each situation, but separate the truth from the unrealistic negatives. Ask yourself how it would affect the bottom line of your company if everyone had the same attitude as you. Do you like the answer? Carefully distinguish between what's actually happening and what you think is happening and what you think about it.

- Don't make a self-fulfilling prophesy out of your negative thoughts. A self-fulfilling prophecy is when you don't want something to happen so bad that all you think about is the negative until it actually happens. It is like the coach who told the baseball pitcher not to throw the fastball inside to the next hitter. All the pitcher could think about was not throwing the fastball inside, and sure enough he threw it inside and the batter crushed it for a home run.

- Don't sit around the office doing nothing. Do get moving. Do something–anything. You could drive by neighborhoods and look for signs saying "for sale by owner" or investment properties. Better yet, fast walk those same neighborhoods. Physical activity is a natural mood lifter, as well as a helpful diversion.

- Don't be too harsh a judge or expect perfection of yourself. Do be as patient with your shortcomings as you are with those of your best friends. Recognize and reinforce in yourself and others the behavior you approve of before criticizing faults.

My motto is:

Learn from your mistakes and leave them behind.

Learn from your successes and keep them with you.

- Don't be a target for the negative people in your life. Do avoid such people when you can and when you can't avoid them, refuse to be affected by their depressive conversation and attitude.

Circumstances may be (and often are) matters of chance, but the moods that accompany them are, for the most part, matters of choice.

> **"Never despair, but if you do, work on in despair."**
> —*Edmund Burke*

Activity literally breeds activity and that breed's productivity! A top executive was asked what advice he would give a person looking to be a success. The executive answered: "fail faster." Failure is not the problem; the problem being so afraid to fail that you do nothing. And nothing gets no thing.

Professionalism, a Checklist

A checklist on how to act professional is in the appendix on page 390. Some of the items are simple and need no explanation. The checklist is to keep you focused.

One last thought on attitude: don't think of yourself as inferior to others, regardless of who or what they are. Do see yourself as a very special, unique, and worthwhile human being. According to Eleanor Roosevelt: "No one can make you feel inferior without your consent." These beliefs about yourself are your own affirmations.

Affirmations

Don't accept unhappiness as a normal, unavoidable state of affairs. Do remind yourself that when you are unhappy it is because your thoughts and self-talk are inappropriate. (Happiness is the normal state of being, and any deviation is abnormal!) You control the things around you. I once heard that you are where you are because that is where you want to be. Your thoughts, positive or negative, put you where you are today. If you actually do not like your place in life, all you have to do is mentally change it.

Affirmation is a sophisticated way to say "self talk." Everyone talks to himself or herself, whether or not they choose to admit it. Napoleon Hill states, "Whatever a person can conceive and believe, he can achieve." This clearly notes Hill's belief in self-talk.

The brain is made up of a complex bunch of neurons that direct the way we feel, act, and react. The brain can be broken into two parts, the conscious and the subconscious. The conscious brain is the thinking brain. You are reading this material and understanding it with the thinking brain. The subconscious is active under the control of the conscious brain. The subconscious brain is always listening and observing. Right now, is there a clock, fan, or some other noise going on while you are reading this? Could you hear it before I mentioned it? If not, it is because the subconscious brain is filtering those noises out. The subconscious motivates us. So we need to ask how can we motivate the subconscious, which in turn will motivate ourselves. The interesting thing about the subconscious is that it cannot tell the difference between imagination and reality.

One summer I worked with my dad at a manufacturing plant that made the paint for the stripes on roadways. It was a powder paint that when heated would melt for spraying on the roadway. The yellow paint had lead in it. I wore a hardhat, a coverall for my clothes, work boots, gloves, and a facemask. The average temperature in the warehouse was over a hundred degrees in the summer. I had to be at work at 6 a.m. and worked till 4 p.m. My job was taking 50-pound bags of this powder and placing them on pallets. That was it, and I hated every minute of it—with a passion. I was in college at the time and this was the best summer job I could get. I endured this torture day in and day out. I did not even have the energy to eat and lost a lot of weight. One day I noticed a rash on my left arm. After a couple of days it spread down my side to my left leg. I finally went to the doctor. He did a series of tests and then asked me: "What is going on in your life?" I wasn't sure where he was going with the question so I just began talking. When I finally mentioned how much I hated my job he asked me why I didn't quit. When I told him that I didn't want to embarrass my dad (he was in management, not on the line), he wrote a prescription that read, "Quit your job." He explained that I was not allergic to anything, that the rash was all in my head. I created it by my thoughts.

I challenge you now to look at your arm and try and get a rash. It can't be done. But I did it. My sincere affirmations gave me what I had asked for.

Affirmations do not need to know how, but what, and what I wanted was out of that job.

Affirmations program the subconscious by relating information to it that has not yet become reality. "I feel good, I feel fine" repeated often will make you feel good even if you did not feel that way in the beginning. Affirmations must be:

1. stated in the present tense.
2. stated with intense emotion.
3. stated repeatedly through the day.
4. stated in positive format.
5. believable.

You have many beliefs about yourself, not just one. These beliefs are what control the real use of your potential, at the level of your self-esteem and self-image. When you learn to change these beliefs, you can expand the use of your skills. You have an unlimited potential within you. The way you think determines the way you act. If you grew up thinking of yourself as shy, then you are shy. If you see yourself as naturally overweight, you might lose a few pounds. But soon you will creatively gain back those pounds you lost because you see you as an overweight person.

At one time in my life I believed that I could not remember people's names. My subconscious mind granted me my belief. I could be introduced to a person and ten seconds later could not remember his or her name. What is interesting is that my subconscious mind had done what I had commanded, even though it was not actually what I wanted.

Do not underestimate your sarcastic humor; your subconscious mind does not get it. Have you ever seen a person that continues to say something about himself in a sarcastic way and becomes more and more like that? The reason is because the subconscious mind gives you what you ask for whether or not you really want it. My subconscious mind would interrupt my thinking with other thoughts like: "What should I say next?" or "I wonder if there is spinach in my teeth?" All of these thoughts limited my ability to remember the name. One day I determined that I would remember people's names. I began working on my self-talk. I concentrated on telling myself that I was great at names. As a result, I began listening different.

Someone would say a name and in my mind I would repeat it several times. Every time I saw that person, I would repeat the process. In a short period of time I was great at remembering names. Now I can enter a classroom and within an hour I have every person's name saved in my memory.

Many professional athletes use affirmation and visualization along with practice to help them play at peak form. They visualize the perfect athletic feat over and over again.

The same can be true for you and business. If you rehearse the future over and over in your mind and see yourself performing perfectly, you will dramatically increase your chances of making that future reality.

Affirmations work on you, but you should not neglect your service to others. The best way to think of others is to ensure your service is of the highest quality. Always strive to improve your quality service.

Quality Service—Client Advocacy

Improving quality is on everyone's mind these days, but you don't need a major crash course to upgrade the quality of your efforts. A slow but steady approach is more likely to be effective in the long run. There are many programs out there, including Total Quality Management, Quality Control, Quality Service, Continuous Quality Improvement, but the main point is to ensure that your clients are not only satisfied with your service, they are thrilled with it.

Stanley Marcus's father, the founder of Neiman Marcus, gave Stanley some valuable advice early in his career. It was advice that later helped build Neiman Marcus into a first-class store. A woman ruined a dress she had worn just once and wanted her money back. While Stanley argued that the woman had obviously abused the dress herself and that the manufacturer wasn't going to help pay for it, Stanley's father told his son to give the woman her money back. He said that the woman wasn't doing business with the manufacturer; she was doing business with Neiman's. His father told Stanley that it had cost more than $200 to get the customer, and that he didn't want to lose her over a $175 dress. He also told Stanley to refund the money with a smile. During the years, the woman spent more than $500,000 at Neiman Marcus.

Having thrilled clients means they will not only come back but they will tell their friends to use you. Here are a few ideas:

- **Begin by beginning.** Don't procrastinate; look for whatever you can do to increase your quality and efficiency. The hardest part of reworking yourself is to start. Many reasons come up that hinder you from doing your business better. If you don't start now, the question is when?

- **Keep an open mind.** I once read that the minds of many people were like concrete, "thoroughly mixed and permanently set." Don't be that person. Working on one project may trigger ideas that will help improve quality in other areas of your work. Put your new ideas into action and test them.

- **Start simple.** Don't put too much pressure on yourself by over-preparing or tackling a huge problem. Try to get a realistic feel for what you can do. Real estate is a personal business, so concentrate on how to make you better.

- **Practice continual improvement.** No matter how efficient you become, always look for ways to get better. Minor improvements might have beneficial effects on other areas of your work. Remember that the process never ends. To be successful, you've got to dedicate yourself to pursuing quality endlessly. It's not easy, but in these tough competitive times, it's necessary. This book has been revised many times and will continually be improved.

The following are some aspects and examples of quality:

> **PERFORMANCE**—*Primary Operating Characteristic*
>
> ("I know that my real estate salesperson performs and behaves just as he or she should.")
>
> **FEATURES**—*Services Offered*
>
> ("The features, characteristics, and attributes of my real estate salesperson are all that anyone could ask for.")
>
> **RELIABILITY**—*Trust in the Service*
>
> ("I can rely on my real estate salesperson to get the job done.")

CONFORMANCE—*Meets Standards for the Industry*

("My real estate salesperson satisfies the requirements that have been set.")

DURABILITY—*Service Life*

("I know that my relationship with my real estate salesperson is long lasting.")

SERVICEABILITY—*Ease of Handling Problems*

("If something goes wrong, I know that my real estate salesperson will correct the problem.")

AESTHETICS—*Experience of the Sense*

("I feel my real estate salesperson has done a fine job.")

PERCEIVED QUALITY—*Reputation*

("I perceive my real estate salesperson is of high quality and integrity.")

TIMELINESS—*Prompt Response*

("I receive the service in a timely manner.")

ACCURACY—*Exactness or Preciseness*

("This transaction is free from errors.")

Professional real estate salespersons must be of high quality and should know how their businesses are conducted and how they earn their living. Some real estate salespeople get confused on the difference between professional service and doing things for free.

> "The trouble with a great many of us in the business world is that we are thinking hardest of all about the dollar we want to make. Now that is the wrong idea from the start. I'll tell you the man who has the idea of service in his business will never need to worry about profits. The money is bound to come. This idea of service in business is the biggest guarantee of success that any man can have."—*Henry Ford*

The best way we can determine that our service is of the highest standard is to look at other professionals, like people in the legal profession.

Attorney's Contingency

I have been accused in my real estate training classes that I do not like buyers. This is true, I believe buyers tend to be a waste of time *IF* they are not handled properly (more on this later). So I began to analyze my treatment of buyers to determine whether it was just in my decision-making. My brother is an attorney and sometimes it is easier to learn from other industries on how to do real estate business. Let's ask questions to an attorney: Will you take a case on a contingency-fee basis as we do buyers in the real estate business? The answer is yes, *IF:*

1. **The case is a sure win.**
    Easy enough, the facts are clear and we will win.

2. **The case has a sure paying defendant.**
    For lawsuits this means the defendant is capable of paying and would pay if challenged. Attorneys' like insurance companies because they are sure paying defendants.

3. **The case has significant sums of money.**
    No attorney takes an insignificant case for little or no money.

I became curious on how I could use this in dealing with clients of mine in the real estate business. Here's the answer:

1. **The seller or buyer transaction is a sure win.**
    The seller is motivated to sell and the buyer is motivated to buy.

2. **The seller or buyers are sure paying clients.**
    In real estate, we have a sure paying client when the client is financially qualified to buy or sell a property. Buyers must have the resources necessary to pay cash or get suitable financing. The salesperson must obtain this information before showing the buyer one house. Never show an unqualified buyer a house. It wastes your time and the buyer's time. Qualifying a buyer will be discussed later. Sellers must have the right to sell and the ability to pay. A seller who must price a property out of the market to have enough money to pay us is not a qualified seller.

3. **The seller or buyer transaction involves significant sums.**
    I think this is the one that bothers most salespeople. For some reason the real estate "sales" profession has skewed quality service into free service. This is not true. National sales trainer Tom Hopkins

frequently says: "If you take time from my family you will pay dearly for it." I like that! Stated simply, get paid for your services. I believe that your spouse should make the decision to give your money away. My wife is not that close to my clients and she likes for me to get paid. She would not like it if I were gone from the evening meal working for clients and came home with no money. She would be just in her thinking. I have seen countless salespeople work hard for a sale that nets them a couple of hundred dollars or worse—nothing. I heard one salesperson say, "If I help them now maybe they will remember me."

Everyone is a potential client of yours; why spend time with those who will not or cannot pay you? Check the section of this book on alternate fee arrangements for other ways to get paid and still help people. Back to my brother for another question:

If you have a really nice person that does not meet all three contingency criteria, would you still work for them? Yes, *IF:*

The client is willing to pay for my services by the hour.

So in real estate, if the client was willing to pay by the hour or maybe a flat fee I should work with them? The answer is, YES! Now the only question is how much am I worth?

No matter what you do or how you do it is of little concern to customers if they refuse to work with you. Our job is not to just sell property, but to get the customer to buy that property *through* us. The first thing we must do to get them to buy through us is to build rapport and learn their wants and needs.

A Little TLC

One of the most important aspects of relating and selling to people is TLC. In real estate sales, the letters mean:

T—Trust

L—Like

C—Close

A potential client must *Trust* you and *Like* you, before you can ever *Close*. I find that, far too often, clients are resistant to do business with you because you have rushed into the sale without knowing them. People want to do business with people they like and trust. I was talking with a single, elderly lady about the sale of her home. I was energetic and enthusiastic. I talked fast. I moved quickly. I failed to recognize her needs. I asked her to market her home through me. She told me she wanted to talk it over with her son before she made a decision and she would let me know the next day. Then I understood. I closed my marketing materials and set back in my chair. I said "Tell me about your son." And she did—for nearly one and a half hours. Afterward she said, "O.K., I will go ahead and market my home with you." What changed? I did. I stopped doing what I wanted and did what she wanted. I showed her I cared. She now liked and trusted me. As life improvement expert Zig Ziglar always says, "People don't care what you know until they know you care."

The following is a diagram of what a real estate salesperson should remember and follow. The problem is that very few actually do.

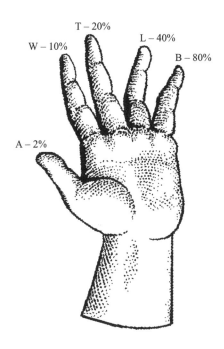

The "B" stands for "Be familiar with you." The client must know you and know of you. If all you do is sit home and watch daytime soap operas, you will not be known. If you consistently provide quality service, you will be known the way you want to be known. Eighty percent of real estate sales-people know what the "B" is and spend a great deal of time and effort in being known.

The "L" stands for "Like you." After the client knows you, he or she must like you. You can only build long-term relationships with clients who like you. People want to do business with people they like. A real estate professional must be cognizant of the fact that he or she must be liked. Only 40 percent of real estate salespeople understand and do this.

The "T" stands for "Trust you." The client must not only know you and like you, he or she must trust you. You must earn a client's trust and then work to maintain that trust. Only 20 percent of real estate salespeople go this far to complete client advocacy.

The "W" stands for "Wants and Needs Analysis." It is the basis of knowing a client. The better you know your client the better you can serve him or her and the greater the client advocacy you build. (This will be explained later in more detail.) Only 10 percent of real estate salespeople ever get to a wants and needs analysis.

The "A" stands for "Advocacy." When you develop client advocacy, you have built a lasting relationship. The client who is your advocate will promote you, recommend you, and return later for additional sales. Ben Yeatts, manager and real estate trainer with a prominent real estate company, says, "An Advocate will swear by you not about you." Very few (two percent) of real estate salespeople build client advocacy.

A salesperson of mine came into my office to complain that a customer would not sign a required agency disclosure form. He said he had met this single woman at a vacant house to show her the house and she refused to sign the document. The next day he showed her another vacant house and she still refused to sign the document. What was he to do?

Let's take a look at this from the buyer's side. A man who she did not know met her at a vacant house and asked her to sign a document. She has no

TLC for the salesperson. I told him to get her into the office and do a wants and needs analysis, and then discuss the disclosure form with her. The next day he came into my office with a smile on his face and declared that she signed the document and would buy a property through him within the week. What had changed? He did. He built "like and trust" before he closed for her signature.

One of the best ways to build "like and trust" is to use the customer's name over and over. This can be hard to do if you don't remember his or her name. Calling a customer "dude" over and over will not build rapport.

Institutes, Societies, and Designations

Being a professional entails more than the way one dresses and speaks—it also includes an active role. Being active does not just serve as a means to get clients; being active in your professional community enables you to interact with other real estate salespeople. It opens a door of opportunity for sharing or for possibly taking a leadership role. The real estate industry includes many societies and associations. They offer courses or training that come with a designation to make you stand out among your peers. The following list shows several professional organizations and some of the designations they offer.

Institutes and Societies	Designations
Commercial and Investment Real Estate Institute (CIREI)	Certified Commercial Investment Member (CCIM) Eight-hour exam
Counselors of Real Estate (CRE)	Counselor of Real Estate (CRE)
Institute of Real Estate Management (IREM)	Certified Property Manager (CPM) Accredited Management Organization (AMO) Accredited Residential Manager (ARM)
National Association of REALTORS® (NAR)	Graduate, REALTORS® Institute (GRI) Residential Accredited Appraiser (RAA) General Accredited Appraiser (GAA)
Real Estate Buyer's Agent Council (REBAC)	Accredited Buyer Representative (ABR) Accredited Buyer Representative Manager (ABRM)

REALTORS® Land Institute (RLI)	Accredited Land Consultant (ALC)
REALTORS® National Marketing Institute (RNMI)	Certified Real Estate Brokerage Manager (CRB)
	Certified Residential Specialist (CRS)
Society of Industrial and Office REALTORS® (SIOR)	Specialization in industrial and office real estate
Women's Council of REALTORS® (WCR)	Leadership Training Graduate (LTG)
	Referral and Relocation Certification (RRC)

Fair Housing

A professional real estate salesperson is also a person who handles his or her business in the correct manner. No professional real estate salesperson would even consider violating anyone's rights to buy, sell, rent, or lease real property based on personal bias.

The most important law protecting fair housing was adopted in 1866. The Civil Rights Act of 1866 only prohibited discrimination base on race. In 1968, another fair housing law was adopted as part of the Civil Rights Act, which prohibited unfair treatment in housing based on color, national origin, race, and religion. An amendment in 1974 included a person's sex as a protected class, and in 1988, familial status and handicap persons were added. Familial status refers to the relationship of people in a family, and handicap persons are those with physical conditions that impair them, including those with AIDS. Under this law, a handicapped person may make minor modifications to allow safe access and use of a property. Investigation of practices that violate fair housing laws are filed with HUD-FHA. To test your fair housing knowledge, take the Fair Housing Self-Assessment located in the Appendix on page 395.

Ethics

Everyone hears the term "ethics" and cheers and believes if everyone had more ethics the world would be a better place. Ethics is very different. Ethics is not for everyone else. Ethics is for the individual. Ethics is the way you behave in relation to others. Ethics is doing the right thing even if it is the difficult thing.

Definition

Ethics comes from the Greek words "ethickos" and "ethos," meaning Moral Character. Ethics in real estate is the way we treat others. It is the way we conduct ourselves in private and in social groups. Ethics has been a source of interest since early Greek times and will continue to be of interest for eternity. —*Stanford Encyclopedia of Philosophy*

NAR Code of Ethics

The National Association of REALTORS® (NAR) was founded as the National Association of Real Estate Exchanges (NAREE) on May 12, 1908. Its mission was "to unite the real estate men of America for the purpose of effectively exerting a combined influence upon matters affecting real estate interests." These were lofty words, given the state of affairs at the time. Real estate salespeople were writing contracts on sheets of paper and hiding property defects. As a group, they were considered unscrupulous. To combat that image and further the reputation of the real estate professionals in the economy, in 1913 the NAREE adopted a code of ethics with the Golden Rule as its theme. A requisite for membership in the NAR, this code sets the standards in writing by which its members abide. In 1916, the organization's name was changed to The National Association of Real Estate Boards (NAR) and the term "REALTOR®," identifying real estate agents as members of the NAR and subscribers to its code of ethics, was first used. Only real estate salespeople who belong to the NAR can use the REALTORS® designation. The NAR currently has a membership of over one million. To learn more, visit the NAR Web site at *http://www.realtor.org.*

Personal Code of Ethics

A personal code of ethics is simply what you would do if no one was watching. It is the way you behave when you are alone. People have an inherent knowledge of right and wrong. Personal ethics is how we act with that knowledge. Ethics is taking money back to a restaurant if you were overpaid in change. Ethics is returning a lost wallet with all the cash money intact. Ethics is being honest in your dealings with others. Ethics is always doing those things that you know are right.

I purchased an entrance mat from a distributor at a real estate conference. I paid for it and I took it. About 6 weeks later I was shipped another one. I laughed and started putting it back in the box. My administrative assistant said, "What are you doing? We need one for the back door." Without hesitation I finished boxing it up and it was shipped back the next day. My personal ethics would not allow me to take advantage of another person's mistake. I never thought about it until now, but can you imagine the precedent I would have set if I had kept it? No one could trust me to make the right decisions. You never know who is watching, maybe no one, maybe your boss. What would you do in the following situations?

1. A buyer gives you $600 dollars for earnest money, thinking he only gave you $500.
    A. Return the extra $100.
    B. Buy yourself lunch with it; you deserve it.
    C. Keep the extra $100, if the buyers are that stupid they didn't want it.

2. While showing a property you break a valuable vase.
    A. Clean up the mess and call the listing salesperson immediately.
    B. Run, they will never know it was you.
    C. Break the back window and steal some stuff; the sellers will think they were robbed.

3. A seller's water well will not pass a water test.
    A. Disclose this issue to the buyer and try to work out a solution even if it means losing the sale.
    B. Get water from a different well and pass it off as the seller's well. You can later claim something just went wrong with the water but it was fine during inspection; meanwhile you have put a down payment on that new car you want with the handsome commission you made on the sale.

C. Forge false documents that indicate the well has no problem, so the seller can sell the property and you can get paid. Remember your duty is to represent the seller's best interest.

All answers are "A" and given. While not all personal ethics questions are that simple, don't let a hectic schedule or desperation lead you astray. You would be surprised how many people are embarrassed, in court, or even worse because of a lapse of thinking. Don't be that person. I once saw a sign in a store that read, "You can take anything that God does not see you take." That is ethics. The following situations are a little more challenging.

1. A buyer calls your office and asks for Colleen. You are on phone time at the up-desk, and you say, "Colleen is not in, may I take a message?" The buyer then tells you that she received a flyer from Colleen and would like to buy a house.
    A. Put the caller on hold and check your office policy manual on how to proceed.
    B. Help the caller yourself.
    C. Take a message for Colleen.

2. You are representing a buyer, and you notice a small crack in the bedroom wall of the house your are showing. The buyers are obviously interested in the house.
    A. Disclose the crack and recommend further inspections.
    B. Don't say anything. You are not a structural engineer.
    C. Let the buyer beware. It is not your job to discover structural defects.

3. You hear a real estate agent in your office tell a buyer that a property is not in a flood plain. You know this agent is a good friend and you know he has seen and understood a report stating that the house is in a flood plain.
    A. Discuss this with your broker.
    B. Address this issue immediately before it is too late.
    C. Keep quiet to save your friendship.

These are not as easy as the first set of situations, but again all the "best" answers are "A." Personal ethics will give yourself the true meaning of success. Having all of the money in the world and not believing in yourself is not worth it. You always know yourself.

In developing moral character, consider the following:

- Practice being a mentor; treat everyone with love and respect.
- Practice moral discipline; use rules and moral reasoning.
- Practice moral reflection; read and discuss issues.
- Practice conflict resolution; solve conflicts fairly and without force.

Chapter Summary

This chapter mainly deals with the way we feel about real estate. Real estate can be a mean business if our attitude is not correct. We must believe in ourselves because others might not. We sell ourselves in the real estate business. We don't sell houses. A buyer will buy a property with or without us, but it is our job is to have that buyer buy through us. To accomplish this goal we must believe that we are the best real estate people for the client. To that end, we must provide the best, most professional service to fulfill their needs.

Ethics is how we respond when no one else is looking. It is our innermost being and our integrity. It is what sets us apart from unscrupulous salespeople. It is how we want to be treated. Keep your ethics up and you can sleep at night.

Summary Questions

1. What is the mark used to denote a real estate salesperson affiliated with the National Association of REALTORS®?
    A. Realator
    B. NAR
    C. Agent
    D. REALTOR®

2. The National Association of REALTORS® was founded as the National Association of Real Estate Exchanges on what date?
    A. May 12, 1908
    B. July 4, 1776
    C. January 1, 1996
    D. February 5, 1962

3. What trade association has over one million members?
   A. National Real Estate Commission
   B. National Association of REALTORS®
   C. International Association of Real Estate Agents
   D. The Global Real Estate Sales Group

4. Ethics comes from the Greek words "ethickos" and "ethos" meaning what?
   A. "Thick" and "ethics"
   B. "Moral" and "character"
   C. "Strong" and "ethics"
   D. "Silent" and "truth"

5. The NAR preamble is measured by what rule?
   A. 80/20 Rule
   B. Ethics Rule
   C. Rule of Thumb
   D. Golden Rule

6. Kimberly, a real estate licensed salesperson, fails to log in a customer's call per the established office procedure. The customer calls back on licensee Brittany's opportunity time but doesn't mention Kimberly's name. Brittany establishes a relationship with the caller and eventually sells him a house. When Kimberly finds out about the sale, she demands at least part of the commission as procuring cause. In this case, the broker should:
   A. Tell Kimberly to get a life.
   B. Tell Brittany to split the commission with Kimberly.
   C. Pay Kimberly out of the brokerage commission to avoid an in-office dispute.
   D. Refer Kimberly to the policy manual and advise her to follow office procedure.

7. You have given your current broker two week's notice that you will be transferring your license to a competing broker. On your last day of opportunity time, you get an incoming call from a buyer interested in buying a million-dollar property. What is the best course of action?
   A. Assist the buyer and ask your current broker to assign another salesperson after you leave.
   B. Assist the buyer and ask him to follow you to your new broker when you leave.

C. Assist the buyer and ask your new broker for guidance.

D. Assist the buyer with your current broker's permission and guidance.

8. You have written an offer from a customer for your sellers for $270,000. You could get both sides of the commission. Just when you are about to leave the office, the telephone rings with another competing agent who has an offer for your seller's house for full price at $275,000. What is the best course of action?

   A. Ignore the first offer because it is not in writing yet.

   B. Pretend you never received the agent's call. It is that agent's word against yours.

   C. Present your first offer and tell the seller another one may be coming in.

   D. Call your buyers and tell them they need to up their offer by $5,100 because you need to be higher than the other offer.

9. You have a commission dispute with another agent from a competing real estate company. What should you do?

   A. Call for a duel at ten paces with single-shot pistols in the parking lot of the local association of REALTORS®.

   B. Sue the other agent in a court of law.

   C. Consult your broker.

   D. File a grievance with the real estate commission.

10. Which of the following is not an unethical practice?

    A. Selling your own property.

    B. Failing to remove the real estate yard sign after it has expired.

    C. Calling sellers from MLS data to see if they will change real estate companies before their exclusive listing has expired.

    D. Using imaginary houses to fill up advertising space.

11. A client wants to show her appreciation for your efforts by giving you a $100 at closing for you and your wife to have dinner somewhere. What is the best course of action?

    A. Put the money in an envelope and take it to your broker.

    B. Politely refuse because it is a fiduciary breach to take more money than agreed to in a listing contract.

    C. Do what your client demands and take the money to buy your wife dinner.

    D. Split the money with the title officer to keep her quiet.

12. Which educational designation allows a licensed real estate salesperson to specialize in industrial real estate?
    A. SIOR (Society of Industrial and Office REALTORS®)
    B. CCIM (Certified Commercial Industrial Member)
    C. CRE (Industrial Society of Real Estate Counselors)
    D. PID (Professional Industrial Dealer)

13. As a professional real estate salesperson you should ask yourself which of the following questions?
    A. Am I too old to sell real estate?
    B. Why should someone choose me?
    C. Is my car good enough to show people houses?
    D. Who's buying donuts for the office meeting?

14. Which of the following things can we change?
    A. Our past.
    B. The way people act.
    C. Our attitude.
    D. The inevitable.

15. Which of the following are examples of an unsuccessful attitude?
    A. Arguing with a client.
    B. Following through after the sale.
    C. Knowing what to do every day.
    D. Full knowledge of the client's needs.

16. What should your attitude do?
    A. Show genuine concern.
    B. Convey trust.
    C. Show confidence.
    D. All of the above.

17. According to this book, what do the initials TLC stand for?
    A. Too Little Cash
    B. Trust, Like, Close
    C. Temporary Loan Contingency
    D. Tender Loving Concern

18. What is incorrect with the following affirmation?
    "Every day I will try to better myself in some way."
    A. "Try" is an excuse for failure.
    B. "Will" is future tense and affirmations must be in present tense.

C. "Some way" is not exact enough to be an effective affirmation.

D. All of the above.

19. Which of the following is not the correct match with the abbreviation?

    A. GRI—Graduate, REALTORS® Institute
    B. CRB—Commercial and Residential Brokerage Manager
    C. CRS—Certified Residential Specialist
    D. WCR—Women's Council of REALTORS®

20. Which equation comes from attitude?

    A. I win = You lose
    B. Hard Work = More income
    C. What you think = What you bank
    D. Egotism = Self-love

21. Which of the following best describes the word "work"?

    A. Doing something when you would rather be doing something else.
    B. What you have to do to get a paycheck.
    C. Real estate.
    D. An alien from Ork.

22. What should your attitude consist of?

    A. Genuine concern.
    B. Undivided attention.
    C. Conveyance of an attitude of trust.
    D. All of the above

Characteristics of Successful Salespeople and Time Management

Chapter Overview

This chapter is an overview of what successful real estate salespeople do. Successful salespeople set goals. This chapter includes what to wear, what to drive, and what to learn. It even talks about what to do with your money once you have earned it. The chapter's objective is to show you the traits of successful salespeople. Once you see what other successful salespeople do, you can do the same things and be more likely to get the same results.

You will also learn about time management and a few ways to help get things done. You will learn that time management is doing the simple things, and how to plan out a day, week, and a year.

Key Words

Budget: An itemized summary of estimated expenditures for a given period.

Business Plan: A proposal requiring concerted effort.

Conventions: A formal meeting of members of an industry.

Financial Planning: The management of money, banking, investments, and credit.

Goal: The purpose toward which an endeavor is directed, an objective.

Investing: To commit money or capital to gain a financial return.

Personal Assistant: Holding an auxiliary position, giving aid.

Productive: Yielding favorable or useful results.

Qualify: To describe an individual by financial capabilities.

Seminar: A small group of students in study under the guidance of a professor for the purpose of exchanging ideas.

Success: The achievement of something desired, planned, or attempted.

Time Management: The managing of one's time. Analysis of the operations required to create a service with the aim at increasing efficiency.

Characteristics of Successful Salespeople

Introduction

The characteristics of successful real estate salespeople can be categorized in three groups:

1. The vast 80 percent of real estate salespeople aren't sure they're going to make it in the business and are just "giving real estate a try." I bought a real estate office once. The first thing I do when I acquire an office is to interview each salesperson. One woman came into my office for an interview and casually plopped down in a chair. She started by exclaiming, "I've heard about you. You want people here that are serious about the real estate industry. Well I am not sure I want to work that hard. I just want to *try* the business to see if I like it. So I don't think I will work out here." I agreed, stood up, and motioned her to the door. She looked at me like I was rude. Can you imagine talking to your new broker like that? I guess she wanted me to beg her to stay. The word "try" is not allowed in my office. The word breeds failure. When you do something you *do it*. If you try something you can always say, "Well, I tried it and it did not work out." Notice the blame is somewhere else. Instead, say this: "I took action and the action I took failed." This is much better because you can always change your actions; don't blame yourself–just modify your actions. If you do the things you need to do consistently, you will not fail.

There was a company vice-president who made a mistake that cost a million dollars. When he faced the president the next day he said, "You don't have to fire me, I will quit." The president responded, "Fire you, heck I just gave you a million-dollar lesson!" This president knew this vice-president would never make that mistake again. It is not bad to fail, it is bad to fail and not learn from it.

If you are not sure real estate is for you, I understand. Do it right though, and give it your all. That is the only way you will really know. I have seen so many new salespeople who get into the business and wait for it to come to them. It doesn't work that way. You must get out there and work. I once worked for a real estate company where seven of the salespeople were driving brand new Cadillacs. The problem, however, was that no one in that office was making any money and it eventually went out of business. Their spouses bought all the Cadillacs. No one actually earned them.

2. The top 15 percent of real estate salespeople make 80 percent of the money. These salespeople are totally committed and know they will reach their goals. These people are working and making money but they lack the passion necessary for long-term success. They tend to burn out because they see the work as just a job and eventually they lose their desire.

Are you a good real estate salesperson or a *great* real estate salesperson?

The "GREAT" ones follow this formula:

G—Gap (Wants and Needs) analysis needs to be performed to determine the client's desires.

R—Respect. Earn respect.

E—Ethics. Must follow an ethical path.

A—Accept the leadership role. You must be perceived as the leader in the transaction.

T—Trust. The ultimate goal is to have a trust relationship.

3. The top 5 percent of real estate salespeople—are highly skilled, totally committed, and have an overwhelming love for the real estate industry. These are the "winners." Here are some of the characteristics of the top 5 percent:

- They have something to prove. They want to prove they can be a success. That is why brokers are careful in firing salespeople. The person fired may get it in his or her head to prove the previous broker wrong and that motivates him or her to succeed.

- They have an overwhelming desire to achieve, and they refuse to accept mediocrity. They will never accept second place.

- They love people and use money instead of using people and loving money.

- They operate like a business. They have a business plan even though they are salespeople. They work their plan and if the plan fails they modify it until they achieve success.

- They pay attention to details and yet they don't get bogged down with the small, unimportant stuff. They are organized. They track their business numbers. Persistence is the most essential ingredient for a successful career in real estate, with organization being next. The salesperson who believes he or she can get organized later will never see later.

- They strive to keep balance in their lives, to reach goals in all areas: financial, emotional, physical, and spiritual. Take time to be at your son's ball game, at evening meals, at school events, and sometimes just hanging out. The real estate business allows you to schedule your own time. I remember going to my daughter Brittany's school and spending the day with her. I sat in those little bitty chairs just to be by her. She would beam her happiness to all the other students. It meant so much to me. To this day I would trade no amount of money for that time. One of Brittany's teachers told me it was great to have me in class because so many of the children don't ever get to see their dads. Strive to keep balance because that is the only way to "true" success.

- They deliver a proven sales strategy with a non-sales-type personality. They are professional salespeople as well as ordinary people.

- They realize real estate is nothing but a big numbers game, and they must play the percentages.

- They have learned to love the word "No."

They have goals. So let's learn about goals.

Goals

> "Winning is a habit, so is losing. Which habit are you forming daily?"
> —*Dirk Zeller*

Make a decision about what you truly want. Once you do, you can stay away from things that prevent you from making your goals. So many people don't know what they want. They meander through life and end up somewhere they never intended to be. If they had only asked themselves this question, "What do I truly want?" they could have designed their life to achieve it. If you follow your current direction, where will *you* be in a year? In five years? In ten? And is that where you really want to be? Be honest with yourself. What if you got on a ship sailing to Europe and asked the captain, "Got everything planned out to get us there?" And the captain said "Oh, no, I am just gonna head that-a-way and see where it takes us." How fast would you get off that ship? Don't run your life like that captain.

Goal setting requires five important items:

1. **The goal must be attainable and realistic.**

   If your goal is to be 7'4" tall but you are 5'9" and have stopped growing, you will not reach your goal. If your goal is an annual income of $100,000 and the most you have ever made in real estate is $28,000, it may not be attainable. The problem is that if you have any doubts about your goal's viability, you won't work toward it. The goal will not motivate you. If you set more realistic goals and achieve them, then reset a higher goal next time. A goal should stretch you. A goal of $28,500 for next year when you already made $28,000 this year is not stretching you enough.

   When Douglas MacArthur entered the U.S. Military Academy at West Point, he announced two goals: to lead his class and to one day become Chief of Staff. Leading his class was a short-term goal and becoming Chief of Staff was his great vision—what he thought, at the time, was to become the greatest achievement for a West Point cadet.

   In his four years at West Point, MacArthur met his short-term goal by setting scholastic records. He later won fame as a front-line general in World War I, and in 1930, he met his long-term goal when President Herbert Hoover appointed him army Chief of Staff.

   MacArthur went on to become the Supreme Allied Commander in the Southwest Pacific in World War II. He headed the occupation government in Japan and later led U.S. forces successfully against the Communists in Korea.

   Goals must stretch you as they did for MacArthur.

2. **The goal must be measurable.**

   How do you know when you have met your goal if you cannot measure it? When I ask real estate salespeople about their goals I hear things like, "I want to be happy." How do you know you are not happy now? Your goal could be helping the American Cancer Society (ACS). That would make you happy. Great, I can measure that. When you make a certain amount of money in real estate you give a donation to ACS.

3. **The goal must be flexible.**

   In real estate opportunities come up all the time. If it is not in your goal plan to go on a listing appointment and a seller calls you, change your plans. Do not step over a dollar to pick up a penny.

4. **The goal must have a specific time frame.**

   Goals without a specific time frame will never become more than a dream.

5. **The goal must be in writing.**

   Your goal should not only be in writing; you need to review it at least twice a day. I always ask new recruits to show me their written goals. Time after time I get blank looks or they tell me they keep their goals in their heads. If your goals are not written down, they will stay in your head and never develop. Writing them down clarifies them and helps you commit to seeing them through.

> **Your goals are the road maps that guide you and show you what is possible for your life.** *—Les Brown*

Steps for Successful Goal Setting and Achievement

Goal setting is an extremely powerful technique for accomplishment, but effective goal setting requires more than just writing a list of dreams and filing it away. The following is a step-by-step process to develop goals.

1. **Well-formed goal declaration**

   The goal declaration forms the basis for the entire goal-setting process, so pay careful attention to formulating a clear and accurate goal declaration.

   The goal should be

   - Specific enough so that you know exactly what you are striving for.
   - Measurable so you know exactly what is to be accomplished.
   - Scheduled so you know when to reach it.
   - Action-oriented declaring positive activity that will produce results.
   - Realistic in that it is practical and can be achieved given a limited availability of resources.
   - Tangible meaning concrete and not vague.

   The goal declaration "Increase listings 25 percent by the end of the fiscal year without increasing advertising spending" is an example that follows these rules.

2. **Breaking down goals into manageable steps**

   Once you have a well-formed goal declaration, you need some direction to achieve this goal. While the goal "Increase listings 25 percent by the end of the fiscal year without increasing advertising spending" is a great goal declaration, this is a monumental task without being broken down into smaller detailed steps. The creation of goal steps gives an "Action Plan" that when completed will lead to goal achievement. Steps also allow for tracking of progress toward the goal. Goal steps should be positive and not used to list obstacles that must be overcome. This will force you to focus on the negative, and negativity can kill motivation. There is power in positive thinking.

3. **Motivation and commitment**

   Motivation and commitment are what make us strive for achievement. They give us the push, desire, and resolve to complete all of the other steps in the goal process. This motivation can be obtained by developing a personal statement that creates a high level of emotion and energy that guarantees achievement. Zig Ziglar says that as a child he was kicked out of his local country club pool because he was not a member. In response he later made a goal of one day having a pool that is one foot bigger than that country club pool. The motivation of being asked to leave the pool provided the necessary fuel for him to achieve this goal. Commitment creates more accountability and is what sets us on a direct course to reach our goals. Failure to attain a goal may create costly negative consequences. Making a commitment is like having invested your savings in your new business. If the business fails, you will lose your savings. Motivation and commitment are specific to your situation and life, and only you can form statements that will ensure you reach your goal.

4. **Reminders and keeping on track**

Reaching goals requires persistence and regular attention. You need some sort of system to keep you reminded and accountable. Use a combination of reminder e-mails, calendars, and reports to keep organized and on track. Sharing your goals with others who can help and support you is a highly effective way to increase your chances for success. If some accountability system is not used, then you are likely to lose sight of your goal and fail.

5. **Frequent review and reassessment**

When you first sit down to define your goals, it can seem like a difficult task but over time it begins to get much easier. Patience is required. Goal setting is definitely an ongoing process that is accomplished over time. Any goals program that defines goals and then ignores them will fail. All goals due in the next year should be reviewed at least weekly and daily, if possible. The great thing about frequent review is that this forces you to make big decisions and determine priorities in life. You should keep watch for goals that are not being achieved on time or for goals on which you keep extending the deadline.

Additional Goal-Setting Tips

- Determine the value of your time. How much are you actually worth to your clients? Anyone can make more money if he or she trades more time for it. Calculate your net earnings for the past year and divide that by the number of hours you worked. Be sure to add in all the time you spent driving around and doing odd jobs. You may be shocked at how low your "hourly wage" is.

- Develop a philosophy. Set guidelines for doing business and define clearly your world of business. For example, determine the type of sellers and buyers you want to work with, including their price ranges. When a buyer or seller is out of step with your philosophy, refer him or her to somebody else. Be sure before you profile a customer that you do so as a marketing technique and are still in compliance with Fair Housing. Fair Housing law prohibits target marketing based on race, color religion, sex, handicap, familial status, or national origin.

- One of your goals should have to do with production in the real estate industry. Don't hurt your chances for success because of the little things like how you dress.

Dress for Success

It is said that you should dress so as not to be noticed. Perhaps a better way to say that is do not let your clothes speak for you. You have heard "Dress to Impress," but be wise, because what you perceive as impressive may not be impressive to your customer. I've always worn ties to work. But when I purchased a real estate office outside of the city, all of the real estate salespeople in that office started begging me not to wear a tie. It was making them feel uncomfortable.

What you like might not be what someone else likes. Don't wear a $600 pair of dress shoes to show a cow pasture. Don't let your perfume arrive before you do. Don't have a haircut that makes you look like a freak. Which brings us to two more things:

> **You only have four seconds to set a good impression and the customer is always right.**

There was a real estate salesperson who went up against me on a listing appointment. The other salesperson went first and now it was my turn. I covered my services and explained why this seller (single male) should list with me. Finally, I looked at the seller and said, "Put me to work for you." The seller agreed. After he signed the listing agreement, I locked it in my briefcase (make sure they can't get it!). I asked why he decided to list with me and not the other salesperson. He told me that the other salesperson looked like the devil and he didn't trust him. Interesting analogy. The seller was right; he did look like the devil. He had a flat top haircut that wasn't that flat because it stood up on the sides (looked like devil horns) and he had a scruffy goatee. The other salesperson asked me why I got the listing over him, so I told him. He did not like what I had to say. He said, "The way I look is up to me." He is correct but it was costing him a lot of money. For the next several months this salesperson struggled financially. He finally shaved his beard and restyled his hair. Now he is one of the top producers in the area. I don't care what you look like, but is what you look like costing you money? When you are at home dress for home, but when you are working dress for work. I have seen real estate salespeople show up at work in a pair of shorts and ratty t-shirts. They usually explain that they aren't really working; they just needed to do some computer work. They don't consider that the rest of staff there is working and it would be embarrassing if clients saw them dressed inappropriately. It's always import to have respect for those around you.

Dressing for success includes dressing with career apparel. Career apparel can be as simple as a nametag to embroidered shirts and jackets. You should never be a "secret agent." "Secret agents" are real estate agents in such good disguises that no one would know they sell real estate. Wear your nametag everywhere. I was once paying for groceries and a manager walked up to me and asked me if I sold real estate. My nametag said I did, but I didn't want to make a potential client feel stupid, so I said, "I sure do." You never know when a small thing can give you big results. This also goes for the car you drive.

Drive for Success

Drive for success does not mean driving the latest, biggest, most expensive car on the road. It does mean keeping what you have in the best condition. Keep your car clean and waxed. Keep the interior clean and neat. Fix any minor dings or nicks. People don't care what you drive as long as they know you care. When I was first in the real estate business I drove an old beat up, two-door Mustang. I loved the car, but it wasn't the best car for real estate. I would show houses and joke with the buyers, "Do you want to take mine or do you want to drive?" They always drove. The buyers liked and trusted me; they did not care what I drove. Let me tell one more story about that Mustang. I would go on listing appointments and park down the street to avoid the seller seeing my car. I did this once to a particular seller. When I was finished with my listing presentation I told the seller to list with me and the seller agreed. I asked that seller why he listed with me and not my competition. The seller told me that the first salesperson arrived in a brand-new Cadillac and proceeded to tell the seller what to do. The second one was driving a brand-new Lincoln Continental and also told the seller what to do. I drove up in a beat-up Mustang and parked it down the street. The seller said, "I saw you park down the street in that *car* and figured you must be hungry!" I don't believe the Mustang got me that listing; I got it because out of all three real estate salespersons I was the only one who took the time with the seller and showed him I cared. But the Mustang did not eliminate me either. I now drive a better car, by choice, because I have earned it. Don't sweat the small stuff. If you want a newer or better car, then budget for it and when you have earned it, buy it.

Read for Success

It is amazing to me the number of people who never read. Do you have a current library card? Did you know your local association of REALTORS® has a real estate library? I have been in those libraries and the material has not been checked out in years. Most real estate salespeople do not have or use the public library. If you do not find real estate related reading material, they have tons of books on sales and marketing that are also helpful. You should read at least two books per month to stay ahead of the game. You must read all of the real estate trade publications you can get your hands on every month. However, do not read while you should be making money; read at night or while you are doing other odd jobs. I like to read while I am on the stationary bike. The best-educated real estate salesperson that has no clients is called "Broke." Do not take this lightly; your competition is reading and will leave you behind.

Listen for Success

It is said that you can get the equivalent of a college education in ten years by listening to educational cassette tapes or CDs in your car. I believe it. Listening in my car has changed my career for the better. I am now comfortable with sales techniques and handling objections that I learned from listening to tapes and CDs. I see real estate salespeople singing to songs in their car and they know all the words to the songs they sing. Later, in a sales situation they do not know what to say. My daughter, Brittany, can sing the words to songs of her favorite music groups, and I asked her how much money they paid her to spend her time learning the words. (She doesn't think I am funny!) Which makes you more money, singing to the latest music hit or knowing scripts to use in sales situations?

Seminars and Classes

The real estate industry offers numerous seminars and classes dealing with real estate and making money. You should go to as many of these as you can, but don't let it interfere with your making money. Be smart and selective. The seminars tend to fire you up and get you on the right course. The real estate classes will give you added insight into the real estate industry. Most of the seminars are free because the speakers are trying to sell you their products. The only question is whether should you buy the material. The answer depends on you. Will you use it? If not, don't waste your money on something that will only gather dust. I can tell a real estate professional by his or her library. When I interview brokers to work in my office, I ask to see their real estate libraries. I have hundreds of books and numerous cassette tapes, videos, and CDs. Whenever I need a boost I listen to one of my best tapes or CDs or read a powerful book.

Conventions

Real estate conventions are yearly events where real estate salespeople get together to share, learn, and receive awards. Most large real estate organizations, such as the National Association of REALTORS®, have annual conventions. They are generally in different locations. These are rewarding and valuable if you go to develop referrals. No better place to ask for referral business than at a convention. One real estate salesperson from California meets a real estate salesperson from New York. Now they can pass referrals back and forth. So if you go, go with the right attitude, press some palms, ask for referrals, and learn something new. I went to a convention in Las Vegas. The next scheduled event was due to begin in a few moments, just enough time for one or two hands of black jack. The small talk began when I sat down. "What do you do?" I asked the guy next to me,

"Real estate," he said. "So do I," said the woman just down from him. It turned out everyone at the table was in real estate and in town for the convention. Interesting note, I was the only one who left the table for the convention event. Go with the right attitude.

Ask Questions

The best way to receive knowledge is to ask questions. Too many people are afraid to ask questions because they do not want to look dumb. Well it is dumb not to ask. If someone does not want to help you, you do not want to learn from that person.

Safety in Real Estate

The real estate profession is quite safe. Several stories of bad things happening to good real estate salespeople are frequently heard about but rarely occur. It is more likely that an individual will be mugged shopping in a mall than selling real estate. However, it does happen and efforts should be taken to prevent any such chance.

The salesperson is never alone with a client, especially at the first meeting. This seems logical but is quite often overlooked. The salesperson gets a buyer call on the telephone in the office and the call goes something like this:

> **Buyer:** "I would like you to meet me at the vacant house on Elm Street."
>
> **Salesperson:** "Sure, I'd love to!"

Almost every salesperson makes this mistake, and it creates an avenue for trouble. The section of this book on telephone answering techniques will help with the proper way to answer the real estate telephone. Avoiding being alone with a stranger is especially critical in dealing with buyer clients. With seller clients the salesperson will go to their home, creating much less chance for trouble. Incidences of trouble tend to occur separately, away from others. The salesperson should always meet the buyer at the real estate office. If the buyer is far away, the salesperson should meet him or her a public place like a restaurant before showing property. Trouble is often avoided in a public place with witnesses around. Persons wanting to cause trouble do not want to be seen. If the buyer is reluctant to meet in a public place, choices need to be made. Consider if the potential sale is important enough to risk trouble. The answer is No. It only takes once.

Some people recommend making a copy of a buyer's driver's license. Remember, if this is done it MUST be done for ALL buyers or risk a violation of Fair Housing.

Here are some other tips for safety's sake:

- Keep the car's gas tank at least half full.
- Have a cellular telephone.
- Notify others of your whereabouts.
- Dress with personal safety in mind.

Business Plan

The professional real estate salesperson should have a detailed business plan for a real estate career. A well-laid-out plan helps establish the goals and how to accomplish them. It tells the owner of the plan whether or not he or she is on track. It then is broken down to yearly, monthly, and daily events. Each event should lead you closer to your goals.

Each daily event should be put in your daily planner. The most essential tool of the trade for a real estate salesperson is the daily planner. Most planners list the days in the year. My favorite is a "week at a glance." This allows me to view my entire week so I won't forget an appointment. Personal Digital Assistants (PDAs) also have great planning capabilities. See Chapter 3, Technology for the Real Estate Professional, for more details regarding PDAs.

Financial Planning

The real estate business is tough unless you have some type of financial planning. The average real estate salesperson receives large sums of money at different times per month. This makes any planning difficult.

Your plan should include a budget and some type of investment portfolio. It should also allow you to track statistics and do tax planning. All of these are addressed next.

Budget

Real estate salespeople must have a budget or they will find themselves frequently without money. I suggest you place all of your real estate money into an account and pay yourself a regular fixed salary out of that account and pay your bills from the salary. If there is more money left in the account after your salary, you should invest that money. However, you should always pay yourself first. That simply means put some money away for investments before you pay your first bill. If you don't, chances are you will never invest. If there is not enough money left after your salary for investing, you need to make more money.

Some real estate salespeople get in a situation where they receive a commission check for several thousand dollars and place that money down on a car. That creates two problems: first, a new car payment increases your monthly expenses, and second, all of the commission is used up in one situation.

The fluctuation in income is what I call the roller-coaster effect of real estate. One minute you are on top making money and the next minute you are broke and have no listings. The only way to level the income stream out is to budget, and all money goes into that budget. I have seen a multitude of good real estate salespeople quit because they didn't have the discipline to budget their income.

How to Set up a Personal Budget

- Start with a budget worksheet.
- Go through your checkbook or bills from the last two to three months. Add and delete categories from the worksheet to fit your expenditures.
- Think about your hobbies, entertainment, and habits. Be sure to add categories for these expenses.

- Go through your pay stubs or bank deposits and calculate your average monthly gross pay.
- Calculate any interest income, dividends, bonuses, or other miscellaneous income.
- For each expense category, determine a budget amount that realistically reflects your actual expenses while setting targeted spending levels that will enable you to save money.
- Once you're comfortable with your expense categories and budgeted amounts, enter expenditures from your checkbook from the last month.
- Keep track of cash expenditures throughout the month and total and categorize these at the end of each month.
- Subtotal the income and expense categories.
- Subtract the total expenses from the total income to arrive at your net income.
- If your expenses are greater than your income, your net income number will be negative. Your situation can probably be greatly improved by changing your spending habits.
- If you have a positive net income, transfer most of it to a savings or investment account at the end of each month. Extra cash left in a regular checking account has a way of getting spent.
- After you've tracked your actual spending for a month or two, analyze your spending to identify where you can comfortably make cuts.
- Once the budgeting process is in place, take an in-depth look at your largest spending categories, brainstorm about ways to reduce spending in specific categories, and set realistic goals.
- Update your budget and expenses monthly.

Budgeting Tips

- Don't try to fit your expenses into somebody else's budget categories. Tailor the categories to fit your own situation.
- Make your categories detailed enough to provide useful information, but not so detailed that you become bogged down in trivial details.
- Think of your budget as a tool to help you get out of debt and save money, not as a financial diet.

Tracking

Real estate salespeople should track their statistics to determine their current status. The items that should be tracked include:

- **Number of sales**—Are you increasing the number of people you are helping?

- **Dollar amount per sale**—Are you increasing your average sale? The higher the price range, the more money you make.

- **Time on the market**—How long does it take for you to sell a listing? What can you do to sell the properties faster?

- **Number of appointments per week**—How many face-to-face appointments do you have per week? How can you get more?

- **Number of prospecting calls per week**—How can you get more?

- **Ratio of appointments to sellers (buyers)**—How many sellers (buyers) are you getting from your appointments? How can you improve that ratio?

- **Ratio of sellers (buyers) to solds**—How many of your sellers (buyers) are actually selling (buying)? How can you improve that ratio?

- **Ratio of number of hours spent in the business to your income**—How many hours does it take to make money? How can you improve that ratio?

- **Number of outgoing referrals sent to other real estate salespeople in other areas of the country**—How many referrals do you send? How can you improve that number?

These statistics will show you where you stand in the real estate business and the areas in which you need to improve.

Taxes

This is a tough subject, but if you do not pay your taxes the IRS gets really mad. A problem with the real estate industry is that taxes are not normally withheld from your commission paychecks. This means that at the end of the year you must pay a large sum of money to the IRS for taxes for the year (actually you are to pay quarterly or pay a penalty). My only suggestion is to set up an account for taxes and pay the share from each commission check. Keep this money separate and only use it to pay taxes. All other information on taxes should be attained from a tax authority.

Investing

When the average person hears the term "investing" it strikes fear because of risk and most people do not like to take risks. To be a profitable investor you must assume some risk. Each investment has a relationship between the risk and the return. You need to determine your risk tolerance.

The key to any successful investment is time. The more lead-time on an investment the more money it will likely make. If you wait until you need money before investing, it will be too late. No one else will invest for you; you must do it. Paying yourself first means setting aside an amount for investments first and then paying your bills. As a result, you will pay all your bills and in years ahead you will thank yourself because you are financially secure.

Savings

Saving is not really investing; it is providing a safety net. You should have enough in your savings account to cover your living expenses for six months. Invest this "safety" money in some secure mutual fund and forget about it.

Stock Market

Many fortunes have been made and lost in the stock market. You invest in other companies you believe have a marketable product or service. As the company you invested in does better, you do better. The two main ways to make money in the stock market are by capital appreciation (the stock value goes up) and income (through dividends or sharing of the profit with investors). The drawback of the stock market is the time it takes to really follow the market–the time it takes to study trends, information, terminology, and the actual trading action. You can hire a professional investor, but the expense would limit your profit. In addition, you have no control in the company you're investing in. The company may look good on the outside, but on the inside, the managers may be embezzling money. If the company goes bankrupt, you lose your investment.

Real Estate

Real estate has consistently been the best investment for the long run. Everyone wants real estate. I have always said you can make a very good living selling real estate; you can also become wealthy investing in real estate. The two main ways to invest in real estate are capital appreciation (the investment property is worth more than you paid and every month you pay down on the note, assuming you are amortizing your note) and income (the investment property with positive cash flow). You can invest in residential real estate, commercial, industrial, agricultural, or any number of other type of real estate. The most popular way to invest is to buy an undervalued, small, single-family property that is in need of repair. Buy it, fix it up, and sell it for a profit. Some investors buy property and rent it for income and long-term capital appreciation. The reason I like real estate investing better than the stock market is because I have control. I get to make the decision on which property to buy and when to sell. I don't have to trust others with my nest egg.

Retirement

The real estate industry typically does not provide any retirement. You must do this on your own. You do not want to wake up one day and realize you're not interested in real estate anymore but you have to do it anyway because you do not have any investments.

Personal Assistant

A personal assistant helps you with your everyday busy work. Whether or not the assistant should be licensed is based on the type of work you have. Check with your state for guidelines. I believe you will never reach your potential if you do not have at least one personal assistant. He or she can help you with marketing, promoting, and follow-up, which will allow you more face time with your sales prospects. Don't get an assistant so you can goof off. Having an assistant only makes sense if you are out using your time prospecting. Don't do $5 an hour work if you are worth more. Remember: If you don't have an assistant, you are an assistant.

Time Management

Have you ever had too many things to do and no time to do them? This could be a time management problem. Time management can be misconstrued to be cumbersome, but it should not be. Time management is doing what you are currently doing but doing it better.

Your time is to be decided by you. It is not to be decided by your broker (if it is, maybe it is because you are not doing anything by yourself). It is not to be decided by your spouse or significant other, and it is especially not to be decided by your clients. Too many times in the real estate business a client needs us immediately, or at least they believe they do. In turn, we jump. We drop whatever important business we were doing to meet them, show them property, or straighten a crooked yard sign. Don't mistake me here, I am not promoting ignoring your clients. I am saying control your time. Imagine you want to leave for Las Vegas at 3:00 p.m. today, so you call the airlines and request that the airplane be fueled and ready for take-off at 3:00 p.m. They say the next flight is not booked to leave until 5:15 p.m. What do you think are your chances to get the airline to change the schedule? Why is that? It is because it is a *professional* airline. We call ourselves professional and then meet a client on a whim. What are we saying to the client? "Call me anytime, I have nothing to do."

Time Planning

Now the question is how should you plan your day? The first step is to determine all that you want to accomplish in a day and put those items on a list. Next you must set priorities. You need to determine that if you only get one thing on the list done, what would that one thing be. Then do that one thing first.

The to-do list should be written and flexible, yet thorough. If you can get several items on the list done in one day, figure which item you hate to do and do that one first. Along the same line, determine what time of the day you are most productive and do your least favorite and most difficult items during that time. For example, if you have a closing coming up, you should have a checklist to make sure you accomplish everything necessary. The checklist will include items on it that are fun and easy to do and things that are difficult to do. Be sure not to put off the difficult things and do just the fun things. There are several sample checklists in the Appendix of this book.

One great tool for time planning is the telephone. It should be used to screen unwanted calls. Do not prolong conversations. Try to control interruptions.

Here are some additional time management hints:

- Create a time log (task analysis). Go through a day and document everything you do.
- Review the time log and determine what processes and/or services can be streamlined or eliminated.
- Determine the services you offer that can be eliminated or reduced without affecting your bottom line.
- Determine what services or new ideas you can implement. By implementing them, you will reduce time you spend on each client. [Things like a new computer software program can help you complete a (CMA) faster.]
- Determine tasks that can be delegated at a reasonable cost. Maybe to the homeowner, lender, title company, or the other agent.
- Schedule your days, weeks, and months, and then stick to your schedule.
- Separate personal and professional time. Work at work and play at play.
  Waste time honestly. In all the offices I've worked in, there have been "nesters." These are real estate salespeople who have built themselves a nice "nest" at their desk. They have family pictures, old sales awards, novelty items, and the like. They are comfortable at their desks and wouldn't leave for anything, including a prospect. They now are wasting time. They could sit for hours remembering the "good ole days." If you're going to waste time, don't act like your working, waste it honestly. Go to your car and just sit. Stay there as long as you need before you realize you are wasting time. You may get some strange looks when you come back in the office, but at least you are wasting time honestly. Now get back to "real" work. I might not just sit in

my car (especially in Texas in August) but I have left the office for a while to get my head straight. Sometimes the telephone gets so heavy that I cannot seem to pick it up. This is the time that I leave.

No home number on your business cards. If you include your home number on your business card it just screams "Call me at home!" Your family needs to know that when you are with them business is a distant second.

- Sometimes the business has to wait. An appointment with your family should not be interrupted by business. Tell the potential client that you have an appointment that cannot be broken, even if the appointment is for your child's soccer game. Most clients will reschedule. If they refuse, question whether they the type of people you want to work with and consider referring them to another real estate salesperson that would accommodate them.

- Sometimes the family has to wait. If there is an important appointment, your family may have to wait.

- Get help if you need it. Talk to your broker, a title company, or your real estate commission when you need help.

- Establish family goals. Be careful here though. I once set a financial goal for myself and wanted to involve my family. So I asked Brittany (my daughter who was 5 or 6 at the time) what she wanted if I accomplished my goal. Without hesitation she said she wanted to go to Disney World. I said O.K. Well, a few weeks went by and I was working late one evening and came home dragging. Brittany walked up and demanded that I go back out and work because she wanted to go to Disney World!

- Do things you hate most early in the morning. It makes the rest of the day better.

- Use a communication log for your client files. Record your calls. That does not mean with a voice recorder. Just make a note and place it in the files. I know a real estate salesperson who used to make notes on the file inside cover. She wrote the date and what she and her client had discussed. No matter how trivial the call, she put it on the file. She got involved in a lawsuit. The sellers were claiming she said all kinds of things she did not say. Because she had the conversations recorded on the files of all her clients (it was her standard operating procedure) and the sellers had no such recordings, the suit was dropped. Learn something here.

- Set aside some alone time. Work only five and a half days per week. This will lessen burnout. If all you do is work, it tells your mind that you cannot complete the work in the time given.

- If you don't have an assistant, you are an assistant! If you cannot afford an assistant, perhaps you can share time with another real estate salesperson who also needs an assistant. You can also hire a temporary assistant.

- Handle paperwork only once. Do it, Delay it or Discard it. Real estate salespeople tend to be the biggest pack rats I have ever seen. I bought a real estate company and after the transaction closed I began to investigate what I bought. In the attic I found boxes of real estate files dating back 15 years. There were so many boxes I believe it was weighing down the support structure of the building. I began trashing the outdated material by placing the boxes outside to be picked up on trash day. My real estate salespeople began complaining that those files might be important some day. Remember, they hadn't been used or opened in over ten years. So I said, "Great, you can take home as many boxes as you want, but they must be taken home." No one took any boxes. It was O.K. to junk up the office but not their homes.

- Find a good mortgage and title people and then let them do their jobs. Tell them your expectations of them up front.
  - Have them pick up contracts.
  - Don't courier papers for them.
  - Give them contact numbers for everyone involved in the process.
  - Give the title company complete papers, including the listing agreement.

- Use the fax, mail, and e-mail for negotiating and prospecting.

- If you must do busy work, combine the activities.
  - Put up a sign, riders, flyer tube, and a lockbox at the same time. Keep one of each item in your car if you are allowed.
  - Make cold calls and do computer work or paperwork while on floor time.
  - Do some prospecting while cleaning your car and filling it up with gas.

- Start the day early.

- Never let your gas tank go less than half full.

- Always have an educational book in your car to read if something comes up and you have to wait.

- Pay someone to do for you the things that are not enjoyable and take up your personal time, like mowing the grass, washing the car, or cleaning the house. Some people like doing yard work. It is a form of relaxation. For me it is unnecessary work and I delegate it to others.

- Learn to say "No." We want to be nice, so we say "yes" to things we do not have time to do. This puts us under more time pressure. Pretty soon we give up and don't do anything.

  – Refuse to do the other agent's jobs.

  – Delegate meeting inspectors and appraisers. You do not have to be there with inspectors and appraisers.

- Promise a little, deliver a lot. It is a simple time management philosophy.

- The last thing you should do every day is review what had happened that day and then look to tomorrow and plan what should be done. I call this review/preview. Review the day by writing down all of your thoughts about the day's business. This is your business journal. Include things like conversations with potential client. How did it go? How did you happen to get them as potential clients? Do not include the incidences such as Mary making you mad because she took the last jelly donut at the morning office meeting. Then preview what things need to be done tomorrow and itemize and prioritize the list.

Allocating Time to Build Your Business

> To find the number of hours you have available for building business:
>
> _____ Hours sleeping
>
> _____ Hours with family and friends
>
> _____ Hours eating
>
> _____ Hours driving
>
> Total time _____ Hours committed to personal life

Subtract

from 24	_____ Hours available for work
Divide	
by 2	_____ Hours for building your business

Why is time planning important? Time is money. Time planning prevents future problems.

> **Twelve Words to Live By:**
>
> **I must do the most productive thing possible at every given moment.**

Build "tickler files" for both buyers and sellers and use them for:

1. **For Sale By Owner (FSBO) or Specialized Area Leads**—Whether you specialize in FSBOs, expired listings, certain types of professions, etc., keep contact names in your files.

2. **General File**—Everyone you know, including friends, relatives, and social contact–anyone you meet.

3. **Past Buyers and Sellers**—Keep in touch. Then, when they think of real estate, they'll think of you. You'll get to resell many homes this way. If you keep records on the entire past transaction, you'll be prepared to handle their needs at any time.

4. **Expense File and Tax Records**—Keep all receipts and business expenses.

   All of these files should be on your computer in a management software system. If you don't have one you should budget to get one. Until then, create a file using 4" × 6" cards.

Invest time in high-payoff activities. How much is your time worth? Once you know this, make sure you're investing your time wisely. Decide what activities give you the highest payoff in your business, and then have the self-discipline to focus on these activities every day. Ask yourself if you are doing the most important thing you can do at the given moment. If your answer is no, then stop doing what you're doing and do the most important thing. Identify your top three income-producing activities and how you spend your time each day. Then shift your resources to where you get the highest return. As a salesperson, your job is to outthink your competition. Then outwork them, if you desire.

Qualify the potential client. This is crucial to success. The goal in qualifying is to eliminate customers who aren't truly motivated. They will waste your time and eventually drive you out of business, both emotionally and financially.

Create strong systems and delegate. Develop systems that create the results you desire without your involvement. You need systems for listings, escrows, buyers, sellers, leads, other agents, presentations, negotiating, and following up on leads. Put these systems in your day planner and keep them with you at all times.

Day Planner

The most critical tool for success for a professional real estate salesperson is a day planner. The best one for me is a "week at a glance." It shows all of my appointments for the week so I don't forget any. I can't imagine how anyone can operate effectively without one. Currently the popular way to track appointments is with a personal digital assistant (PDA). These are great, but the best tool for you is the one that works best for you.

Before you go to sleep at night, have in your planner the six most important things in order of priority that you must do the next day. Be sure to include all scheduled appointments, time for research, family, and social engagements.

Create a schedule. Block out specific times each day for key tasks, including prospecting, qualifying buyers and sellers, negotiating contracts, returning phone calls, giving listing presentations, and showing property. Plan your day and then work your plan.

Chapter Summary

If it is your goal to be successful in the real estate business, you first need to determine your definition of success. One person might want to be the top producer of the world and another might want much less in money but more in time with his or her family. Both goals are possible in the real estate industry if you act professional and are determined.

Time management allows you to solve your problems more efficiently. Time management is professional and can be a huge stress reducer. Daily planners will help set and maintain your plan. Listing and prioritizing your tasks for the day will also help.

Summary Questions

1. How many days should you work per week?
    A. 8
    B. 5
    C. 3
    D. 5

2. What is "nesting"?
    A. When agents keep personal items at their desks, books and files all around them, and enjoy sitting there instead of leaving the office to go prospecting.
    B. The actual day a buyer moves into his or her new "nest."
    C. A type of knitting that agents give to buyers as house warming gifts.
    D. When an agent gets listings only from friends and family.

3. Goals must be
    A. Attainable or realistic.
    B. Completed within six months.
    C. Rigid.
    D. Oral.

4. Which of the following is a characteristic of the top 5 percent of the professional real estate salesperson?
    A. Loves people and uses money.
    B. Chooses work over family.
    C. Overspends to create motivation.
    D. Loves money and uses people.

5. Choose the best "dress for success" statement:
   A. Do not have your hair in spikes longer than 6 inches.
   B. When the paint on the wall curls up it is time to take a shower.
   C. Picking your nose is a good "ice breaker."
   D. Do not allow your appearance to speak for you.

6. Persistence is the most essential ingredient for a successful career in real estate. What is the next most important ingredient?
   A. Negotiating skills.
   B. Being good with people.
   C. Organizational skills.
   D. Likes to look at houses.

7. What is a real estate agent's most essential tool of the trade?
   A. A leather briefcase.
   B. A high-end laptop computer.
   C. A four-door car.
   D. A daily planner.

8. What should you do to avoid being a "secret agent"?
   A. Don't be seen at the office.
   B. Wear a nametag.
   C. Cold call from your office.
   D. Take a place of service with your local association of REALTORS®.

9. What determines how successful you will become?
   A. The car you drive.
   B. The clothes you wear.
   C. The way you sell yourself.
   D. The friends you have in the business.

Chapter 3

Technology for the Real Estate Professional

Chapter Objectives

This chapter covers the effects of technology on real estate. It includes information on personal computers, laptop computers, personal digital assistants (PDAs), digital imaging, virtual tours, handheld computers, contact management, Web sites, and digital cameras. Other information covered includes using e-mail as a marketing tool and using the Internet to increase your income.

Introduction

Technology can help you do your business better, faster, and with more efficiency. The technology field is constantly changing and as a professional real estate salesperson, you should be able to keep up with it, otherwise you may be left behind. While I've always prided myself on staying up-to-date, I once believed that the Internet was just a fad. How good was that belief?

Database

A database is the best way to keep up with your prospect leads. The best type of database is a contact manager software program designed to store all the information about your clients and your current listings and sales. The contact manager also makes it easy for you to retrieve and manipulate all of this information and to do mail-outs to your entire client base.

> "Past Trend: More and more mail-outs and see what sticks."
>
> "Future Trend: Less number of contacts, more often."
>
> —*Rolf Anderson, National Real Estate Speaker*

As far as a time saver, a database is a must. It allows you to input time-stamps on leads that will notify you when to call a client. Further, you can make call notes that become a permanent part of that person's record. This is extremely valuable if there is a conflict at some point. You can input duties to be performed on your listings and closings and have each item on the list automatically appear on your daily calendar. You can have the contact manager notify you of reminders such as when it's time to install a sign or a lock box or to send mail-outs.

You can also use the database to target buyers or sellers. For example, you can select a group of people who might be interested in a particular new listing, then call or mail them a postcard with a picture of the listing. You can print out mailing labels for any or all persons in the database or for a select group. You can organize a bulk mailing by zip code or by any other field. Be careful about others managing your client base because this is your career.

The contact manager can also prepare a variety of reports, including contact, listing, and closing reports, which will come in handy during tax time.

Database Records

Information is stored in your contact manager database through the use of data records. Each record contains individual fields or input areas that contain specific information related to the person or the property. This allows you to find a person or property instantly based on information you have entered. You can search the database using a person's first name, property address, number of bedrooms, or any criteria you have entered into a field.

The ability to search your database will help you market more directly. Say you find an article about area grade schools; you can search the database for potential buyers with children and mail them the article.

While talking to someone on the phone, if you hear a dog bark, ask for the dog's name and enter it into your database. The next time you talk to that person, you can ask about the dog. Follow the same procedure if, for example, the caller says she has to hang up to get to her daughter's soccer game. Record the information in your database for future use. Most contact managers allow you to assign a contact type or category to your records. The contact type is your connection to that person or some way to identify the contact. You can enter how you came in contact with the person, such as call-in-buyer, referral, or For Sale By Owner, or according to hobbies, employment, or address. If you take a new listing, you can mail it to all of your clients you think might be interested (buyer type). Once you create the group in the database, you can work with just that group, including making phone calls or printing letters, postcards, or labels. There is no limit on how you can manipulate the database.

Once you have called up a group from your database, you can sort them to better use the data. If you want to send mail to past clients, you can call them up on your contact manager, then sort them according to their zip code to help in bulk mailing.

Follow-Up

A good contact manager program makes following up on clients efficient and easy. The contact manager will synchronize with other software so you can better conduct a follow-up program. A follow-up program allows you to conduct a series of activities for a prospect, listing, or closing. A contact manager allows you to create a customized follow-up plan for each type of prospect. You can then instantly attach the plan to every similar prospect you have. When you attach a particular plan to a prospect, each event is tied to the calendar in your contact manager.

Here's an idea. Volunteer to maintain the database for your local civic club. Ask to maintain the database and send out a monthly newsletter. (Of course, you will have your advertising banner on the newsletter.) Now you have contact with the entire club. (Note: You should not join a civic club for leads, but if you are available and the leads come to you, that is good.)

Personalized Mailings

Using your real estate contact manager program gives your mass mailings a greater impact than other types of mailings. With the contact manager you can use the "merge codes" to personalize each of the letters or cards you send to a group. A merge code is a special instruction inserted into a document that brings into the document information from a particular field in each record selected for the mailing. For example:

Dear <First Name>:

Just wanted to thank you for being a client of mine and remind you that tax season is approaching. If you need help filing for your homestead tax exemptions, please let me know.

All of the finished letters will have the first name from your chosen database field in the proper place.

Reminders

Another fun feature of contact management software is the ability to set reminders for specific events. You can set a reminder of a client's birthday, anniversary of a home sale, or any other important date. If you send a birthday card, use this script in the body of the card:

> **"You're not getting older, you're building equity!!!"**

A good way to learn someone's birthday is to ask, "What month and day were you born?" Ask slowly, and never ask for the year. People will respond to you much better than if you simply ask for their birth date. You can set the reminder to remind you on an annual basis. (Smart real estate salespersons can also use this function to remind them of their *OWN* wedding anniversary.)

Notes

An interactive contact manager allows you to take notes regarding a person, listing, or closing and to attach the notes as a permanent part of the individual's record. You can print these notes at any time. These notes form an important part of your business "paper trail" for each transaction.

Reports

The contact manager software can produce a variety of reports for your use. You can print the latest activity for a listing and mail it to the seller as a progress report. You can print a report detailing the year's expenses for tax purposes. Several reports are generic to most software. Some software programs will allow you to integrate the local MLS data for custom listing presentation reports.

Computers

When you mention the word "technology," most people think about computers. Virtually every facet of our lives has some computerized component. The appliances in our homes have microprocessors built into them, as do our televisions. Even our cars have computers. But the computer that everyone thinks of first is typically the personal computer (PC).

Personal Computers

A PC is a general-purpose tool built around a microprocessor. It has lots of different parts, such as memory, a hard disk, a modem, that work together. "General purpose" means you can do many different things with a PC. You can use it to type documents, send e-mail, browse the Web, and play games.

How Computers Help in Real Estate

Computers help us access information and use databases in ways that streamline what used to take hours of work. I can remember spending a couple of hours putting together a listing presentation. Today, that same information can be produced by one of the real estate software programs in 10 to 15 minutes and the presentation is more comprehensive. Yet, I still see many agents who aren't using this time-saving tool.

Your computer allows you access to e-mail and get the word out to the folks that count! Ten percent of the agents in your area probably sell 90 percent of the homes, so compile an e-mail list of these sales associates so that you can get the word out when you have a listing. Get the sales associates' permission to add them to your e-mail list, and then e-mail them photos of the listing. If you have an open house, e-mail these people in advance or, better yet, invite them to view the virtual tour of the home on your Web site.

Laptop Computers

Many real estate salespeople are considering buying a laptop computer instead of a desktop computer. Today's laptops have just as much, or more, computing power as desktop computers, without taking up as much space. You can take a laptop on the road with you for computing or making presentations. Perhaps you prefer working comfortably by the pool instead of sitting at a desk. Maybe a laptop is for you.

How Laptops are Like Desktops

For the most part, laptops have the same major parts as desktops:

- Microprocessor
- Operating system
- Solid-state memory
- Disk drives
- Input/output ports
- Sound cards and speakers

Other laptop features include:

- Some laptops have more than one bay built into the case for disk drives.
- Some laptops have one bay that you can swap or interchange various with drives to use either floppy disks or CD-ROMs. You just pull one drive out and put another in.
- Some laptops have no internal drives. All drives are external and connected to the computer by cables. This feature allows the laptop to be very small and thin. To avoid the hassle of all those cables, a docking station lets you slide the laptop into the docking station and work on it like you would a desktop without having to plug in cables. Computers need to talk to other devices, such as printers, modems, and networks.

How Laptops Differ from Desktops

Laptops differ from desktops in the following features:

- Power supply
- Displays
- Input devices
- Docking connections

Like desktops, laptops can be plugged into the wall to receive AC power from the electric power through an AC adapter. But what makes the laptop unique is that it is portable; so, batteries also power laptops.

Modern laptop computers have 800 × 600 pixel resolution, which makes for a clear screen; anything less than this resolution should be avoided.

For a desktop computer, you typically use a keyboard and mouse to enter data. However, because using a mouse takes up room, other devices are built into laptops to take its place. Laptops come with one of three input devices:

- **Track-ball**—rotating the ball allows you to move the cursor on the LCD screen.
- **Track-point**—pushing your finger over the point allows you to move the cursor.
- **Touch-pad**—moving your finger across the pad allows you to move the cursor.

All of these devices have buttons that act like the right and left buttons on a mouse. Also, most laptops include a port for hooking up a mouse if you wish.

Personal Digital Assistant (PDA)

PDAs fall into two major categories: hand-held computers and palm-sized computers. The major differences between the two are size, display, and mode of data entry. Compared to palm-sized computers, hand-held computers tend to be larger and heavier. They have larger liquid crystal displays (LCD) and use miniature keyboards, usually in combination with touch-screen technology, for data entry. Palm-sized computers are smaller and lighter. They have smaller LCDs and rely on stylus/touch-screen technology and handwriting recognition programs for data entry.

Regardless of the type of PDA, they all share the same major features:

- Microprocessor
- Operating system
- Solid-state memory
- Batteries
- LCD display

- Input device or buttons in combination with touch-screen or keyboard
- Input/output ports
- Desktop PC software

Like standard desktop and laptop computers, PDAs are powered by micro-processors. The microprocessor is the brain of the PDA and coordinates all of the PDA's functions according to programmed instructions. Unlike desk and laptop PCs, PDAs use smaller, cheaper microprocessors.

A PDA doesn't have a hard drive. It stores basic programs (address book, calendar, memo pad, and operating system) in a read-only memory (ROM) chip, which remains intact even when the machine shuts down. Your data and any programs you add later are stored in the device's ROM. This approach has several advantages over standard PCs. When you turn on the PDA, all your programs are instantly available. You don't have to wait for applications to load. When you make changes to a file, the changes are stored automatically, so you don't need a Save command. And when you turn the device off, the data is still safe, because the PDA continues to draw a small amount of power from the batteries. The PDA's power can be recharged by setting the device in its charger.

Battery life can vary from two hours to two months depending upon the PDA model and its features. If the batteries do run completely down, most PDAs lose all their data, which makes backing up a PDA on a desktop or a laptop extremely important.—*How Personal Digital Assistants (PDAs) Work,* by Craig Freudenrich, Ph.D.

How PDAs Help in Real Estate

- Coordinate and manage your schedule and contacts.
- Remind you about important meetings through an alarm system.
- Ensure all of your important numbers are with you at all times.
- Track your commissions.
- Track your tax liabilities and deductions.
- Track comments and problems that arise in real estate situations.
- Keep notes on property inspections.

- Draw floor plans at the listing.
- Minimize handling and potential information loss.
- Store all of your lock box serial numbers and codes.
- Track the hours you have accumulated in Continuing Education and how many hours you still need to complete for your license renewal.
- Maximize customer service and business efficiency, which in turn provides sales opportunity and improved profits.
- Carry with you detailed property information.

Digital Cameras

The digital camera is truly different from its predecessor. Conventional cameras depend entirely on chemical and mechanical processes–you don't even need electricity to operate one. All digital cameras have built-in computers, and all of them record images in an entirely electronic form.

The key difference between a digital camera and a film-based camera is that the digital camera has no film. Instead, it has a sensor that converts light into electrical charges and displays images on a screen like a computer.

The amount of detail that the camera can capture is called the resolution, and it is measured in pixels. The more pixels your camera has, the more detail it can capture.

Some typical resolutions that you find in digital cameras today include:

- **256 × 256 pixels**—You find this resolution on older or less expensive cameras. This resolution is so low that the picture quality is almost always unacceptable. This is 65,000 total pixels.
- **640 × 480 pixels**—This is the low-end on most "real" cameras. This resolution is great if you plan to e-mail your clients pictures of your latest listings or post them on a Web site. This is 307,000 total pixels.
- **1216 × 912 pixels**—If you are planning to print your images, this is a good resolution. This is a 11 mega-pixel image size—1,109,000 total pixels.

- **1600 × 1200 pixels**—This is "high resolution." Images taken with this resolution can be printed in larger sizes, such as 8 × 10 inches, with good results. This is almost 2 million total pixels.

If you take pictures in JPEG format at 640 × 480 resolution, you can download them to your computer and e-mail them to your real estate buddies without having to do anything to the picture. There's no need to get film developed or scan the developed picture. Just take the picture, transfer it to the computer, and e-mail it.

You may or may not need lots of resolution, depending on what you want to do with your pictures. If you are planning to do nothing more than display images on a Web page or send them in e-mail, then using 640 × 480 resolution has several advantages:

- Your camera's memory will hold more images at this low resolution than at higher resolutions.
- It will take less time to move the images from the camera to your computer.
- The images will take up less space on your computer.

On the other hand, if your goal is to print large images, you definitely want to take high-resolution shots and you need a camera with lots of pixels. —*How Digital Cameras Work* by Karim Nice and Gerald-Jay Gurevich.

How Digital Cameras Help in Real Estate

One of the best aspects of a digital camera is adding photographs directly into your laptop listing presentation. Can you imagine the seller's excitement when seeing his or her home on the listing presentation you are giving? You can have professional graphics of the seller's home with a picture already on your computer ready for print. All you need is the seller's authorization to get started.

You can take panoramic shots of a property for a wide-angle view. Some cameras allow you to take multiple photos and then put them together (stitching) into one final image that is actually wider than a computer screen. The customer can pan across to see the full image.

Use digital cameras to involve prospects that seem interested in the home. If you have someone who starts expressing interest in a home, offer to let him or her use your digital camera to take photos. Tell them you'll e-mail the photos to them and that they'll be waiting for them when they get home.

Technology "To Have" List

Rather than thinking about buying all the technology you need at once, you probably need to start thinking about it as an ongoing investment and budget accordingly. Successful businesspeople invest in education, marketing, and technology on a continual basis. Like it or not, technology is an ever-growing part of our future in real estate, and the future is not something you buy all at once or only one time.

The amount you invest every year depends on where you are on the technology curve right now, where you want to be, and when you want to be there. As a rule of thumb, I'd suggest you budget at least 10 percent of your income for technology-related items to build your business.

Here are some suggestions on what to put on your list. The most important to your career are listed first, but depending on your needs you must determine what is best for you.

- Laptop computer
- Real estate management software
- Seller and buyer presentation programs
- Digital camera
- Personal Digital Assistant (PDA)
- Broadband Internet access
- Scanner
- Personal Web site
- Portable printer
- Business mobile telephone with voice mail (not for personal use)
- Home office fax machine
- Home office copy machine
- Professional print capabilities

Responsible Use of Technology

Technology gives greater access to people and places, and with greater access comes greater power. Greater powers brings with it responsibility. No one likes junk mail–either in print or electronic form. Ask for clients' permission before adding their e-mail addresses to your contacts list; otherwise, they may consider your message unwanted or what is known as "spam." Ask for the seller's permission (preferably in writing) before taking a digital picture of his or her house and putting it on your Web site. Otherwise they may feel like their privacy has been violated, and that's no way to build client trust.

Chapter Summary

For more direct and updated information on the latest trends in technology and products, use the Internet. If you do not know how to use the Internet, you need to learn. Technology should support you, not the other way around. Do not buy the latest gadget just to have gadgets. Don't buy a product unless it will work for you. Be tech smart.

Summary Questions

1. What is the best way to track your leads?
    A. Don't have any leads; then you don't have this problem.
    B. Write them on pieces of paper.
    C. Enter them into a computer database.
    D. By memory.

2. Which of the following number of pixels offers the best in resolution from a digital camera?
    A. 65,000 pixels
    B. 307,000 total pixels
    C. 1,109,000 total pixels
    D. 2 million pixels

3. Which of the following is not a laptop input device?
    A. Track-ball
    B. Think-pad
    C. Track-point
    D. Touch-pad

4. What is the purpose of the real estate contact management software?
   A. To organize data on all of your people, listings, and closings.
   B. To teach management skills to brokers.
   C. To confuse real estate salespeople.
   D. To run an office from home.

5. Examples of searches in a typical database include which of the following?
   A. High-priority prospects.
   B. Buyers looking for a house in a certain price range.
   C. Buyers looking for a house in a certain neighborhood.
   D. Members in your sphere of influence.

Chapter 4

Psychology of
Marketing

Chapter Objectives

Marketing is putting something out there and hoping someone will buy it. The chapter focuses on the psychology of marketing in real estate sales. You will learn to determine a person's needs and how the individual processes those needs.

Key Words

Behavior: The actions or reactions of persons or things in response to external or internal stimuli.

Ego: The division of the psyche that is conscious, most immediately controls thought and behavior.

Enthusiasm: Great excitement for or interest in a subject or cause.

Physical: Of or relating to the body as distinguished from the mind or spirit.

Profit: An advantageous gain or return.

Social: Living together in communities.

Spiritual: Of, concerned with, or affecting the soul.

Introduction

Marketing has changed drastically in the last few years. We now must analyze not only the service we provide but we must analyze the client also. The real estate business is made up of many different aspects, but the main thing you sell is you. A buyer will buy with or without you. Your job is to have the buyer buy that house through you. The same applies to sellers.

The following are some tips for strengthening yourself as a salesperson.

Get tough with yourself. Real estate success demands hard work and lots of hours. Make a commitment to yourself to succeed; it's not as difficult as it may seem once you make a firm, unalterable decision to do it. You must learn to schedule your time and discipline yourself.

Don't fear the competition, because the only true competition you have is yourself. When I teach students often ask me if I hold back the really good information for myself. The answer is no. The reason is that the only competition I have is myself. Real estate isn't a "limited pie" business. There is enough business for all of us. If I ever need more money all I have to do is work harder and more money appears. I don't fear competition, I don't fear the economy, and I don't fear the end of humankind. I know the only thing I can control is myself and if I do that, well, I win.

You need to abandon old ways and be open to new things. You don't just "go to" work or work slowly and still get paid. My dad got in the business at the same time I did, although he never figured out real estate sales. One day I saw him cleaning up his desk and putting things in his briefcase. When I asked what he was doing, he said it was time to go. It was only 4:55 p.m. He was still on corporate business time. In this industry, the best hours to work are the hours when others are off work. You have to devote more time to real estate than you have devoted to any job you've ever had, but it's different, you're working for yourself! I never thought much about minor holidays or weekends. Those days off are for the working stiffs. We salespeople might have to work them because that is when our client is available for previewing prospective homes to purchase. But remember, it is always *our* choice to work or not.

Get yourself in the right frame of mind to succeed. You must develop and maintain a good attitude or you won't survive. Attitude is infectious. If it's bad it will destroy your best efforts. Top producers are enthusiastic about their careers!

You must discover procedures that produce results and then follow them over and over again, day after day until you become so good at your career no one will be able to compete with you. Don't give up on real estate if you do not make a sale in the first month. If you combine perseverance with singleness of purpose and you continue learning, you cannot fail. I am frequently asked for one word that describes success in the real estate business. That word is persistence.

The one overriding factor to your success confidence. You're a licensed professional in the business of selling homes. Look on a listing as a contest, one in which you, the listing agent, will be victorious, because you can anticipate the owners' moves before they make them and you know what to do to counter each objection. As a professional, everything is in your favor. You know what you're talking about. You have a broad perspective of the market.

If you don't know something when asked, you can go out and find an answer. I find that the number one reason that new real estate salespeople fail is the fear that they will be asked something and they will not know the answer.

Hint: Doing something is better than doing nothing.

Always be proud of yourself. Think of what you have done to get where you are right now.

- You made the initial decision to get into real estate and you did it. Many people think about changing careers, but most never get farther than dreaming.
- You studied hard to take the licensing exam.
- You took the exam and passed it. (If you haven't yet you will.)
- You survived office training.
- You bought this book and are reading it.
- You are in the real estate business for yourself.
- You are demonstrating courage calling a potential client.
- You are prepared for the call because of the knowledge and information that you have gained.

Be proud of yourself and your accomplishments. You can only sell what you believe in, so believe in yourself.

You have to like to compete with others to do well in real estate. You have to make a firm commitment to outlist everyone! It's part of getting tough with yourself. Make up your mind to get more listings than anyone else. There's no reason you can't. Perseverance alone will eliminate most of your competition. Ultimately you are your only real competition; however, competition with others is fun and challenging.

Last but not least, you must generate enthusiasm. People like to do business with enthusiastic people. Enthusiasm makes people interesting. I once went on a field training exercise with a new real estate salesperson to his first listing appointment. While I was thinking about the weather, that I needed to wash the car, and whether the Dallas Cowboys would win the football game on Sunday, the new salesperson was literally shaking from his enthusiasm. I miss that.

Do you want to beat the top listing salespeople of the industry? Then be more enthusiastic. A thorough professional licensee who knows the real estate business and is excited about how it benefits his or her clients is someone people want to work with.

Reasons Buyers Buy

A good salesperson understands human behavior and the emotional and physical reasons that motivates buyers to buy. The four basic needs of human behavior include physical, social, ego, and spiritual needs. The more you know about your customer, the better you can tailor your sales approach and inventory to fit your buyer's needs.

Reasons Sellers Sell

Sellers typically sell because they want a change. A multitude of sellers will stay in the same general area. Yes, the list provided in the "Reasons Buyers Buy" section of this book also applies to sellers. Sellers are motivated by greed in that they want the most for their houses that they can get. Is that a surprise? I will address the motivations of sellers in the objection handling section of this book.

Chapter Summary

In this chapter we studied the average consumer's buying motives. Each marketing effort should be targeted to the specific group you are trying to reach. Probably the best marketing is through public relations stories in the local newspapers. These cost no money and carry a lot of meaning.

Summary Question

1. Which of the following is not one of the four basic needs human seek to fulfill?
   A. Physical
   B. Ego
   C. Social
   D. Sensual

Chapter 5

Marketing & Advertising

Chapter Objectives

The main objectives of this chapter are to gain an understanding of how marketing and advertising affect real estate. You will understand marketing strategies, learn how to write an effective real estate ad, and learn how to avoid the pitfalls of the legal aspects of advertising and marketing.

Key Words

Advertising: The activity of attracting public attention to a product as by paid announcements in print or on the air

Marketing: The commercial functions involved in transferring goods from seller to buyer.

Networking: An informal system whereby persons having common interests assist each other, as in the development of professional contacts

Introduction

Marketing is the overall concept of offering a property for sale to the general public. Good marketing reaches more people than if nothing is done. However, poor marketing reaches no one and is a waste of money. The more people who know a property is available, the better chance the property has of selling for the most money in the fastest amount of time. Marketing does not sell an overpriced property but it will help sell properties that are priced correctly. Advertising is just one aspect of marketing but it is probably the most recognizable.

Personal Marketing Strategies

A marketing strategy is your overall marketing direction. It should guide you in your decision making for spending money and time. Your marketing strategy should include projections for what you want to accomplish by marketing. It should be written out in detail but contain very little in numbers and finite dates. Those items will be included in your marketing plan.

McDonald's dominates the fast-food market. The main reason they are the leader is because they recognized their client is actually the children when it comes to choosing where the family will eat. McDonald's strategy is to specialize in what the decision-maker wants most, and in the case of children it's a hamburger, French fries, and soda.

McDonald's targets advertising to children, and it works.

Personal Marketing Plan

The marketing plan should organize your marketing strategy. A compete stranger should be able to pick up your marketing plan and understand all aspects of it.

Detail each step of the plan with exacting standards. (Analyze each step to determine its purpose and whether it aligns with the overall marketing strategy. If it does not, delete it or rework it until it fits with the plan.) Include beginning and ending dates with each step, as well as costs and contact people. If you are directly involved in any step, your time needs to be analyzed.

Also include all types of promotion, marketing, and advertising in your marketing plan. These may be planned promotional events, direct mail campaigns, or advertising in your local newspaper. If you do advertise you will need to separate name recognition advertising from prospect generating advertising.

Finally, compare the entire marketing plan to your what your competition is doing.

Name Recognition vs. Prospect Generating

Name recognition is the type of advertising that gets people to know your name and what you do. The objective of name recognition advertising is not to make a prospect call you on the telephone. That is the purpose of prospect generating advertising.

These two efforts are often misconceived. For example, a billboard ad may say, "Call me at 817-555-1212." We think this is prospect generating advertising, but it is not–even though you might get a call. Your pretty face plastered on a billboard will help people get to know your face, your name, and what you do.

Name recognition advertising is critical in making your job easier, but it takes a long time to work and it is expensive. Most national real estate companies spend millions per year on name recognition advertising. Some examples include television advertising, radio advertising, bus stop benches, airplane trailer banners, personal brochures, shopping cart cards, name badges, career apparel, and car signs.

Prospect generating advertising is meant to make the telephone ring. Ads showing houses for sale in the newspaper make the phone ring. If you are on a limited budget, consider concentrating on prospect generating advertising to get the most for your money and let your company worry about name recognition advertising. Other examples of prospect generating advertising include listing yourself in telephone directories, sending direct mail, installing yard "for sale" signs, and passing out your business cards.

Determining which type of advertising is right for you will be part of your marketing strategy.

Writing Effective Advertising

Before preparing ad copy, analyze the property and identify its features and benefits. Decide who your target buyer might be.

In addition to your personal appeal, which is critical to the success of your ad, every classified ad should carry the reader through four selling steps. These steps are Attention, Interest, Desire, and Action, or AIDA, as they are known through the advertising community.

1. **ATTRACT ATTENTION.** You need to catch the prospects' attention with the first few words of your ad or your will lose them forever. A catchy headline may do the trick. In fact, the headline is probably the

most important part of your ad. Other tips for attracting attention include:

- Use sincerity, not clichés.
- Include the price. People shop by price. If you feel including price is a problem, try running the ad without it. Always document your results to determine the best use of your money.
- Use a lot of white space (that space where nothing is written). White space in print advertising attracts attention to your ad.
- Occasionally ask questions in your ad. People have a natural tendency to be attracted to questions.

2. **AROUSE INTEREST.** Once you've got a reader's attention, use the interest stage to pull him or her in for further reading. Otherwise the prospect will stop reading and move on to the next ad. Create interest and desire with features on lower-priced properties and with benefits and emotions on higher-priced properties.

3. **CREATE DESIRE.** This stage creates desire. In your case, the desire to have the property. Writing skill here is necessary to create the right atmosphere for the prospect. If space is available list the property's most desirable features so the prospects will able to see themselves living in that house. Anything less and you will not receive a phone call.

4. **CALL FOR ACTION.** To get the sale, you must ask for the sale. Ads are written and sold exactly the same way. In ad writing you must ask for the call.
   A. Research has found that you will receive a greater response if you close the ad with a request to call, using your full name. Be active. Tell your readers to "Call now!"
   B. Research has found that by using the word "please," the close is softened and greater response occurs. So please call for action in your ads.

If your ad copy tells all the essential facts clearly, holds the reader's attention from start to finish, and makes a specific call to action, it will be successful. The following is a checklist for writing the ad:

1. Organize all the facts from the viewpoint of the reader, not your own. Buyers are looking for pictures of houses not information about you.
2. Appeal to emotions, for example: love of comfort, status, and family responsibility, etc. The higher the price, the more emotional the buy;

> **Buyers are looking for real estate houses not real estate salespeople.**
>
> *—Luella Blaylock, Manager, Real Estate Office*

the lower the price, the more practical the buy. The higher the price, the more emotions you place in the ad; the lower the price, the more features you list in the ad.

3. Keep It Simple and Short (KISS). Avoid long-winded sentences; however, do not abbreviate or use real estate jargon. If it is important enough to put in an ad it is important enough to spell out. Sometimes we get so close to real estate and we forget what it is like to be a consumer, so create the ad from another direction. Remember that mini-pick-up truck I wanted to buy? I noted some newspaper ads would include "OBO" at the end. I wondered what a musical instrument had to do with buying a truck? O.K., so I knew they were not talking about a musical instrument, but I really did not know what the letters "OBO" meant. Guess what? I never called on those ads. I may have missed out on buying the best truck but I would not call and be embarrassed by my lack of knowledge. I have a friend with a used car lot so I asked him about "OBO." He got a big laugh and told me it means "Or Best Offer." My point is don't eliminate your potential client by using cute abbreviations because a potential buyer might not know their meaning.

4. Use meaningful words that stir emotion. Make the readers "smell" the steaks "sizzling" on the grill or feel the "cool" water across their skin when they jump into their new swimming pool.

5. Inspire confidence. Don't use overexaggerated descriptions that are not believable.

6. Avoid clichés and overused words, such as "super," "great," "Mrs. Clean lives here," and "Gingerbread house," etc.

7. Sellers buy people and buyers buy houses.

8. Differentiate your marketing. Advertise for three different markets:
   A. To get buyers and sellers.
   B. To get other real estate salespeople.

C. For self-promotion (normally to get listings, except for buyers brokers). Ads should never be written to satisfy a seller.

9. People first select housing by price, then they eliminate properties by comparing features and benefits.

10. A majority of buyers shop price first, then area, and then physical attributes of the property.

11. Describe the most saleable feature in the headline. If the house is located in the most desirable part of town, say so. If it is a bargain, say so.

12. Stick to the truth. Misleading advertising is illegal and unethical.

13. Finish with a call to action: "Call today" or "Call now." Follow this with a phone number that is answered during the day.

14. If you want to use a slogan, keep it at seven words or less or it becomes counterproductive. For even better results, keep the slogan to three words or less.

15. An average person retains 1 percent of what he or she sees each day. An average person inherently mistrusts and sometimes fears things and people that are not familiar.

16. Advertising campaigns should appear no less than weekly for a minimum of three months.

17. Consider these additional points:
    - Do people like your ad?
    - Is your ad memorable?
    - Does your ad give you personality?
    - Does your ad provide a simple message?

R. J. Wrigley commented on advertising:

> "Tell them quick and tell them often. You must have a good product in the first place and something that people want, for it is easier to row downstream than up. Explain to folks plainly and sincerely what you have to sell, do it in as few words as possible, and keep everlastingly coming at them."

Research has found that the more meaningful the message the more it is received. Research has also found that there is an inverse relationship to the amount of messages in any given ad to its results. Here are a few things that get attention:

> **Babies, animals, old news photos, odd situations**
>
> **Most popular color: Red and Blue**
>
> **Most associated item in the home: Couch or Chair**

Once an ad has run, you should do the following:

1. Change the ad layout and words each time you rerun it. You don't want a potential buyer to skip over your ad because he or she has seen it before. Maybe a different message will spark a potential buyer to call.

2. Experiment with features of the ad. If it ain't workin' change it!

3. Document the calls received with each change. This will track the correct changes and the ones that did not work. Don't make the same mistake twice.

Fair Housing Law Guidelines

Fair housing laws were passed to be sure that everyone has the same right to buy and rent real property as everyone else. The law does not look at your intent. Do your actions indicate a discriminatory behavior?

Race, Color, National Origin

When running an advertisement for real estate, the salesperson must be sure not to indicate any preference to a group of people based on their race, color, or national origin. Advertisements that indicate a "type" of person that the particular property would suit (based on any protected class) would be a violation. Phrases such as "master bedroom," "rare find," or "desirable neighborhood" are not in violation.

Religion

Advertisements should not indicate a preference for any religion or religious reference to direct members of that protected class to or away from a piece of property. An advertisement that reads, "down the street from a Catholic Church" could be a violation.

Sex (Gender)

Advertisements cannot indicate a preference for or exclusion of persons based on their gender. Advertisements that offer a multiunit apartment for lease for "women only" could violate the law.

Handicap

Real estate advertisements should not show bias against a person with a handicap. Describing a property's amenities like, "great for lovers of tennis" would not violate the act.

Familial Status

Familial status refers to the members of a family, especially those members under the age of eighteen. Advertisements may not state a preference or exclusion, based on the number or ages of children, or state a preference for adults, couples, or singles.

Fair Housing Law Guidelines for Acceptable Wording

The following words will not violate the law if they are used in advertising.

Close to downtown, schools, generic places

One-bedroom apartment

Den

Family room

No smoking/drinking

Number of bedrooms

Play area

Private setting

Privacy

School district

Secluded

Security provided

Seniors (property must meet HUD [Housing and Urban Development] guidelines for senior housing)

Square footage

Townhouse

Traditional (style of home)

View

Walking distance to . . .

Questionable Wording

55 and older (property must meet HUD guidelines)

Older persons

Executive

Female roommate

Male roommate

Neighborhood

Remember: Describe the property, not the seller, landlord, or appropriate buyers and tenants.

Unacceptable Wording

Adult (adult building, adult park, etc.)	Adults only/Adults preferred
Age, any specification	Bachelor/Bachelor pad
Any use of girl, lady, or woman	Any use of boy, guy or man
Black	(Blank) need not apply
Blind	Board approval
Catholic church	Christian

Couple (couples preferred, only, etc.)	Crippled
Deaf	Drinker(s)
Ethnic landmarks	Executive, exclusive
Family	Female
Gentleman's farm, ranch, etc.	Grandmas' house
Gender (except ads for roommates)	Handicap limitations
Hispanic	Integrated
Jewish	Male/Man
Marital status	Mature or mature person
Membership approval	Mentally handicapped/ Mentally ill
Mormon temple	Name of school
Nationality (Oriental, Hispanic, etc.)	No children
No family problems	No play area
Number of people	Older person
One child	Oriental
Perfect for 2	Physically fit (ideal for, limited to)
Private, private community	Race
Religious landmark	Religious name
Restricted	Retired
Senior citizen, senior discount	Sex
Single, single person	Smoker(s)
Traditional (settings)	Two people
Unattached (referring to personal relationship)	White woman
Words descriptive of landlords or tenants	Young, energetic person

Ads that Comply with REG Z

The Truth-in-Lending Act (REG Z) was enacted in 1969 to "assure the meaningful disclosure of credit terms so that the consumer will be able to compare more readily the various credit terms available to him to avoid the uniformed use of credit." The Act refers to the fact that advertisers must tell the public all details of financing if certain "trigger" words are used. For fixed-rate loans if you advertise any of the following loan terms you must also advertise the rest of the terms:

I. Annual percentage rate

II. Simple interest rate

III. Down payment

IV. Monthly payment

V. Loan term (length)

REG Z only applies to the advertising on one- and two-unit residential real property.

REG Z only applies to advertising where the potential consumer will use the property as a principal dwelling.

Personal Marketing

Personal marketing is marketing yourself rather than the real estate company you work for. Be sure to follow local laws and directions of your broker in respect with personal marketing.

Business Cards

If you do not have or have run out of business cards, you are no longer in the real estate business. This is the backbone of business communication. Order your business cards as soon as possible and reorder before you run out.

How the business card is laid out is of personal interest but it should include your picture and should not be too "busy." What I mean by that is do not have little words all over and only provide two main contact numbers.

I have seen business cards that have the salesperson's office number, home number, cell phone number, voice mail number, personal fax number, office fax number, a Web page, and e-mail address. I know the salesperson wanted to be hip having so many ways to be contacted, but it became "busy" and intimidating.

Use the business card at all times. Give one to everyone you meet. Set a number of cards you want to pass out a day. Mine was fifteen, which doesn't sound like much until you factor in that you must give the card only to someone you have not given one to in the past. You start dreaming of people to give cards to . . . neighbors, relatives, etc. I even gave one to a policeman that was writing me a speeding ticket. Another rule I made for myself was that if anyone took my money they took my business card. This means every time you eat lunch the waiter gets your business card. When you are grocery shopping the checker gets your card. When you mail your monthly bills you should include a business card in each envelope. I went to fill my car with gasoline and when I paid I left my business card. I handed the clerk my card and he bought a house through me. How's that? I gave him $13 (back when you could fill-up for $13!) for gas and he gave me $1,300 for a real estate sale.

When you hold an open house, make up special business cards for the open. Do a business card with your standard information on one side and a photo and information about the home on the other side.

Another idea is to put financing information for buying the home on the reverse.

Personal Brochures

Personal brochures are usually tri-fold type letters that introduce yourself and your accomplishments. Use these sparingly. Their cost prohibits mass mail-outs. Instead, send them to any appointments you may have and leave them with anyone you talk to about real estate. The difference between a brochure and a business card is that everyone gets your business card and only serious prospects get your personal brochure.

You can create a personal brochure using your personal computer, if you have that capability. Be sure that if you do it yourself you do it well. A cheap brochure means a cheap real estate salesperson. There are companies that will create personal brochures for you, but the cost is high.

Networking

Networking is meeting of people for the purpose of spreading business contacts. If you are in real estate and you meet someone who sells new cars, you should put that person in your network. If you sell someone a house and he mentions that he will buy a new car, refer that person to your new contact and vice versa. Join any networking groups that you can. These groups sponsor events where the only purpose is to meet people. This is not "network marketing" where people try to sell you something, so be careful. It is also not a dating service, so stick to business. This is also called sphere of influence (SOI) marketing. It is mentioned here as a marketing technique.

Public Relations

Public relations is getting the media to notice you in a positive light. Your objective is to get media attention at least once a month. When a newspaper writes an article on one of your achievements it becomes truth to the reader. If you pay for an ad, the consumer discounts that because it was paid for.

Submit weekly public relations stories to the newspaper. The worst that could happen is the article is not used. Newspaper people need to fill in sections of their papers with stories. If you have stories handy for them, they might use them to complete the newspaper.

The stories you submit can be on virtually any subject. For instance, I once submitted a story on how our real estate office rescued a kitten that was trapped. No kidding, it made the front-page news complete with pictures. It sounds silly, but we got many calls thanking us for our kindness and concern. Here are some other suggestions for PR stories:

- New associate in the office
- Top listing salesperson
- Top selling salesperson

- High-dollar listing
- Any charity event
- Any award or recognition received

You never know what will be used or rejected; your job is to submit.

Chapter Summary

Marketing is in almost every area of real estate. We cover it throughout this book, and this chapter covers the parts of marketing not mentioned elsewhere.

Summary Questions

1. What do the letters AIDA stand for in the advertising community?
   A. Alternate Institutional Diversified Advertising
   B. Absolute, Individual, Demand, Actual
   C. Attention, Interest, Desire, Action
   D. AIDS Association

2. When you write an ad, what should you do?
   A. Change the ad layout and words each time run.
   B. Experiment with features of the ad.
   C. Document the calls received with each change.
   D. All of the above.

Chapter 6

Law of Agency and Alternative Representative Agreements

Chapter Objectives

This chapter is an introduction to real estate agency law. While you may obtain further details from other sources, our objective is to keep agency law on the forefront of your mind as you work your real estate career.

In this chapter you will learn about representative agreements that are not used regularly in the real estate industry. Whether you actually use these agreements is not as important as is the knowledge of their existence.

Key Words

Agency: A business or person authorized to act for others.

Alternative: Espousing or reflecting values that are different from those of the establishment.

Broker: One who acts as an agent for others.

Client: The party for which professional services are rendered.

Customer: The purchaser of goods and services.

Dual: Having a double character or purpose.

Representation: The act of representing. To stand for.

Retainer: The fee paid to retain a professional adviser.

Law of Agency

Introduction

Agency law is common law, meaning it applies to everyone. We tend to look at agency law only from the aspects of real estate. Sometimes we get more insight by looking at law from the lawyer's point of view. Attorneys know who their clients are. Both parties know whom they're working with. The attorneys spend a great deal of effort making sure their clients know about how they are being represented. We in real estate should do the same. We should disclose to interested parties our agency relationships.

Agency Relationships

An agency relationship exists when one person or business acts on behalf of another person or business. In real estate, an agency relationship typically involves a broker who acts on behalf of a seller. The broker is the agent, and the seller is the principal.

The purpose of the arrangement is for the broker to find a buyer and arrange the sale of the property on behalf of the seller. A similar arrangement exists when a broker acts on behalf of a landlord to find a tenant. The broker can also act on behalf of a buyer. In this respect, the broker finds a house for the buyer. This is called a "buyer's brokerage."

Brokers who help tenants find space or housing are called "tenant reps" in commercial situations, "apartment locators" for finding apartments, and a buyer's broker when finding houses for tenants. Tenant reps are extremely common in major cities for larger commercial lease spaces of around 10,000 square feet or more.

Only brokers (and attorneys) are paid commission directly by the seller, buyer, or principal. Salespeople are not required to become brokers. In practice, a real estate firm is often set up as a corporation, which holds a broker's license in its own name, and the corporation, as a broker, sponsors and holds the licenses of its salespeople.

Duties Brokers Owe to Clients

There are certain duties a broker owes to a client, including the duty of reasonable care, the duty of obedience, the duty of loyalty, the duty of accounting, and the duty of notice. These duties are obligations of the broker, and failure to fulfill any of them can lead to the loss of commission and maybe worse. Key distinctions between duties given to a client versus those given to a customer are advice, opinions, and advocacy. These are general categories with specific duties that include care, obedience, loyalty, accountability, and notice. These five duties form the acronym COLAN.

Care

The duty of reasonable care requires the broker to display reasonable care for his or her clients. This includes but is not limited to:

- Keeping the property secure.
- Keeping the seller from legal harm.
- Pricing the property correctly.
- Filling in the purchase agreement correctly.

Obedience

The duty of obedience requires the broker to follow the lawful instructions of his or her client. This means that if the client directs the broker in a certain direction the broker must follow the client's wishes. The only exception to he duty of obedience is when the client directs the broker to do something that would violate a law.

Loyalty, Fiduciary

The words "loyalty" and "fiduciary" are sometimes used interchangeably. "Fiduciary" loosely translates as "putting the clients' wishes above your own." The salesperson must act in the client's interest even if it would jeopardize a commission. If a seller rejects a risky offer and you insist the seller take it so you will get your commission, this is a violation.

Accountability

You are accountable for your client's money that is involved in the real estate transaction. You must be accountable for any earnest money.

Notice

The duty of notice requires the broker to be informed about the real estate industry and communicate related information to his or her client. It requires the broker to tell the client anything that a reasonable person would find of interest. This includes any negotiating position, environmental concerns, or market analysis.

Office Policies on Agency Relationships

Most real estate commissions require each brokerage company to have a written office policy on how they will deal with agency questions. The following are five typical office policies:

Seller Only

In the "seller only" office the real estate broker and the salespeople all represent the seller only. Under no circumstance would the broker represent the buyer, which is called a traditional agency. A real estate salesperson can work *with* a buyer but cannot work *for* a buyer. The salesperson must treat a customer with honesty, integrity, and expertise.

Buyer Only

In a "buyer only" office, the broker and salespeople only represent buyers, never sellers. A real estate salesperson must follow all applicable laws (agency and state licensing laws) and must follow the lawful direction of the buyer.

Seller Only with Buyer Representation

In "seller only with buyer representation" office policy the broker and salespeople represent the seller only; however, if the buyer does not want a listing held by the broker, the salesperson might show the buyer other property and represent the buyer. Because it is not an in-house transaction, the salesperson is not obligated to represent the seller. If the buyer wants to buy an in-house property, the seller must be represented.

Buyer Only with Seller Representation

In this office the broker and salespeople all represent the buyer. If a seller wants to market his or her house, the listing agent is required to represent the buyer. In other words, if a buyer comes in the office to see the seller's property but decides against buying it, the agency may represent that buyer and show him or her other properties. If a buyer not represented by this company wants to buy the sellers house, this company now can represent the seller.

Intermediary

Under the "intermediary" office policy the broker may act as an agent for both the buyer and the seller, but with reduced representation to both while negotiating a transaction between the parties.

Alternative Representative Agreements

Most real estate representative agreements have real estate salespeople being paid by commission. Here are a few alternative representative agreements and working arrangements. Take a look at each on its own merit. Don't dismiss them without seeing the possibilities. The future of big time real estate income hinges on the real estate broker being open-minded about alternative working arrangements. If you are not the broker, consult with your broker before attempting any of these arrangements. These arrangements are legal but your broker must approve any income and all actions.

Dual Agency

If a broker represents a seller, it is the broker's duty to meet the seller's objective. Generally, the seller is wanting to get the most money for the property, but sometimes achieving a quick sale is more important. If a broker represents a buyer, the broker's duty is to meet the buyer's objective. When a broker represents the seller and the buyer in the same transaction, it is called dual agency. If the broker represents both the buyer and the seller in the same transaction, to whom is the broker ultimately loyal? The broker must disclose this relationship and get approval to move forward in the transaction from both principals. This type of agency is rarely used in today's market because of the inherent conflict of interest.

Nonagency

A nonagency relationship is one that allows a real estate broker or salesperson to work with a buyer or seller, providing administration-level assistance, but not offer any representation. Some other terms that are synonymous with nonagency are consultant, counselor, facilitator, and transactional broker.

Not too many customers want to pay a real estate professional if that person is not representing them. Why pay for nonagency when you can get full representation for the same money? I do see a place for nonagency and that is if you are to do limited service. For example, if you were to do a fee-or-service type transaction (discussed later) you would need to be a nonagent.

I was a nonagent once. I received a call from a "For Sale By Owner" who disclosed that she had found a buyer. She asked if I would do the paperwork for a percent of the transaction. I agreed. I met the buyer and seller at the seller's house. I brought out the purchase agreement and looked at the buyer. "In what name would you like to take title?" About twenty minutes later I had signatures on the agreement and was out the door. I made about $800 for 20 minutes work, not bad. In this case I represented neither party and only did the paperwork. The reason I could not represent the seller is because that representation meant more than I agreed to do. Generally we do not hear of nonagency because it is usually reserved for high-dollar properties–in the millions of dollars. No one cares about paying a hundred thousand dollars for the advice of a real estate counselor on a $40 million housing complex. But there might be trouble paying the same hundred thousand dollars on a single-family property valued at $75,000. A better way to pay for real estate counseling is the "fee for service."

Fee for Service

A fee for service type listing is one in which the seller picks from a smorgasbord of services and only pays for the ones he or she uses. This arrangement works well for sellers who believe they can sell their homes themselves, like "For Sale By Owners" and new home construction (builders). This allows sellers to get what they need and not pay for those things they can do themselves. Several companies' entire businesses are set up under these terms. Sometimes the services are bundled together and sold as packages.

Bonuses

Bonuses, in which the seller agrees to pay a little extra to a cooperating broker for bringing in a buyer, are not new in the real estate business. These are called "bonuses to the selling agent." The name is somewhat misleading, as all monies paid must go through the selling broker, not the agent. In my experience, these can generate a few more showings but I would rather see the seller price the property correctly in the first place. That way no bonus is needed. A properly priced property will sell without any further incentives.

That said, I have seen some great bonuses. The highest percentage I have seen was a $20,000 bonus on an $180,000 sale. Other bonuses I have seen include vacations, cash, and the most unusual: a brand new, cherry-red Lamborghini plus a $135,000 commission ($4.5 million sale).

Transaction Fees

Transaction fees are charged by a broker for expenses incurred in a real estate transaction. The fee usually amounts to a few hundred dollars paid at closing, although some brokers will bill the real estate salespeople if they do not charge the fee. It is somewhat like an origination fee charged by mortgage companies for processing mortgage loans. Real estate salespeople demanding a higher split while wanting the broker to pay more for more and better services are squeezing real estate brokerage firms' profit margins. As a result, transaction fees are higher to offset those costs. Some brokers and state agencies feel that these fees could be more than the client agreed to pay and are unconscionable.

Trades

Trades (when you give real estate services and receive in return something other than money) don't happen often, but twice in my career I have traded for services. Once, I took part of my commission as a timeshare on a lake and another time I traded for legal advice. No trade can be made unless all parties are aware of the cost of the trade and the trade is approved by your broker.

Tote a Note

Occasionally a seller will not have enough equity to pay the entire commission owed on a transaction. Instead of giving away your commission to make the deal work, tote a note. Have the title attorney (most will do this for little or no cost) draw up a promissory note to you for the amount owed.

For example: A seller agrees to pay the listing broker 6 percent of the sales price to sell his house. The listing broker finds a buyer, but at the closing the seller is short $500 for the broker fee. The broker may choose to take a promissory note for the $500. The terms of a note are negotiable but mine are simple: Pay $100 per month until the total amount without interest is paid.

If a seller chooses not to pay me, I won't do a thing. The notes are a promise, nothing more. I have taken notes three times: one was for $700 of which I received $500; another was for $1,500 of which I received $600; and the third note was for $500 of which I received nothing. Ultimately, you deserve your money because you have done your job. Taking a note is one way that could help your bottom line.

Rebates

A rebate is money returned that has already been paid.

I will give a rebate on the listing commission to a seller who guarantees to buy his or her next house through me. There are a couple of criteria before I agree to a rebate. First, the next house the seller buys must be significantly higher in value than the one he or she is selling; and second, the seller pays me *all* of my commission from the sale. It is not until then that I rebate the money. This helps keep the seller honest. It ensures that the only way the seller gets the rebate from me is upon closing of the second house. Some real estate brokers will reduce their listing commission to get the buy side without using a rebate. The problem with that, however, is that there is no incentive for the buyer to remain loyal.

Hourly Fees

Here is a novel idea, charge by the hour. It is interesting that when I ask a class of students for the amount a real estate salesperson is worth per hour, I hear anywhere from $10 to $30. How cheap are we? If I were to work for someone on an hourly basis, I would require $200 per hour. Here's why: I have to support a family and myself. If I work for $20 per hour, what happens when I only work ten billable hours per week? Get it? I go broke! Real estate salespeople do a whole lot of work that isn't actually billable.

Now, I don't believe we should gouge the consumer for our benefits, but we have to live. I also know the consumer might not be too happy paying the salesperson $200 per hour. That's why commissions are the most popular method of payment. The consumer likes paying us only when we perform and we make the money we need to survive.

Let's look into hourly fees in more detail because they can make sense. If a seller wants you to help on an open house but can handle most of the rest of a sale, charging by the hour for the open house makes sense. If a buyer can find a home himself but needs you to help with the contract, charging by the hour for contract writing makes sense. If a builder wants you to be on-site for a new construction property, charging by the hour makes sense. So don't dismiss hourly fees outright without thinking it through first. The best way to ensure you are paid your hourly fee is to charge a retainer fee.

Retainer Fee

A retainer fee is generally thought of as an attorney's fee. It is paid in advance of services rendered, ensuring that the payment is received. In real estate, a buyer pays this fee before the salesperson shows the buyer a house.

Flat Fees

Flat fees are charged in advance. For example, a real estate broker may agree to sell a property for a flat fee of $3,000 regardless of the amount the property actually sells for. A flat fee makes sense if the property is not worth much or if a variable commission would be too confusing.

I once agreed to sell a tract of land for a commission. Out of desperation the seller kept reducing the listing price. By the time the lot was sold the commission was so low that I lost money. I should have charged a flat fee.

Chapter Summary

Be alert to all of the changes in the way a real estate broker can be paid. Do not be afraid of the changes. If you are, then seek out more information to determine what is best for you and your client.

Agency law can be very complex. This introduction into agency law is by no ways intended to be complete. If you feel you need more information about agency law, please seek council from your broker and refer to the back of the book for additional information. Real estate salespeople must be certain of the people they represent. Salespeople must disclose all of their relationships to their clients. Salespeople must give their clients all of the duties (care, obedience, loyalty, accounting, and notice).

Summary Questions

1. What type of agency exists when a broker represents two principals in one transaction?
   A. No agency.
   B. Double agency.
   C. Dual agency.
   D. This type of agency is illegal.

2. A seller agreed to pay a flat fee of $2,000 to a broker on a property that was worth $40,000. The seller took 8 percent less than the sales price. If the seller has $4,900 in additional closing costs, what is the broker's commission?
   A. $1,840
   B. $1,600
   C. $1,355
   D. $2,000

3. A real estate buyer's broker hired to locate a property for a buyer must comply with all of the following except
   A. Lawful instructions of the buyer.
   B. Lawful instructions of the seller.

    C. Law of agency.

    D. State licensing law.

4. Which of the following are key distinctions between the duties given to clients versus customers?

    A. Advice, opinions, and advocacy are given to clients, not customers.

    B. More advice and opinions are offered to customers.

    C. Customers get advice and opinions for free, while clients must pay.

    D. Clients must have a contract to receive services, while customers do not.

5. A real estate broker, acting as an agent for another in a transaction, has a primary duty to:

    A. Get the transaction closed successfully.

    B. Help the parties reach a mutually beneficial agreement.

    C. Treat all parties impartially.

    D. Represent the interests of his or her client.

6. Which of the following is the responsibility of a buyer's agent?

    A. Provide advice on how much money to offer on a property.

    B. Disclose any latent structure defects.

    C. Show the buyer suitable property.

    D. All the above.

7. If you work for the seller, your relationship with a buyer customer is best characterized as:

    A. A fiduciary relationship.

    B. A common law representation relationship.

    C. A caveat emptor relationship.

    D. A relationship of honesty, integrity, and expertise.

Chapter 7

Prospecting for Seller Appointments

Chapter Objectives

In this chapter you will discover ways to get business. You will learn of the many opportunities to come in contact with possible clients and how to convert those opportunities into money for you. This is an exciting chapter that you will want to review over and over.

Key Words

Active: Being in physical motion.

Appointment: An arrangement to do something or meet someone at a particular time and place.

Clear: Free from obstruction or hindrance.

CMA (Competitive Market Analysis): The separation of the real estate market whole into its constituent parts for individual study.

Fair deal: An exchange of one thing for another at equal prices or for accurate fees.

Listing: An entry in a list or directory of real estate properties.

Passive: Receiving an action without responding with an action in return.

Presentation: Something such as a lecture that is set forth for an audience.

Prospecting: Searching for a potential customer or client. Something expected, a possibility.

Introduction

Prospecting is the key to success in the real estate business. One of the most dangerous aspects of this business is the free business. I employed a new real estate salesperson who began her career with over eight sales in her first two months. She made almost $25,000 in 60 days. Maybe that is not a lot of money to you but for someone brand new to the real estate business it is incredible. It was also the worst thing possible for her. This business all came from her family and friends. They had waited for her to get her license and then bought and sold their properties through her. She did not have to prospect for the business; it was given to her. This salesperson has since left the real estate industry. Do not ignore free business but learn to earn.

> **An appointment a day keeps the creditors away.**

Another real estate salesperson who worked for me knew practically everyone in our small town. She makes her money on referrals and word of mouth. My fear for her is the chance of a change in her situation. What if she had to move? What if the economy in the small town dries up? The town is, in fact, changing. New people who she doesn't know are moving in and her business is moving out. She's not prepared to go anywhere else and make money in real estate because she doesn't know how to prospect.

Don't let outside influences dominate your career—learn how to sell anything anywhere.

What real estate activities will help bring you long-term career success? There are several: good evaluation skills, closing skills, listing presentation skills, referral activities, etc. At the forefront of all these skills and activities is prospecting. According to Webster, the word "prospect" means "a possibility; an anticipation." The infinitive "to prospect" means "to explore, to search."

In the real estate profession, "prospecting" means exploring and searching for a possible buyer or seller of real estate. You become a "prospector," combing your territory for customers and clients, just as those in olden days panned the rivers and streams in search of gold.

Your willingness to prospect consistently has a great deal to do with how successful you become. In addition to seeking out current business, prospecting is a means of building a network of clients and customers to ensure future business. For this reason, prospecting is perhaps the most important part of the real estate business.

Here are a few "truths" about prospecting:

1. Prospecting should be *listing-based.* The real estate salesperson that lists is the one that lasts. If you have no listings you have no income.
2. Prospecting should be based on your real estate *goals.*
3. Prospecting methods should be *varied.*

A salesperson's primary focus should be salable, exclusive-right-to-sell listings.

1. Salable listings attract buyers.
2. Salable listings attract sellers.
3. A signed listing represents the seller's commitment to work with you.
4. Salable listings allow you to control your time.
5. Salable listings allow you to control your income.
6. Salable listings are like gold.

If you are going to be active and you do not have a lot of friends and family to "give" you business you need to have listings. One real estate salesperson wanted my personal training so he chose to work in my office. He took a two-week training course with the national company we worked for. He also took a professional 11-week training course that he paid money for and I personally trained him. All of the training concentrated on attaining salable listings. He walked into my office one day and announced, "I have a great idea, I am going to concentrate on buyers." He lasted only a month and had to quit to get another job that actually made him money. He was given all that advice and he paid attention to none of it.

Clear-Cut Listing Appointment

A clear-cut listing appointment has all the essential elements to get a listing if you want it. We need to change our thinking. Most real estate salespeople have so few listing appointments that when they actually get one their attitude is to get the listing at all cost. A successful real estate salesperson has enough listing appointments that his or her attitude is, "Do I want it?" This attitude allows the salesperson to be objective. If the seller is reasonable the salesperson takes the listing, if not the salesperson walks away. This is truly the definition of a clear-cut listing appointment. If you go out to a client's property and you do not have a clear-cut listing appointment, you are *playing* real estate. There is nothing wrong with playing real estate, but it doesn't pay much. A clear-cut listing appointment is as follows:

- **Both**—Both or all of the people involved in making the decision to sell a property are present at the listing appointment. Do not go on an appointment unless everyone is there. If a husband and his wife are selling the property together, they both must be there. If the property for sale is an estate, the heirs must be there. It is even better if one heir has power-of-attorney for all other heirs. That way you only have to deal with one person. If you do not get all sellers together, you have a snake. And when do you kill a snake? Before it bites you. When do you make sure both people are there? Before it bites you. No matter how good your presentation, if one of the sellers is not present at the listing appointment you will not get the listing. Here is a conversation at the property without one of the parties present:

    Salesperson: "Put me to work for you."

        Seller: "Sounds good, just let me talk with my spouse and we will probably list with you."

    Salesperson: "Forget him and list with me now!"

What do you think the odds are that you will get that listing? The chances of getting that listing drop to around 20 percent. This is a snake and it just bit you.

So how do you get a clear-cut appointment when you are talking to the client on the telephone? Ask.

    Salesperson: "Are you the only one making the decision on the property?"

        Seller: "No, it is my husband and myself, but I will decide who to list with because he is so busy."

    Salesperson: "Understood, will your husband be with us tomorrow night?"

        Seller: "No."

Salesperson: "When would be a better time so everybody will be there?"

Seller: "My husband is busy until the weekend."

Salesperson: "Is Saturday or Sunday better?"

Seller: "Sunday afternoon."

Remember, you cannot win if only part of the selling party is at the listing appointment.

- **Two Hours**—You must have at least two hours to do a listing appointment. It takes from twenty to ninety minutes to give a good listing presentation. You can devote the remaining time to answering the sellers' questions. The worst thing that can happen is when you are doing well and the seller looks at his watch and says he must pick up his daughter from band practice. There goes all your preparation. Kill this snake early. How do you get a clear-cut appointment when you are talking to the client on the telephone? Ask. Sound familiar? Be careful here, though, because who wants to talk to a "salesperson" for two hours?

Salesperson: "Great, Mrs. Seller, I look forward to meeting with you and your husband tomorrow at 7 p.m. Let me ask you a question, If I am running a little bit late working on some other real estate business, how's the rest of the evening looking to you?"

Seller: "Oh, we will be home the rest of the evening."

Now what time do you show up? On time. What other real estate business are you working on? It doesn't matter. You should always be prospecting; that can be your "other" real estate business. I am not telling you to lie to gain an advantage. Lying is not ever necessary. Someone once told me, "I never lie so I don't have to remember what I said."

I once went with a real estate salesperson on a listing appointment to field train. During the listing presentation, the seller asked the salesperson the number of listings available in his price range in his area. Now the salesperson and I both know we don't have any and have never had any. The salesperson smiled and looked the seller in the eye and said, "Several." The seller naturally asked, "Where?" The salesperson now stammered and looked at me and said, "You tell him." I looked at the seller and stood up. I reached out my hand to shake his. I said, "I am sorry for him lying to you" and we left. The reason we left is that the seller had lost the "Trust" part of "Like and Trust" (Chapter 1) and we had no chance. I asked the salesperson to pack his stuff and leave my office. If he lies to a seller he will lie to me.

- **Competitive Market Analysis (CMA)**—While on the telephone with the seller you need to obtain enough information to do a Competitive (Comparative) Market Analysis. You should have a list of questions to ask a potential Seller while on the telephone. There is a list of questions in the appendix on page 347. By asking questions about the house, you show your professionalism and concern. I asked a seller once why she listed with me. Her answer was that I was the only real estate salesperson who asked her questions about the house on the telephone. What she really meant to say was that I was the only one who showed I cared.

- **Why**—You need to know why the seller wants to sell. Is it because of a transfer and he needs to move in 60 days or is it the spring and he always wants to sell his house in the spring? This shows motivation. This important because it tells you if the seller is willing to negotiate.

- **Price**—You have to know the price the seller wants for his or her house. You cannot go to a listing appointment without this knowledge. How do you get the price? Ask. Sometimes the seller believes that if he can convince you, you can convince others and the seller gets more money. This is why the sellers always give you a price more than it's worth. There is more than one way to get the price as you can see:

> **Salesperson:** "Mr. Seller, how much do you want for your property?"
>
> **Seller:** "You are the professional, you tell me."
>
> **Salesperson:** "How much do you owe on your property?"
>
> **Seller:** "I don't owe anything."
>
> **Salesperson:** "After all your expenses resulting from the sale, how much money do you want in your pocket?"
>
> **Seller:** "As much as I can get!"
>
> **Salesperson:** "Would you be happy to get $30,000?"
>
> **Seller:** "No way! I want at least $50,000!"

I would like to point out several things about the previous script. First, by just asking how much the seller wants for the property, you will get an answer. At this point on the telephone all you need is a price; it is not the time to challenge the seller's number. Some sellers believe by keeping this number secret, they will somehow get more money.

At this point you have to move to the next script, which is the "net" script. You find out how much the seller owes on the property and then how much he or she wants to make. Then you can back into the price.

If that doesn't work you move to the "shock" script, in which you give the seller a ridiculously low figure and out of shock the seller will tell you what he or she wants.

Not all techniques work all the time, but in my entire career with these three scripts, I have never failed to get the price from the seller.

The last key point is not to buy into the sellers if they say they don't know what the property should sell for. Most of the time, the sellers know! They at least have a ballpark idea and that is the number you need to get from them.

I will show you how important it is to get the price before you get to a listing appointment. An associate of mine in a real estate office where we both worked was on "opportunity time" (explained in the book on buyer prospecting). He got a call from a someone wanting to sell her house. Once my associate made the appointment he hung up and began to dance around the office singing out loud, "I got a listing appointment! I got a listing appointment!" This was his first listing appointment in five months and he was excited. The actual date of the appointment was for over a week away. He spent that week doing a Comparative Market Analysis. I can do a CMA in seven minutes. He was not working; he was *playing* real estate. He went to the appointment on a Monday night and on Tuesday morning he arrived at the office and silently sat at his desk. Did he get the listing? No, If he had, he would have been singing, "I've got a listing! I've got a listing!"

At our weekly sales meeting, I asked my associate to tell us how his listing appointment went." He said, "The sellers were stupid." Notice he did not blame himself. He did not know how the sellers wanted to price their property and he insulted them and they threw him out. How come he didn't get the listing? He wasn't prepared. And being prepared does not take a week.

The clear-cut listing appointment will give you the best opportunity to get the appointment if you want it. If you fail to get all five aspects of the clear-cut appointment, you will struggle in your career.

Active versus Passive

There are basically two types of real estate salespersons: active and passive. I have thought long and hard for better, more politically correct words; however, I feel that active and passive best describe the prospecting methods we will discuss.

Active prospecting is going out and getting the real estate business and bringing it back to the company. Passive prospecting is marketing yourself and the company and waiting for real estate business to come to you.

Which is better? It depends on you. During my years of teaching real estate marketing, when I bring up the subject of active and passive prospecting, almost all of the students claim they will be active prospectors. The say this because they view the word "passive" as "weak," but it is not.

Some people are good at cold prospecting while others are good at building relationships. To be a success in the real estate business you must determine who you are.

I have seen new real estate salespeople get in the business and begin to cold call prospective real estate business. They hate it, and it shows. They do not get the results and soon quit. It doesn't have to be this way. I blame the brokers and managers at the sales meetings because they continue to preach cold calling as the way to make money. Cold calling is just one way to make money, and it's a great way to make money, if it is who you are.

The advantage of being active is that business and money are fast—fast for real estate, that is. The salesperson actively goes out and gets business by making telephone calls, knocking on doors, calling on For Sale By Owners and numerous other means to get business. The active salesperson is on the lookout for more and more business and burns on through the day. These people do not have a lot of time to be social.

The disadvantage of active salespeople is that they tend not to be good at long-term relationships. They do not have time or the need to build those types of relationships. They can miss out on business because they do not follow up on the business as well as they should. They have long, stressful careers because they must continuously seek out new business, as they have not constructed a business that returns leads to them.

The advantage of being passive is that the business is not as stressful. People call passive people just to do business with them. Most of their business comes from referrals from friends and past clients. The passive salesperson can make a lot of money.

The disadvantage of being passive is that it takes a long time to make significant money. The passive salesperson must mail-out, run advertisements, and press palms until a prospect needs his or her service and asks for it.

Active

While the following prospecting ideas are for the "active" types of real estate salespeople, some "passive" real estate salespeople believe they can do these as well, and they can, if they force themselves.

Telemarketing

Telemarketing (sometimes called cold calls, warm calls, and gold calls—just get on the telephone and call) is the random calling to homeowners to determine if there is any interest in selling their homes. This is the best type of prospecting for new real estate salespeople because of the following factors:

- Prospects are easy to find. All you provide is effort.
- More contacts with less time.
- Can call in any weather.
- Unlimited market.
- No competition from other real estate salespeople.
- These sellers don't know you are new.
- Perfect to practice on, both telephone techniques and listing techniques.
- You can prove that you can always get listings for the rest of your career.

- The basis of all real estate sales.
- When you perfect cold calling you gain confidence.

There are certain categories of owners:

1. Not interested
   No prospect
2. Not interested now but maybe in less than two years
   Lead prospect—keep up with
3. Interested soon, but not now
   Possible prospect—need to create an urgency
4. Interested now
   Grand prospect

Expect 1 out of 100 calls to be grand prospects or possible prospects.

Expect 4 out of 100 calls to be lead prospects.

Telemarketing Procedure

When using the telephone to prospect, you should call from the office. There are several reasons for this, but the main reason is your connection with a business environment. You are near your broker or manager in case you have questions. You are near other real estate salespeople and feed off their energy. And you do not have the distractions of home.

I hear new real estate salespeople say they have a home office and they feel more comfortable there. In my career, I have never known any of those people to become successful. It is too easy to avoid making the calls. You don't want to work at the office and be embarrassed if you sound stupid on the telephone. That is all the more reason to be in the office, to get help sounding better. How can your broker or manager help you if you are never around? Remember, business is business and home is home. Do not blend the two.

The following are the actual steps in telemarketing:

1. Choose an "active" area in which several real estate sales are happening on a continuous basis. You can check the activity through your Multiple Listing Service.

2. Call anytime. Do not be afraid to call for fear of interrupting some family time. With the following script you do not interrupt because you are not on the telephone long. (**Be sure to follow local and national "do not call" laws.**)

3. Look up addresses and phone numbers in the cross directory, which lists contacts by street names. Do this quickly. Don't be too detailed. This is not rocket science. Just call. A new real estate salesperson entered the real estate business from the engineering field. I have no problem with engineers except they may overanalyze. This particular salesperson spent all of his time deciding who to call and never called anyone. He was out of the real estate business in 30 days. Again, just call, and do it quickly.

4. Follow these guidelines once you get an owner on the telephone:
   a. Establish rapport.
   b. Give the owner your reason for calling.
   c. Qualify the owner's need to sell his or her house.
   d. Gain the seller's confidence.
   e. Close the conversation by making an appointment.

Telemarketing is a "numbers game"; the more you play, the greater your chance of winning. The more calls you make, the more listing appointments you should arrange. You should block out time in your day for prospecting. I used to hang a $ sign on my door whenever I was making money. If someone interrupted my prospecting time I typically yelled at him or her. I never won the office popularity contest but I also made more money than everyone else. It's good to be a nice guy, but work is for work and play is for play.

General Approach

Salesperson: "Hello, is this Mr. or Mrs. _____? (Pause, wait for answer) My name is Dan Hamilton with Acme Realty. Have you thought about selling your house now or in the near future?"

Homeowner: (No)

Salesperson: "Thanks. Bye."

Homeowner: (Yes)

Salesperson: "Do you have a second to tell me a little about your house?"

Specific Property Approach

Salesperson: *"Hello, is this Mrs. _____?* (Pause, wait for answer) *My name is Dan Hamilton with Acme Realty. I am calling to see if you have considered selling your house either now or in the near future. Have you?"*

Homeowner: (No)

Salesperson: *"The reason I ask is that we recently listed/sold a house near yours at _____ and as a result of our extensive advertising, we have generated quite a bit of interest for homes in this area and we need more properties. Do you know anyone thinking about selling? How about yourself?"*

Homeowner: (Yes)

Salesperson: *"Do you have a second to tell me a little about your house?"*

Specific Person Approach

Salesperson: *"Hello, this is Dan Hamilton with Acme Real Estate. The reason for my call is that I have been working with a buyer who wants to live in your neighborhood. I have already shown her all of the houses on the market and she hasn't found what she's looking for. I told her I would call around the neighborhood to see if I might find someone who is thinking about selling. Are you considering selling your home at this time?"*

Homeowner: (No)

Salesperson: *"Thanks. Bye."*

Homeowner: (Yes)

Salesperson: *"Do you have a second to tell me a little about your house?"*

Second Variation

Salesperson: *"Hello, Mrs. _____?* (Pause, wait for answer) *My name is Dan Hamilton with Acme Realty. Have you thought about selling your house?"*

Homeowner: (No)

Salesperson: *"The reason I ask is that I'm working for a couple by the name of _____ and they're looking for a home in your area. We haven't found anything and I promised I'd talk to homeowners in the area until I found the right house. Do you happen to know of anyone selling? How about yourself?"*

Let's review the advantages of each script. Anyone can use the general approach. You can call any neighborhood at any time. Here are a couple of quick thoughts: First notice how fast you get to your main question—the first question. This is important because people don't want to talk to you anymore than you want to talk to telemarketers. Get to the question and get off the telephone. People don't get mad if you don't waste their time. The faster you get off the telephone with someone not interested, the faster you can find someone who is interested. If you get an answering machine, leave a message with the same script given. Be sure to leave a telephone number so they can return your call.

The question "Do you have a second to tell me a little about your house?" is a great question for many reasons. When homeowners are called from out of the blue and asked if they have ever thought of selling their home, they may be a little skeptical of your motives. As a real estate salesperson, you may be a little nervous talking with a live prospect. This question helps relieve the tension on homeowner's part because he or she knows the house and can relax and tell you about it in detail. While the homeowner talks you have time to gather yourself and get the listing appointment. Besides, you need that information from the homeowner for your property analysis and for pricing the property correctly. For a list of questions you should post by your telephone, see the Appendix on page 351.

A friend of mine and I used to play chess while we were telemarketing with our headsets on. It was great because chess was slow and we could take a break anytime we got a prospect on the telephone. See, you can have fun and make money at the same time.

Be consistent in your telemarketing. You may not get a listing out of your first call, but eventually you will.

Marketing Door-to-Door

Marketing door-to-door is also called door knocking. Some salespeople prefer marketing door-to-door because they come face to face with potential sellers. I agree; however, I find more advantages in telemarketing. With all of the "do not call," spam, and fax laws passing recently, and more in the future, door knocking may come back as the preferred choice of prospecting.

There are some terms to know:

- Territory canvassing: Getting out in a neighborhood you want to continually work and knocking on doors for leads.
- The warm canvass door: You have no real reason to be there, but it's a nice area and you are going to spend a day trying to discover someone with a real estate need.

Basics of Marketing Door-to-Door

1. After you ring the bell, back up a minimum of two feet.

2. Don't stare at the door. Turn up the street and look away.

3. Don't turn toward the homeowner until he or she acknowledges you.

4. Turn with a nice smile. (Be sure to be wearing your real estate name tag.)

5. Open the conversation with the following statements:

   "Good afternoon. My name is Dan Hamilton representing Acme Realty. There has been a tremendous amount of real estate activity in this area, and I am wondering if you've thought of making a move in the near future. Do you know of anyone in the neighborhood who might be interested in moving? Thank you so much for your time. I'm curious. If I find a home today, do you know any friends or relatives who might be interested in living here? Thank you again. By the way, when do you think you will be moving? I'd like to keep in touch. Would you like an evaluation of your equity position in the next few months? It's just a document telling what the homes in this area are worth."

This type of approach can lead to a discussion, during which you will learn more about the community and its residents. Your new acquaintance may know of a neighbor who intends to sell later on and will tell you about it. After all, you have given him something and it is natural to reciprocate by accepting your invitation or volunteering information. Most assuredly, if you have impressed him with your pleasant manner and obvious ability, he will remember you in the event he should ever need the services of a good active salesperson. If there is no answer at the door you should leave a door hanger with information about you if soliciting is allowed in the area.

Here is a fun little game when real estate becomes dull. Get with a real estate friend of yours and go to an area to market door-to-door. You start on one street and use the script given. Once you are through a certain number of houses, you meet the other salesperson who was door knocking in another area. Now switch areas and start door knocking again. Use the following script this time.

Salesperson: "Good afternoon. My name is Dan Hamilton with Acme Realty and I am introducing myself to the people in this area."

Homeowner: "Yeah, a guy named Bob Smith from your company was by a few minutes ago doing the same thing."

Salesperson: "Really! Wow, that is such an honor to you. If Bob wants to sell your property you are in great hands. Bob sure can do you the best. I cannot compete with his talent so I will leave now, it was good to hear you are so well taken care of, thanks now, bye."

You get some strange looks, but the homeowner thinks Bob is something great and will remember his name. Of course, the other salesperson will do the same for you.

For Sale By Owners

The For Sale By Owner (FSBO) is a homeowner who believes in selling his or her house without a real estate broker. Let's take a look at that logically; who wouldn't want to save maybe thousands of dollars if they could? A salesperson's job is to prove his or her worth. Remember, if you do your job right, the letters FSBO change into the "Fastest Source of Business Opportunity!"

One important advantage is that the FSBO is obviously interested in selling. FSBOs believe they can sell their property themselves and if we try to tell them they can't, all we do is irritate them. Most FSBOs overprice their properties, which creates fewer showings and lessens the chances of sell. Eventually FSBOs get the idea that they need help. What we need to do is be there in their thoughts when they realize they need us.

I remember when I was a stockbroker. We would be on the phone from 7 a.m. to 9 p.m. trying to find prospects. If I had a sniff I would bird dog that lead forever. Now I get into real estate and they publish a list of potential clients in the newspaper and real estate salespeople do not want to call them. Of course I am talking about the FSBO section of the local newspaper. I think real estate is sometimes too easy to do nothing. Mike Ferry, a national real estate trainer, tells of a time in his personal office when he was frustrated that none of his real estate salespeople were calling FSBOs. He entered his weekly sales meeting and put a hundred dollar bill on a corkboard. He placed a FSBO newspaper ad on the bill and tacked it to the corkboard.

He then turned to his real estate salespeople said, "Whoever lists that property gets the $100 bill. I don't care if you list it for only a day. I don't care if you list it with no commission to be paid. I don't care if you list it overpriced. I just want you to list it. So the first to do that gets the $100!"

After a couple of days Mike began to feel bad about what he had done to that FSBO. All his salespeople were now hammering the FSBO. Mike felt so bad he decided to call the FSBO and apologize. "Mr. FSBO, this is Mike Ferry with Mike Ferry Real Estate. I am sure you have heard from my company?" FSBO: "Nope." As it turns out, no one had called the FSBO. When Mike Ferry asked his salespeople why, they all thought that everyone else had already called.

In my market area there are probably 300 FSBOs at any time and over 6,000 licensed real estate salespeople. Only about 20–25 real estate salespeople call consistently. You have no competition.

Keys to Working FSBOs

1. You must meet these people face-to-face or you have nothing.
2. Be professional.
3. You must be committed to this program for at least twelve weeks or don't even start.
4. Follow up.
5. Follow up.
6. Follow up.

Furthermore, you must get in the door honestly, which means calling or stopping by. Some real estate salespeople make a big deal of showing the house to a potential "buyer" to impress the seller. The buyer turns out to be a friend of the salesperson and isn't in the market to buy a house. That is dishonest, and the only thing we ultimately sell is our self. If we don't believe in ourselves, how will others believe in us?

You must be committed to this program for at least twelve weeks or don't start. You will waste your time. Why? A majority of FSBOs will eventually list their properties with real estate companies, but they first believe they can sell it themselves. Waiting twelve weeks is a commitment on your part and generally the FSBO will convert his or her feelings in that time.

FSBO Action Plan

1. Get the real estate section of the local paper.

2. Find an area quickly.

3. Call the ad. (See script below.)

4. Go see the property.
   Bring just a notepad. (See script below.)
   Schedule one every 20 minutes.

5. Contact at least once a week.
   Use Fair Deal.
   Close for the clear-cut appointment.

6. Follow up for 12 weeks.

Calling on a FSBO Ad

> **Salesperson:** "Hi, I am calling about the home for sale. Are you the owner? Would you considering working with Real Estate in any way?"

> "Well, my name is Dan Hamilton with Acme Realty. I will be in your area later this week and was wondering if you would mind if I stopped by to take a quick look at your place?"

This script will get you into the homes of six of every ten FSBOs you call. Let's analyze this script. With the first three lines you have not addressed the issue that you are a licensed real estate salesperson. This is acceptable because the conversation has not become substantial. You should be careful, though, and not let the FSBO speak because the FSBO might get excited and give you substantial information. So when you ask about the home for sale, ask the second question, "Are you the owner?" immediately, without pause. You want to find out if they are the owner in case someone else, like a friend, is helping the owner out; you don't want to talk to a friend, you must talk to the owner. The last line, "Would you work with Real Estate in any way?" is a confusing and rhetorical question. You are trying to get the FSBO's attention. Most real estate salespeople make a big announcement that they are in real estate. The FSBO is geared to reject that salesperson immediately. This script allows you time to make an impression. Your response is the same no matter how the FSBO responds. The final question is actually to solicit a "no" response. Read it again: "I was wondering if you would mind?" If the owner says "no," it means he or she doesn't mind you taking a look at the property. Be sure to explain you'll only be taking a quick look. Do not vary these scripts. They are proven. You can change them only after you have called 100 FSBOs.

If the owner resists, try this:

> **Salesperson:** "Is it the fee that is keeping you from listing your property with a professional real estate salesperson?"

If they respond, "No," probe further. If they respond, "Yes," continue:

> **Salesperson:** "Well, If I have a buyer that I have been unable to help, could I send them directly to you?"

Whatever the answer:

> **Salesperson:** "I'm sure you have buyers in your home and they decide not to buy it, don't you?"
>
> "You see, those are still potential buyers to me. If you give me a list of those buyers I would be happy sending a buyer that I couldn't help to you. Now doesn't that sound fair?"
>
> "It only makes sense for me to see the house so I will know which of my buyers might be interested in your home. I'm available tonight or will tomorrow be better?"
>
> This script will get you in nine of every ten FSBOs you call.

Alternate Response:

"I show a lot of homes in your neighborhood and like to be familiar everything that's for sale. It's good business for both you and me when I drive by your home with a client and say, "That home has three bedrooms, two baths, and a lovely kitchen area. It is selling for $100,000. My clients may wish to see your home."

Once you have the FSBO appointment you should send a reminder card.

Door Knocking for FSBOs

Salesperson: "Hi, my name is Dan Hamilton with Acme Realty, and I am doing a quick survey of why people try to sell their homes by themselves. Do you have a second?"

First visit or door knocking questions:

1. Why did you decide to sell your home yourself without a broker?

2. If you were to hire a broker, what would you look for?

3. If you don't sell the house yourself, will you stay here or will you hire a broker?

4. When will you make that decision?

5. What methods of marketing are you currently using?

6. Have you heard of Acme Realty's 21-point marketing plan?

Further FSBO Hints

1. FSBOs have lists of buyers that have seen their houses and have not bought. Remember, we make money with buyers *and* sellers. If you get those lists you can begin working with those buyers. (See scripts in the Appendix on page 352.)

2. FSBOs may list their houses with agents that can offer a variety of options for purchase. For example:

MLS filing	$995
Open house	$225
Yard sign	$75
Mail-outs	$50/100

    All fees are negotiable and must be paid in advance. The above prices are examples only. For more information see Chapter 6 on alternate representation agreements. I know of an agent in Las Vegas who made in excess of $1,000,000 for himself in one year exchanging buyer lists with FSBOs.

3. Follow up, follow up, follow up.

4. If you find resistance to getting in to see the FSBO house, find out if you can help the FSBO find a new home. Call the FSBO as your company's Relocation Specialist and attain a referral to another area. (See the script in the Appendix on page 384.) To achieve the designation of Relocation Specialist see your broker.

5. FSBOs should be *one* area of your business. Don't devote all your time to them.

6. Mean FSBOs are the best FSBOs.

FSBO Stop-By Appointment
When a FSBO agrees to meet with you to show his or her property, you should do the following:

1. As soon as you hang up with the seller on the telephone, put a reminder note in the mail. Be sure to include the date of the appointment and one of your business cards. Also include an agency disclosure form, if one is required by local laws.

2. Take only a notebook and a pen to the appointment. You agreed to a stop-by appointment. Keep your briefcase and any necessary listing material in your car. If the seller wants you to list his house, you will be prepared.

3. Once you're inside the property say the following:
"Show me through and just treat me as if I am a buyer."

4. If the homeowner says something about the house, write it down. If it is important enough for him to say it is important enough to write down.

5. When finished, leave the property. Do not ask a lot of questions. Do not offer any services. Do not even offer a business card. Be professional.

I have seen salespeople walk into FSBO houses and immediately begin to sell. The FSBOs are ready for that and the FSBO starts in on how real estate people don't do anything except take their money. By the time the FSBOs stop, the real estate salespeople are leaving the houses with their tails between their legs. You want the seller to believe you have something to offer. Every other real estate salesperson that the FSBO has invited in has tried to sell. If you don't, you leave the seller with the thought that you are special and have some special qualities. I was calling FSBOs one day and set an appointment with one. I found out later that a new real estate salesperson in my office had an appointment with the same FSBO that day. I asked the other salesperson if we could go together and I could teach on handling FSBOs. I explained to the new salesperson not to say much to the seller, to let them do most of the talking.

When we got to the house I could sense the seller thought of us as typical salespeople stealing money. We said very little but I could tell the seller was expecting the same speech "Here's what we can do for you . . . " that he has heard from every other real estate salesperson. The house tour was over, so I turned to leave and simply said "Thanks." As I walked passed the new salesperson, I could tell he was horrified and wondering how I could go to a potential client's house and not offer services or even my card. This salesperson whipped out a business card and said, "If we can be of any help. . . . " Before the salesperson could finish his sentence the seller laid into him. By the time we got outside the seller was yelling at us. I expected it. I wasn't disappointed. The new salesperson was shocked and never called on an FSBO again.

Here's the analysis of what happened. The FSBO believes he can sell the house himself. The salesperson comes in and tells the FSBO he needs help. This irritates the FSBO and challenges his integrity. It's no surprise that the FSBO now wants to fight. As far as the business card goes, you can mail it to the FSBO with a thank you, *after* the tour!

FSBO Follow-Up Facts
1. Put each FSBO lead from the newspaper on a 4" × 8" index card. Cut out the FSBO ad and tape it to the top right-hand corner of the card. FSBOs will change their ads but they won't change their telephone numbers. Because you have the FSBO's telephone number in the ad taped to your card, if they change the ad you will not be unaware. You call the FSBO back and say, "Noticed you changed your ad, looks good!" That is a lot better than having the seller tell you that you called last week. Print the name, address, and phone number in the top left-hand corner. Use the back of the card to list

your discussions with the FSBO, including the date of each contact. If you have client management software, add FSBO's information to your program.

2. Create a binder for logging FSBO contacts. Label each page in the binder with the three-digit telephone prefix number at the top of the page. Then record this specific FSBO's back four numbers in a column. Before you call any FSBO, check this binder first to see if you have talked with him or her already. Remember, FSBOs will change their ads, but not their phone numbers. Scratch out FSBOs that are off the market. Highlight FSBOs that you do not want to call again. You will call a lot of investors, but keep them on a separate sheet. You may need them later if you find an investment-grade property for which you do not have the capital.

Tracking FSBOs is of the utmost importance. They will not list with the first real estate salesperson who contacts them; they will list with the last real estate salesperson that contacts them and that must be you. How do you ensure that you are the last? Follow up weekly with each FSBO you are tracking. The follow-up date should be on the same day and time each week. This allows the FSBO to remember when you call.

I called a FSBO on the telephone and he slammed me and told me he did not need a real estate salesperson. I stayed in there (remember: the mean ones are the best ones) and made an offer he could not refuse. So he finally told me to be at the house at 2:00 p.m. on Thursday. He would not be there but his wife would. (It is O.K. to meet with only one person when you're only stopping by.) I was on time and as soon as the wife saw my nametag she ranted and raved about how she and her husband do not need a real estate salesperson. I told her I understood but her husband had told me to stop by. She then flung the door open, told me to take a look, and walked off into another room. Well, needless to say I had had enough. I tossed my business card on the coffee table and walked out. When I got back to the office I began to destroy their prospect card. I did it slowly to enjoy the feeling of destroying the last memory of these horrible FSBOs, and I threw it all in the nearest trashcan. We do not have to work with everybody.

The next day I got a call from a person who said he had decided to list his house with me. I told him I'd love to market his house and then realized that this was the FSBO from the day before. I made a mad dash back to the trashcan to retrieve the pieces of his prospect card. I went out and listed the property and later sold it.

Why did those mean and nasty FSBOs list their property with me? Because I was the last to contact them. They were so mean that all of the other real estate salespersons had thrown their prospect cards away, just like me. The difference was I did it right before they conceded to needing professional real estate help.

The FSBO must be called every week. You should call either Sunday night or Monday. If you call on Friday they have no interest because *this* weekend is the weekend they will sell their house. If you call Sunday night or Monday they are less excited and more willing to talk. Also, you want to call at the exact time each time you call. You never know when the sellers decide they need you, and chances are they never kept anything you gave them. Here is a typical conversation:

FSBO #1: "It doesn't look like we can sell it ourselves."

FSBO #2: "Nope"

FSBO #1: "Who should we call?"

FSBO #2: "I don't know."

FSBO #1: "How about the guy that keeps calling?"

FSBO #2: "Fine."

FSBO #1: "Did you keep his card?"

FSBO #2: "Nope."

FSBO #1: "Oh well, it doesn't matter he will call tonight at 6:15."

The dialog with the FSBO is one of a "fair deal." As the words indicate, it is a deal of valuable items. The real salesperson wants an appointment to market the house. The FSBO might need any number of services and the salesperson finds service will trigger the FSBO to act. The services the salesperson offers include MLS, yard "For Sale" sign, professional ad writing, and any number of other services. What you offer as a "fair deal" is not as important as just offering something. You should develop a list of "fair deals" for yourself and post them near where you call FSBOs for review.

Offering a Fair Deal

Salesperson: "Mr. or Mrs. FSBO, it is a proven fact that buyers tend to believe that the price you are asking is more realistic if it is backed by written data. Do you have some evidence proving your home is priced right?"

FSBO: "Well, no."

Salesperson: "I'll tell you what I can do and that is prepare a written report on the fair market value of your house and present that to you to use. Are you available today or would tomorrow be better?"

Several things happened here, so let us examine them separately. First, notice the "fair deal," a Competitive (Comparative) Market Analysis (CMA) for an appointment. Second, if the sellers don't need the CMA, end the conversation with an O.K. and goodbye. Never say, "I'll call you next week," because their natural response is to tell you not to call. If they specifically tell you not to call you cannot (national "do not call" rules) and you have lost a prospect. If you just say goodbye, you can call again next week. Third, notice the close, ". . . today or would tomorrow be better?" An alternate of choice close prevents a "no" answer and gives the seller only two choices. This technique and several others will be discussed later. And last, if the FSBO says something like, "Just mail it to me" or "I can drop by your office and pick it up" you must say: "I appreciate what you are saying but the only thing worse than not having the information is to have it and not to be able to explain it correctly, and I would need to meet with you to explain it. It has been good talking with you. Do you have any other questions? Thanks, bye." Never give a "fair deal" away because that is not fair. Before you do any work for anyone you must have an appointment. I see so many real estate salespeople do this or that for a FSBO and get nothing in return. My services are worth compensation and are not to be given away. If the FSBO is not interested in your "fair deal" say, "Great, it was nice talking with you. Bye."

FSBO Food for Thought

Call until you find a FSBO you can work with. If you only work one FSBO a week for 50 weeks (two-week vacation) you could work with 50 FSBOs in a year. If 70 percent of those eventually list with someone in real estate, that would equal 35 listings. If you list half of those, that would be 17 extra listings per year. If you average $2,000 per sale (I pulled that dollar amount from the air), you earn an extra $35,000. This does not include any other sales from any other sources.

Expired Listings

The expired listing can be another excellent source of prospects. Expireds are sellers who marketed their home with the wrong real estate salesperson (the right real estate salesperson would have been you!) and the home did not sell. The other salesperson has done all the work and all you do is clean up his or her mess. What is already known about the expired listing is that the owners were once interested in selling and not afraid to pay a commission.

Your first task in contacting an expired listing is to determine whether the owners are still interested in selling, and if so, to arrange an appointment to discuss the advantages of listing with you. Talking to expireds is a little tougher (not meaner) than telemarketing because the sellers already know the procedure and they know what they want out of their next real estate salesperson. I do not intend for new salespeople to call on expireds. Pay your dues with telemarketing and then step up to FSBOs and expireds.

Expireds are typically short on the phone, so expect it. It is best to use a lot of questions to get the appointment. Ask them why they think their home didn't sell, how they felt about the listing price, why they want to sell, and what they will do if their home doesn't sell. Keep them on the phone as long as possible to build rapport and keep other real estate salespeople from getting through. When it is time to disconnect, tell them to take their telephone off the hook to prevent being bothered with other real estate salespeople calling. If you get an answering machine, leave a long message so other real estate salespeople can't leave their names.

Some Important Preliminaries

1. Learn and follow your local Board of REALTORS® regulations for contacting expired listings.
2. Do not criticize your competition.

Categories of Expireds

I will break down the types of expireds to specific categories so we can understand them and how we should approach them.

1. **Motivated owners**—There are several categories of motivated owners who have become expireds. These owners are still motivated to sell but have different outlooks on their situation.

   A. An expired will relist with the current office. The real estate salesperson is a personal friend or they have some other relationship. This expired is probably not a prospect of yours, but contacting him or her might be worth a shot. Sometimes a seller may tell you over the telephone that he or she will list with a competitor but if you can get in front of them you have a chance. A typical conversation may go something like this:

   Salesperson: "Have you already signed papers to relist the property?"

   Expired: "No, we are scheduled to sign them tonight."

   Salesperson: "How long was it listed the last time?"

   Expired: "Six months."

   Salesperson: "And you don't feel that was long enough to sell the property?"

   Expired: "PAUSE."

   Salesperson: "Doesn't it make sense to talk with at least one other broker to see what other services are offered, as I am available at 3:00 p.m.? Or will 5:00 p.m. be better?"

   B. Interview alternative offices and current office. An alternative office is one that is not the previous listing office. Good prospect, but you must overcome the seller's loyalty to the current office. This means that you have a good chance at getting a listing appointment, but if you cannot demonstrate the reason to select you over the previous company it might be hard for them to change. The expired believes that if all companies are the same, might as well stick with the one we know.

   C. Interview alternative offices, but not the current office. Major prospect. These are the best. They will list with a real estate company but not the previous one. The reason might be that they were so disappointed in the previous real estate company that they will not list with them again. This seller must be convinced that you will not be like the last one. A guarantee of service is powerful with these sellers.

2. **Nonmotivated owners**
   A. The seller's property is overpriced. The expired may be a good prospect if you can suggest a more realistic price. These sellers believe that their home is better than anyone else's. You might be able to get a listing appointment, but do not overprice it again. You must walk away if you cannot get the sellers to adjust their price.
   B. Waiting for (something). Maybe a good prospect if you can overcome their waiting. The sellers may be waiting on a child to graduate from high school in four months. They are not motivated because they have a long time before they need to be out. You must create some urgency for them to get realistic.
   C. Hate real estate agents. A rarity, but the anger is not personal and this is a good prospect if the anger can be overcome. It is very hard to talk with this type of seller. The key is to show concern by asking a series of questions without telling about yourself or your company. Once you are at the appointment you can tell the sellers about those things.
   D. Don't need agent (currently a FSBO). A good prospect but must show value of services. May offer "Fee For Service" program. When you are out on the appointment you treat these sellers as a FSBO and an expired.

Expect a return of 5 out of 100 expireds you talk with to list with you, which is much better than telemarketing.

Expireds Procedure

Pull up the expired list from the MLS computer and look up the owners from the cross directory. Call every expired (be aware of the national "do not call" rules) owner in the MLS twice a day until you talk with them.

Salesperson: "Mr./Mrs./Ms."

Expired: "Yes."

Salesperson: "This is Dan Hamilton with Acme Realty. I am calling about the property at 1604 Montgomery Street."

Expired: "Yes."

Salesperson: "Is that property still for sale?"

Expired: "No."

Salesperson: "Well, I'd like to stop by and take a quick look at the place, and while I'm there tell you why your property did not sell the last time. So if you do decide to put it back on the market the same mistakes won't be made again."

Leave the following message if you get an answering machine:

> "This is Dan Hamilton with Acme Realty. I am calling about the property at 1604 Montgomery Street, which was taken off the market today. I'd like to interview with you to become your new real estate agent. We offer several different programs, especially in your price range and in your area. So, if you still want to sell your property please give me a call at _____."

The follow-up procedure on expireds is simple: Call twice a day until you actually talk to the owner. You should call first thing in the morning before he or she leaves for work and at night right before dinnertime. I once called an expired for three weeks until I got an answer. The owner had been away on a European vacation and did not know the property was off the market. It was an easy listing; I had no competition.

Real Estate Waif

American Heritage Dictionary defines "waif" as "something found and unclaimed." Real estate waifs are past real estate buyers who have been abandoned by their salespeople. Some real estate salespeople get a sale and never follow up on past clients. Some real estate salespeople get a sale and then get out of the real estate business.

The best way to prospect for real estate waifs is to talk to your broker or manager and ask to go through old real estate sales files. When you find a real estate waif (or several, if you are smart) call them (following the national "do not call" rules) and use the following script:

> "Mr. or Ms. _____, my name is Dan Hamilton with Acme Realty. I noticed that you purchased a home through our company a number of years ago. I am just wondering how you are enjoying the home and if you ever consider moving again?"

Whatever the homeowner's response, you now have a warm prospect. These owners generally have a favorable outlook on your company and now you. They are also a great source of referrals. If their experience was not good and you can make things better, you become their hero. Sometimes people just want someone to listen, as they feel they have been abandoned.

Generally people move every five to seven years. The files you have on these buyers will tell you how long they've lived in their houses. Then, within six months or so of the time you know they should begin thinking about moving (by national averages), you contact them with your marketing approach. In other words, you can get to them before they get the "itch" to move.

If someone has lived in his or her home quite a bit longer than the national average, contact him or her and say: "Are you aware of your equity position? You have been in your house longer than the national average. Maybe we should investigate the possibilities of what it could do for you."

If you stay in touch with these real estate waifs you have a huge source of future business. it is important not to let your past clients become waifs. You need to be in contact with all your past clients at least twice a year.

Obituaries

You won't read much about prospecting obituaries in many real estate marketing books. I've never done it because I choose not to. (Remember, you have choices in this business.)

I do know of one real estate salesperson who prospected obituaries. From the obituary section of the paper, he would take down all the necessary information. Then he would send flowers along with his business card. After a couple of days he would make a follow-up call to the home to learn the status of the property. He found that most widowers no longer wanted to live in the home. Almost all were receptive and appreciated the flowers. He had to deal with relatives frequently but he gained four to six sales per year from prospecting using obituaries. (I don't have a script for this kind of prospecting. You are on your own here.)

On a happier note, you can also use this strategy to find potential buyers and sellers from the newspaper sections for "Job Promotions," "Weddings," and "Baby Announcements." All of these might indicate a desire for new real estate.

Garage Sales

Garage sales are another way to find potential real estate sellers. Now these are fun! I love going to garage sales. I wanted to combine fun things with real estate. The only thing I did different was to use the following script:

> **Salesperson:** "Are you just clearing out some things or are you thinking about selling the house?"

I found out that frequently this is a seller's first step in preparing to put a house on the market.

I look in the newspaper for "Garage Sales" every Thursday night and prepare a map for my tour. The first thing Friday morning I rush to the office and call expireds. (This is a must for me.) Then I leave on my garage sale tour. On the way I study the market, looking for FSBO signs, unkempt properties for investment, and other real estate signs in the area. I drive with my car signs on the door and I wear career apparel and my name badge so there is no mistaking who I am and what I'm doing there. I mill around looking at stuff until I get near the owner. I casually recite the script. If the owner is interested I get his or her name and telephone number and call after the sale. Getting this information is important, as you should not expect the owner to call you. Most garage sales start on Friday, so that is my garage sale day. Many times I've given something like $6 for a garage sale trinket and I get $6,000 in return for selling a property.

Passive

In this section we will discuss the passive side of the real estate business.

Farming

Farming or "neighborhood servicing" is a planned prospecting campaign within a defined market group that delivers a specific message about you and your company. The objective of farming is to have homeowners think of *you* when they decide to sell their property. Farming is planting the seed in homeowners' minds that you are the real estate expert. You can cultivate these homeowners until they produce a harvest of listings for you. Then you harvest the money. (Hence the name, farming.)

Farming is a long-range activity. Major studies conducted in real estate markets show that the average farm will require two years of work before the rewards are substantial. Once your farm starts to produce, however, you should be getting at least 90 percent of all the listings in your farm. Approximately 5 percent of the people will move every year. Be careful, though, this should be a part of your prospecting, not your *only* form of prospecting. Do not get caught up in farming and forget your other prospecting methods. Remember, farming can take a while to develop.

Farming differs from telemarketing in the following ways:

1. Farming is confined to a specific area or group.
2. Farming involves *repeated* contacts.
3. Farming has *long-range* results.
4. Farming is specifically intended to create "top of mind" awareness and to build personal relationships.
5. In addition to the obvious prospecting reasons for farming, another purpose is to compile neighborhood data to help provide your office with complete area coverage.

The most successful real estate salespeople are those who have learned the secret of being "a big frog in a small pond." In other words, they know that it is difficult to be known throughout a large community, but comparatively easy to be well known by a small segment of that community. They also know that a small segment of the community is all that is necessary to produce a sufficient number of listings and sales to achieve the income they desire.

Sphere of Influence Farming

Sphere of influence (SOI) farming was designed to be one of the most powerful tools you will use during your real estate marketing career. It is the key to unlocking many gateways along your journey to financial freedom. This is one of the more significant exercises in this book.

Sphere of influence (sometimes called center of influence) is the group of people that know you by name. It can include your mother, your dentist, the people you grew up with, your friends, people you work with, or people you've simply come in contact with at work or school. These people want to see you do well and will help you if they can. This category of farming is the easiest and the most effective, because these people like and trust you already. They can all be your best contacts if you will simply use them as resources. This personal database list can be the key to unlocking your successful future.

Make a list of as many people as possible. Don't get hung up on a specific number, but think of it as if you are getting paid $100 per name.

As time goes by, you will constantly be adding to this list through referrals, new contacts, remembering old acquaintances, etc.

The following categories should help "jog" your memory. Think about each specific description and who you might know within each one. It's very important not to prejudge anyone while compiling this list. Don't consider their potential interest or whether or not you consider working with them. This exercise is meant to empty your brain of names on paper.

1. Members of your own family
    A. Father, mother
    B. In-laws
    C. Children, children's children
    D. Brothers, sisters
    E. Aunts, uncles
    F. Nieces, nephews, and cousins

2. Your closest friends and those with whom you associate most
    A. Friends, neighbors
    B. People you work with now and in the past
    C. Members of your church or Sunday school class

3. People you met in organizations or clubs
   A. Civic groups, Rotary, Lions, Jaycees, etc.

4. People you do business with (who you buy from)
   A. Doctor, lawyer, barbers, merchants, grocer
   B. Gas station, laundry, postman, insurance salesperson
   C. Beautician, jewelers, favorite restaurant personnel

My brother is an attorney. He had a partner who became a friend of mine. We played softball together and all went out to lunch frequently. He bought a $250,000 home, but he didn't buy it through me. When I asked him why he said that he didn't know I sold in his area. I know if he had known he would have bought through me. I took it for granted that he knew I could sell anywhere. Don't make the same mistake. Every person you know should be on your SOI list and you should keep up with them.

I inadvertently prospected my daughter. When she was in second grade somebody asked her what her daddy did for a living. She told the teacher that her daddy puts up signs and lock boxes. Funny, that's all she ever saw me do because I would take her with me. The teacher translated those activities and was interested in real estate. She contacted me.

Most people have over 120 people in their sphere of influence. Your challenge is to remember all of your SOI names and contact them. Also note that each of the 120 people on your list has a list of 120 people that they know, and so on and so on. Get it? Mail a form letter to them every forty-five to ninety days for the rest of your life.

The following is a script for the letter:

Good Morning!

I just wanted to take a moment to remind you that I'm still in the real estate business. If you or anybody you know if thinking of buying or selling a property, please give me a call.

Have a great day!

If you get a call from someone requesting that you take his or her name off your mailing list, just say, "I'd be glad to, as soon as you give me three good leads. Now who do you know?" You can get away with this because they know you. It is light-hearted and serious so keep it that way.

The members on your SOI list will not mind you calling them. In fact they will expect it. Patrick Wyatt, manager of a Century 21, Judge Fite office, had a salesperson who paid big money to learn that he should end all conversations, including those with people on his SOI list, with a request for real estate business. He found his leads and income increased dramatically. One person said, "I was wondering when you would ask me?" You see this person wants to help; he even expects to be asked.

Prospecting is not limited to the areas we have mentioned. It is an 18-hour-a-day job. (We will let you sleep for six hours a day and then get back to prospecting!) A top salesperson is in love with this profession. The salesperson eats, drinks, breathes, and lives real estate every waking moment. Between 70 and 90 percent of his or her time and energy is spent in this pursuit. Wherever the salesperson goes and whomever she meets along the way, she always turns the conversation toward real estate. Everyone knows she is in the business. She also goes out of her way to meet more people and extend her sphere of influence.

Geographic Farming

This category of farming is effective but time intensive. Unlike SOI farming, geographical farming is cultivating people who you do not necessarily know but are living in a neighborhood where you are an expert. As the expert you should know as much about that area as possible, including the nearest schools, shopping, recreation, and people. You need to know all of the houses that are for sale, sold, expired, or pending. You need to know all the FSBOs, too. You may want to schedule neighbor events, send newsletters, or plan other activity that may make your name available. You should be a member of the neighbor watch program, the homeowners association, and the city council. You need to be seen as the expert, and being the area expert is mostly perception.

The location of your farm will depend in great measure on your personal preference. The farm should be in an area where you enjoy selling and where you feel a degree of personal identification. It is an excellent idea, although not absolutely necessary, to select an area immediately surrounding your own home. The identification is obvious; you live in the neighborhood, you are familiar with it, and you can render better service than an "outsider." The disadvantage of farming in your own community is that the people now know where you live and may disturb your family time, so weigh the pros and cons well.

If you choose not to use your personal neighborhood, you should drive around and look for real estate yard signs. Pick an area with several signs but not one in every yard. Several signs indicates action. Some areas seldom have houses for sale and would be a waste of your time. You also want to look at the real estate salesperson who listed the houses in the area. If the name is the same on almost all the signs, it would be best to find another area. If all the signs have with different real estate salespeople's names, you have an active area but no dominance by one salesperson. Double-check your drive-around results with the multiple listing service to verify activity and dominance.

All of the homes in your farm should be comparable to one another. A homogeneous neighborhood will produce far better results than a heterogeneous one. Age is no factor, as long as all homes are of approximately the same age and will sell for approximately the same amount of money. The maximum number of houses in your first geographic farm area should be no more than one hundred. One hundred houses are manageable. You must contact your farm monthly, and too many houses will become overwhelming. One of the biggest geographic farm mistakes is taking a farm area that is too big. You can always add to your farm once you have the systems down. Don't make this to time consuming. You should spend less than 10 hours a month on geographic farming.

Once you have chosen a farm area, you should track each house in a good-quality, three-hole, loose-leaf notebook capable of holding pages equal to the total number of homes in your farm. Each house should have a full page on which you can identify the owner, important numbers, and personal data like birthdays. Make note of everything you can find out about the owners for future use. As you obtain additional information on a family, the names of the children, in-laws living with them, leases, sales, etc., add to your data page. Always glance at your page before ringing a doorbell to be certain you have all necessary facts. You should have a map of the area and identify all the houses. You can track these on your computer but you will need to print the information to take with you when you visit your farm. You can add a photograph of the house if time permits.

I knew one new real estate salesperson who put together an incredible farm area book. It had pictures of all the houses, research data from the taxing authority, etc. He even called each owner just to verify he had the correct telephone number. This salesperson was out of the business in three months because he spent all his time in development and had no action.

The first time you visit your farm area you should knock on every door and use the following script:

Salesperson: "Mr. or Mrs. Homeowner, my name is Dan Hamilton with Acme Realty. I stopped by to introduce myself as the expert real estate salesperson in the area and conduct a survey. [As you say this, you hold out your business card.] Do you have just a second to answer five questions?"

Owner: "Sure."

Salesperson: "Have you ever thought about selling your house either now or in the near future?"

Owner: "No."

Salesperson: "How long have you lived here?"

Owner: "Six years."

Salesperson: "What made you choose this area to live?"

Owner: "We liked all the mature trees in the neighborhood."

Salesperson: "If you were to leave what would the reason be?"

Owner: "We might retire in Shady Acres."

Salesperson: "And when might that be?"

Owner: "Not for a couple of years."

Salesperson: "Thanks for your time. Would you like a copy of the results of my survey when it's completed?"

Owner: "Sure."

Salesperson: "Thanks now, bye."

Put all five questions on a piece of paper and make copies for each house in your farm area. Put the copies on a clipboard for each house you visit.

You have found out some rich information. The owner might move in a year. Always cut in half what the owner tells you because it is better to be early than late. Mature trees are a selling point in the area. And you have a reason to come back–to bring the results. If the person is rude and tells you to leave, mark them on your sheet. If they continue to hassle you, delete them from your data bank because you do not have to work with everybody. However, this is your farm area so be patient because they may soften up once they get to know you. That is the beauty of farming and that is building relationships.

The follow-up from here is monthly. The homeowners should see or hear your name and what you do every month. The best and easiest way to do this is through the Internet if you have e-mail addresses. If you don't have e-mail addresses, you should use snail mail to send them something once a month. What you send them is not as important as sending them something. Real estate office manager John Lundquist suggests sending "something that is Evidence of Production." Possible mailings include area statistics, notices of houses that have just sold, and upcoming buyer/seller seminars.

You should talk with or visit with the homeowners every six months. On this personal visit you should leave them something to remember you by. Some possible leave-behinds include key chains, candy, mouse pads, a binder of house papers, a CD case, and golf balls. Anything with your name on it that will remind the homeowner of you will work. You may also choose to leave flyers on doors. Some reasons for contacting homeowners include:

- New real estate sales in the area.
- Recipes the homeowners may be interested in trying.
- Upcoming events in the area.
- Services you provide.
- Upcoming community council meetings.
- Real estate news.
- PTA activities of the month.
- News of sports activities.
- Service club news of community interest.
- National holidays.

A monthly newsletter allows you to have an instant welcome into the house, but it can be time consuming to produce. I have seen real estate salespeople spend weeks each month doing a newsletter. Do not do that.

Several companies publish newsletter templates that only require you to add your picture and facts about you. You just print it out and put it in mail.

To speed up the time and lower the cost, you might also consider an e-newsletter. These go over the Internet highway instead of the asphalt highway.

Remember, only spend ten hours a month in your farm area. This is one area of your business, not your *entire* business. The great thing about newsletters is when the homeowners in the area actually look forward to getting the newsletter.

Obviously, the best way to have these in a homeowner's possession is to deliver the newsletter personally. The prospect will be grateful for your time and consideration. You should deliver your newsletter no later than the 30th of the previous month to ensure its maximum use.

Here are some of the important points to remember in developing your newsletter:

- Keep your news full of local people's names.
- Write short, concise sentences.
- Have a "For Sale" column, that is, babysitter services, bikes, etc.
- Use pictures if you can and always include one of yourself.
- Give credit to people who give you stories.
- Always ask a person's permission before writing about him or her.
- Include a section called "Featured Family," introducing new neighbors into the neighborhood.

Include other sections such as local sports, favorite jokes, or upcoming area events. More suggestions for topics of features include:

- Citizen of the month.
- Recipe of the month (a local person's favorite recipe).

- Energy-saving idea of the month.
- Real estate tip of the month.
- Budget tip of the month.

A newsletter is limited only by your imagination. The story of a lost cat and how it was found can be a fun and rewarding project for you. It may be a profitable service to the neighbors.

Another idea that will open up communications with the homeowners in your farm is to plan an area event yourself. These types of events rate high among the owners. Some events you can plan include bicycle safety day, children registration day, a Halloween event, or whatever you could dream up. I once did an Easter egg hunt that included more than 400 children and their parents. The publicity I received for it was amazing. The press even came and did a story on the hunt. I received several thank-you letters and it was fun. Other suggestions for events include:

- Chili cook-off.
- Community-wide yard sale.
- Youth sporting events.
- Game tournament.
- Bring Santa to the neighborhood.
- Pet vaccination.
- Child/bike identification.
- Kite-flying contest.
- Placing small flags along the street on 4th of July or September 11th.
- Food drive, coat drive, or shoe drive.
- Christmas lighting contest.
- Adopt a street in the farm area.

You should be active in the area. You should know every current listing whether it is yours or not. You should take a For Sale By Owner as a personal threat and do your best to list it. You should know each expired in your area and why.

Every weekend during your first year in the farm area you have chosen, you will hold an open house in your farm area. If you don't have listings, borrow them. You can do open houses for listings in your office even if they are not your own; just ask the listing salesperson and the broker.

When a house is sold in your farm, whether or not you had the listing or held open house, you can follow up the sale by personally delivering "Introducing Your New Neighbor" cards. These cards simply state, "New neighbors have moved in at 1623 Brittany Lane." Then tell about their family and if they are going to have a "moving in" party. Always get permission from the new people before you announce anything about them. This can be done because of the careful wording of the "Introducing Your New Neighbor" card. The wording at the top of the mail-out card says, "Listed for sale." Not "I had" or "we had" listed; thus anyone's listing can be used for these cards. Be sure to double-check this with your broker or manager.

The "public service" approach offers a good opportunity to ring doorbells in connection with a local or national election. During the six months prior to Election Day you have a legitimate and logical reason to call on people. For example:

> "Good afternoon, Ms. Homeowner. I am Dan Hamilton of the Acme Realty Company. [Present your business card.] We are making a survey to see if every eligible voter in this precinct is registered. May I inquire if you are?"

An excellent follow-up to the "Public Service Doorbell" is to volunteer your services on Election Day. As each homeowner arrives to vote, and you greet them again and help them with the voting process. They will be reminded of your service and assistance to them.

Always be thinking of ways to contact your farm area. For example, you can send holiday cards, birthday cards, or cards congratulating the owner for something.

An easy way to ascertain a birth date is to bring up the matter of horoscopes by saying, "Say, I'll bet you are a Leo" and the owner replies, "No, I am an Aries." As a natural follow-up you say, "Oh, what month?" and there you have it. When the owner receives your birthday greeting he will not likely recall the conversation but will be impressed by your thoughtfulness.

You might also think differently and send St. Patrick's Day cards. Everybody sends holiday cards, but not as many send St. Patrick's Day cards. If it will make you stand out, why not send both? I have a special card for each month of the year. If you plan to send holiday cards, and custom practically demands that you do, don't settle for the ordinary holiday greeting. Choose something so distinctive and unusual that it will stand out from all others.

Now and then you will have occasion to send an especially thoughtful remembrance. Perhaps, when answering the doorbell an owner will say, "I'm sorry, I can't talk now. My child is sick." You express your sympathy and ask which child it is. The child receives your get-well card and a small gift the next morning, you will have made the child feel much better and made a good impression on the parents.

As a routine matter, you should scan the birth, death, and marriage license columns in the paper to check for addresses within your farm so appropriate cards may be sent. The added results obtained from a program of gift giving and card sending will amaze you.

Eventually you should know every homeowner by name. You should practice naming the owner of each home as you drive down a street. It can be and is being done by the experts. Use flash cards to help: On one side of a blank note card write the owner's name; on the other side, write the address of the owner's house and some identification information. Over time the owners will get to know you and when they think of buying or selling their homes they will think of you.

Multiple Geographic Farming
When you have the geographic farming systems in place and you find you want to expand your territory, you can add more streets to your farm. You can also go to Multiple Geographic Farming (MGF). Here you can select areas that are not adjacent but may be miles apart. Look for different areas of houses and different price ranges to identify sellers in one of your farms that are ready to move up to a different farm area you control.

Business Farming

Business farming is effective, but time intensive. Unlike SOI and geographic farming, business farming is cultivating "business" people who you may not know but who are working in your area. As the expert in the area you should know as much about it as possible.

Business farming can be successful because most people are at work during the day. When a famous bank robber was asked why he robbed banks he simply replied, "That is where the money is." And that is why we farm for prospects where the prospects are–at their place of business.

When approaching businesses you don't want to look like a salesperson. You are not there to solicit sales; you are there only to introduce yourself. So don't wear your nametag or career apparel. Just carry a small note pad and pen or a PDA, if possible, but keep it in your pocket. Walk into the office and introduce yourself to the receptionist. The receptionist is whom you want because that person knows everything about the company.

> **Salesperson:** "Cindy?" [if you saw it on her name plate, if not just say good morning]
>
> **Receptionist:** "Yes."
>
> **Salesperson:** "My name is Dan Hamilton with Acme Realty. I'll be working in the area and just wanted to stop by and introduce myself to you.
>
> **Receptionist:** "O.K."

Depending on the temperature of the receptionist, continue with small talk or excuse yourself and leave.

> **Salesperson:** "I see that you are busy, it has been nice meeting you."

Either ask for a name or ask to take a business card if one is displayed. Do not ask for any business, it is not the time yet. When you step out of the door you should record the receptionist's name, the name of the business, the address, and any other information you gathered while talking with the receptionist. Then move on to the next business, repeating this process at the next ten to twelve businesses that constitute your business farm area. Like geographic farming, do not overextend yourself; keep the area small and grow it as your systems get better.

After you have been through your business farm once, you should return each month on the same day and time, such as the first Tuesday of each month at 9:15 a.m. so everyone knows your schedule. With each visit, try to find out more information. Don't expect the receptionist to remember your name and don't offer any services or ask for business. Continue this at each business for about six months and then bring in a gift. I usually bring donuts with my business card, printed as a sticker, stuck on both the outside and on the inside of the box. It is O.K. if a dozen donuts is not enough to feed the whole company as you are simply prospecting the receptionist. You will find that, on your day to bring donuts, some employees will be hanging around waiting for you. By the way, if you negotiate with the donut shop you can probably cut yourself a deal.

Eventually, the receptionist tells you that she heard Bob from the accounting department is being transferred and will need to sell his house and buy a new one in Seattle. You have now started to harvest this business. Be sure to update the receptionist on the referral and bring her a gift after closing.

How about this bonanza? The company needs to relocate its entire operation. If you are the person who has been there, you get the business of multiple executives.

I find that as long as you keep your visits brief and don't try selling anything, no one gets mad. I also find that it is at least six months before the receptionist knows your name and what you do. Again, business farming should be a "part" of your business, not your entire business. And it is kind of fun.

World Wide Web

The Internet is a great source for prospects. According to the National Association of Realtors (NAR), in 2003 over 71 percent of homebuyers started their searches on the Internet. NAR President Cathy Whatley said, "Nearly 90 percent of Internet searchers used a real estate professional." You need to do your own personal research to find out how extensive your Web presence should and how much it should cost.

Personal Web Site

Give prospects a copy of your Web site. Print out selected pages from your Web site in manual form, as a tri-fold flyer, a brochure, or a booklet. Make sure that every prospect gets a copy.

Nonoccupant Owners (NOO)

Nonoccupant owners (NOO) are the land-owners of real estate who are leasing the properties to renters. Some of these owners are "don't wanters," meaning they own property but don't want it. Some are so desperate to get out from under the burden of the property they become very willing to negotiate. I have said that selling real estate can provide you with a good living but to become wealthy you must buy it. Prospecting the NOO is a great way for you to look for investment grade property.

The five types of NOOs include:

1. **Not interested in selling.** These owners aren't worth your valuable time. Move on.
2. **Interested but has no equity.** These owners may be good prospects if they can sell and have money to pay closing costs.
3. **Interested and has a lot of equity.** Maybe this seller will offer owner financing. If so, you may want to buy the property as an investment. If not, list it and sell it.
4. **Interested but doesn't want to sell at the investment level.** List this property for sale on the open market and make the commission.
5. **An investor in real estate.** Keep these owners on a list for future prospecting. Almost all legitimate investors are always looking for their next deal.
6. **A true "don't wanter."** These are the properties you want to buy for yourself. You must disclose all of the relevant information and work this with the guidance of your broker. If you don't have the money, work out a venture with an investor on your investor list.

You can find NOOs by pulling tax records of the street you are interested in prospecting. Most computers in a real estate office have an online tax database. If not, you must go to the courthouse to search the records. Once you find the tax records, look for any property where the mailing address of the owner is not the same as the address of the subject property. This indicates the owner may not be the resident. Then send the owner the following letter:

Mr. or Mrs. Owner,

My name is Dan Hamilton with Acme Realty. I am wondering if you would consider selling the property at 1520 Westcreek to a prospect of mine?

If so, please call me at 817-555-1212 as soon as possible.

Thanks.

The letter is short and simple. The prospect you speak of is yourself. Remember, you should want to buy property if the owner is a "don't wanter" and you can't know that until they call.

The form letter can be created on your computer. Just substitute the owner's name and the subject property address, print it out, and mail it in a plain white envelope. If you use a business envelope, it may not be opened. You are not violating the Deceptive Trade Practices Act because you address yourself as a real estate licensed professional in the body of the letter. You should also address the envelope by hand, instead of using labels. Out of 100 of these letters sent you can expect the following results:

70%   No response, not interested.

15%   Not interested, just curious.

10%   Investors.

3%   Interested, but has no equity

1%   Interested, but not at investment level

One in every 500 are "don't wanters"

Floor Time

Floor time in a real estate office is sometimes called opportunity time or floor duty. Floor time means taking calls that come into the real estate office. Some offices have receptionists who screen the calls and pass prospects to the floor salesperson. Other offices require the floor salesperson to field and handle original calls.

Property Knowledge

Property knowledge is the knowledge of the property in the salesperson's market area. The only way to gain that knowledge is to view property and show it to potential buyers. If you want to preview property, do it sparingly and only as a break. Your time is better spent prospecting.

Market Specialization

Specializing in one market means concentrating on one main area. It does not eliminate other areas, it just centers your thinking and action.

Third Party Relocation Companies

In this segment of the real estate business third party companies buy or control the selling of the houses for corporate moves. These corporations pay a great deal of money to the third party companies who assign the actual sale of the properties to local real estate companies and their salespeople. The paperwork is intensive but the income is too. Most of this business is already assigned, but it would not hurt to talk with your broker or manager about getting your hands on this business.

Business Relocation

Nobody says you can't create your own relocation business. By prospecting companies you may come across one that is relocating. If so, you can help by providing referrals to the locations they are moving to and selling homes in your area. This type of sales requires a great deal of legwork but it can be highly rewarding.

Niche Markets

You can market your services directly to a niche market. These specific groups of people include any of the following:

- Doctors
- Lawyers
- Businesses owners
- Teachers
- Bankers
- First-time homebuyers
- Police officers
- Low-income homebuyers
- Professional athletes
- Seniors
- Military personnel

Builders

The builders market is unique because builders typically think they can sell a new home without the assistance of a real estate salesperson. If it doesn't sound familiar to you, review the FSBO section of this book. In fact, builders are quite similar to FSBOs. The difference is that builders can give you several properties per year.

There are several ways for you to gain access to builders and their buyers. For example, you can hold open houses for them and provide free advertising. Builders are in the business of building and you are in the business of selling. It is your job to be sure this arrangement occurs.

Real Estate Owned Property

Real Estate Owned (REO) property is owned by banks and lending institutions. They acquired these houses through foreclosure. The banks do not want to hold these properties, so they are great opportunities for the knowledgeable real estate professional. Sometimes they make great investment properties if the bank is willing to finance them. If the bank is really desperate to sell the REO, it might even finance with no money down.

The best way to get into REO sales is to take the bank's REO manager to lunch and find out how the property disposition works. If the manager tells you it is already taken care of, probe farther. (It only takes one screw-up of the current real estate salesperson for the REO manager to look for another.) Once you obtain the information you need, put together a portfolio of services that are tailor made to that particular REO manager and deliver it in person.

Follow-up is critical so keep in touch until the REO manager gives you just one to property to show your worth. If the REO manager is a golfer, ask to go play golf. If he or she enjoys a professional sporting event, come up with tickets. Never just give the REO manager tickets; you need to be there for rapport. Also check with your broker and state and national regulations boards to determine if these activities are considered kick-backs. The Real Estate Settlement Procedures Act is tricky here and continues to change.

Investors

A majority of investors are willing to pay a commission to real estate professionals for the right services. Be careful of these buyers because they can eat up your time and you will get very little in return. You can spend time researching properties and presenting them to your investor just to have the investor give you an offer so low that the seller rejects it. Your time then has been wasted. This could happen many times before a seller ever accepts an investor offer. My question is, "If the investment was such a good deal, why did you not buy it?'

Seller Seminar

A seller's seminar is given by a professional real estate salesperson to help sellers sell their own houses. While you may point out the reasons sellers would have better luck using professional salespeople, the seminar must include good marketing tips that the sellers can use. It is possible to give good and helpful information and still get the sale for yourself.

Each time you hold a seminar you will get better and learn more. You should hold the seminar at different times and on different days to get a feel for what works in your particular area. You must have a participation form attendees must fill out when they come in so you can get all of their information.

The seminar should have a workbook the seller can keep and use to take notes. The workbook should have an outline of the material covered. The book could be paid for with advertisements from local venders.

The class should cover the entire process of selling a house. It should begin with an overview, then cover specifics, and end with a summary and an offer of assistance. The materials should cover marketing, financing, titles, closings, costs, and all the forms necessary to sell a house. The subject matter should be heavily laden with legalities to scare the seller a bit. Make sure there are "gaps" in the presentation so the sellers will realize they need you to fill in those "gaps."

The seminar should include a fee to be determined by you. People see value in a fee. If the seminar is free the public believes it must be worth nothing and who would want to waste their time for nothing? It must be some kind of gimmick if it is for free. The fee is also nice to offset the costs involved in giving the seminar. You may also want to use it to pay for refreshments and printed materials. If you are afraid the fee will scare potential customers, offer free tickets through a local mortgage or title company. Have the company pay a portion of the ticket price for that advertisement.

Be cautious about inviting several important people to speak at your seminar that will make it a huge production. The reason is that if no one shows up you are not as humiliated. I was invited to speak at a seller seminar by a broker and only one seller actually showed up. Now if you think about it, the broker had a legitimate, interested seller; however, because the broker had invited a title officer, a mortgage officer, and myself to speak, she was so embarrassed that she did not even try and get the seller committed. My point is that one good lead is better than no lead at all. I believe it is best to speak yourself because it holds you out as the expert. If you feel you cannot speak, invite only one speaker you can count on.

Be sure to ask the sellers for their business before you end the seminar. Don't make the seminar a waste of time by not asking for the business. Also ask for the buying business. Once a seller sells, he or she becomes a buyer. With all the help you have given them they may feel obligated to buy through you. Take them up on it.

Community Involvement

Well-rounded real estate professionals should give back to their communities. Community involvement should not be contingent upon receiving business; it should be from the heart. If your intentions are not honorable, it will be sensed and you will not only fail, you will disgrace yourself for being dishonest.

I know real estate salespeople who select their places of worship based on the number of licensed real estate salespeople in the congregation. They believe that if they have no competition they can get all the business. I believe you will fail if you choose this approach.

Community involvement will get you business simply by osmosis. You do a good deed and others will want to help you out. (On the other hand, if you do a good deed and *expect* a return, you will receive (and deserve) nothing.) I know of real estate salespeople who have gone to their children's schools and asked to help. They ended up printing school take-home bags for daily information the students were to take home. The school benefits because it doesn't have the cost of the bags and the real estate salespeople put their names on the bags that went into the homes of hundreds of families.

You are the only one who limits the types of community involvement. Volunteers are needed in all types of charity work. I say you should not prospect your fellow volunteer but you can wear your career apparel. But be careful here. I know of many well-intentioned real estate salespeople who ended up so involved in the community and real estate associations that they never had any time to make money. Remember balance.

Association Meetings

The real estate industry offers several support groups and associations. Participation in these groups will not make you money, but the money you get might be easier and more rewarding.

Chapter Summary

As you have seen, there are many ways to make money in the real estate business. You need to practice each of these prospecting techniques to find your favorites and the ones that are most comfortable for you. You should concentrate on those. Do not pass off any of these techniques without putting in effort to master them. You can either be active or passive. Neither is worse than the other, but the better one is the one that is best for you. Market yourself through calls and knocking on doors. Develop your contact list with your sphere of influence and the areas you choose to farm. Call on FSBOs. Get involved in your community. These may not all pay off immediately but in the long term they might be extremely profitable.

Summary Questions

1. Which of the following is an "active" way to prospect?
   A. Call FSBOs.
   B. Offer assistance to the "Welcome Wagon."
   C. Run a personal advertisement.
   D. Join a health club to meet new people.

2. How many weeks should you follow a FSBO system to be successful?
   A. 3
   B. 12
   C. 18
   D. 6

3. What critical goal must be achieved when initiating and then developing a relationship with a FSBO?
   A. Work up a net sheet.
   B. Get an appointment to be face-to-face.
   C. Develop a mail-out campaign.
   D. Do a market analysis to see if they are priced right.

4. How often should you prospect?
   A. 12 hours a week.
   B. Daily.
   C. Constantly.
   D. Depends on your real estate goals.

5. What should you do in your farm area?
   A. Inform the neighbors if minorities are moving in.
   B. Send out a minimum of 12 mailings per year.
   C. Take all of the available listings, even if they are overpriced.
   D. All of the above.

6. How many homes should be in your original farm area?
   A. No more than 100
   B. 800–1,000
   C. Less than 25
   D. 1,500–2,200

7. What are abandoned clients in the real estate business called?
   A. Protected Sids
   B. Revisions
   C. Waifs
   D. TLCs

8. What is it called when a real estate salesperson specializes in one particular geographic area and becomes the expert on property values and sales activities?
   A. Farming
   B. Generalizing
   C. Active prospecting
   D. Sublocation

9. Salable listings are like:
   A. A prison sentence.
   B. Gold.
   C. A ride on a roller coaster.
   D. A yo-yo going up and down.

10. All of the following often result when FSBOs overprice their properties, except:
   A. More agents contacting them.
   B. Higher out-of-pocket expenses.
   C. Fewer showings.
   D. Sells too fast.

Chapter 8

Seller Listing Procedures

Chapter Objectives

In this chapter you will learn about selling listing procedures–everything from taking a listing from a seller, the entire marketing process, and closing. There are many steps involved and you should be sure to check with your broker or manager on the exact procedures specific to your office.

Key Words

Close: To bring to an end.

Improvement: A change or an addition that improves.

Manual: Of, relating to, or resembling a small reference book.

Market: The business of buying and selling real estate.

Needs: Of necessity, something required.

Price: The amount as of money asked for or given in exchange for something else.

Results: To come about as a consequence; an outcome.

Wants: To desire greatly, wish for.

Introduction

No matter how good you are at prospecting, if you can't sell your inventory you cannot help your clients or yourself. If you do a few things right you will be able to market and sell your properties successfully. One of the most important first steps is to prepare properly before an appointment.

Preparing for the Appointment

You need to prepare for a listing appointment. Don't wait until the last minute. You need to have all of your "stuff" together. You should be mentally prepared for the worst, toughest sellers imaginable. If the sellers turn out to be nice people (and most do) you have it made. If the seller is some type of nasty, cruel troll at least you are prepared.

In a real estate office I owned, I had hired a nice young man who was obviously a rookie. One day as he was leaving the office dressed in a pair of jean shorts with a t-shirt, I hollered to him, "Where are you going?" He said that he was going on a listing appointment. This came as quite a shock to me considering how he was dressed (you should be better dressed just being *in* the office). I asked him what was up and he said a friend wanted him to list his house and sell it. I asked if he wanted me to go along. He said no because this friend knew him and it was a sure thing. I asked him if he had done a CMA and he said "no" because they were best friends and would just talk about it.

Sometimes you can't help no matter how hard you try. When he got back, I asked him how it went and he confessed that his friend wanted him to list the house but his friend's wife "knew" the friend. She knew him as a wild party guy, not a professional real estate salesperson. The couple had decided to let him list the property if he showed up and acted professional. He didn't and they listed with someone else.

I remember a couple who had a property on the market that did not sell. I called them up and went out to their home to list the property. At the presentation, they agreed with everything I said. At times they even remarked, "What a nice guy! You would do that for us." It was one of those times when everything seemed to work. I finally said, "Put me to work for you." They said they would but they were going out of town for two weeks and would call me when they got back. I usually would have pressed the matter and had them list with me right then, but in this case I was sure of my position.

Two weeks later I got a call from them saying they were ready. I was certain the listing was mine, considering I said everything they wanted to hear and I was heading back out to list it. As I was getting in my car a little voice in my head said, "Take *everything* with you." I thought, "Nah, the sellers like me, it's in the bag." But I heard the voice again, only this time it was louder. So I brought everything. When I got to the appointment we exchanged pleasantries and I said, "I have filled out the agreement with the terms we already discussed. I just need your authorization and we will make every effort to get you happily moved."

About this time they turned and began to spit fire and asked, "What is it exactly that you are promising to do for us? How much are you charging? How long is the listing for?" I staggered back and said, "Let me go to my car and get my things." I sat down and began the listing presentation over from the beginning. After all was said and done they listed with me.

What if I hadn't listened to that little voice and had appeared unprepared? I think we can guess.

Boy Scout Motto:

Be Prepared

Before you show up at a seller's front door, you need to know the market in that area. Market research will allow you to describe current market conditions so the sellers can sct a competitive price and understand your marketing strategies. This phase involves completing a market evaluation.

Competitive Market Analysis (CMA)

A solid Competitive Market Analysis (CMA) will help you get your listings sold. It shows sellers where their properties fit in the current market and shows that the salesperson has done his or her homework. The CMA determines the maximum price that justifies taking the listing.

Market evaluation data are records of listings and selling prices of comparable properties. These facts of record will help you evaluate a property and determine a salable price range.

A CMA is not market value or an appraisal. Market value is determined by the amount a seller is willing to sell his or her property for and the amount a buyer is willing to pay with open market conditions, all information known, and both parties acting in their own best interests with neither party under duress.

Some real estate salespeople and the general public believe that an appraisal is value or what the property is really worth. This is not correct; an appraisal is only *one* person's *opinion* of the property's value.

I had a listing appointment in which the seller wanted more money from the house than the market would bear. I could not convince the seller that the property should sell for $115,000 because the seller wanted $130,000. I suggested using a professional appraiser. When the appraisal came back at $115,000, the seller agreed to it and we began marketing the house at that price. Within a few weeks a buyer offered the seller $115,000 and the seller accepted.

The buyer was working with a mortgage company that had "staff appraisers" who work for particular mortgage companies that only accept appraisals from their appraisers.

This staff appraiser had to call me for directions to the property. I should have been afraid at this point. He when came back with a value of $100,000, I asked him to review my comparables. The appraiser said, "No," and that was that.

I don't believe the appraiser acted professionally, but what could I do? I thought we had lost this transaction, but the buyer still agreed to pay $115,000 as we had established value four times against the staff appraiser's one time. Numbers and consistent research are legitimate arguments.

A CMA is a tool, not a weapon. Some real estate salespeople use it to beat the sellers over their heads. They don't ask the seller questions to determine needs. They don't use other techniques to help the sellers see value. All they do is wield the CMA like a battle-ax and the sellers tend to fight. Hint: Never fight with your clients, you might win the battle but lose the war.

> **"Every detail of a property is driven by, reflected in, and comes back to PRICE."**
> —*Rex Patton, Manager, Century 21,*
> *Judge Fite Company*

Types of Data for a CMA

There are three types of data that need to be included on a CMA.

1. **Actives**—This data includes properties that are currently on the market for sale. The information gives you a look at your competition. If the sellers insist on pricing their houses for more, they will be priced out of the market. Actives are for reference only. Prices should be based on the prices of houses already sold.

2. **Solds** —This data includes properties that have actually sold. A ready, willing, and able buyer agreed to a price with the seller. We can use the price to determine a price for the subject property. Generally, the real estate salesperson should use three comparables for adequate evaluation.

3. **Expireds**—This data includes properties that were marketed but did not sell, typically because they were priced too high. This is valuable information for the seller. Do the sellers actually want to *sell* their properties or do they just want to market them?

Good Comparables

It is best to drive around a neighborhood to see the area before doing a CMA. You are not doing the seller any favors if you present a CMA but don't know the area. You can learn the neighborhood quickly by looking at the statistics and driving around the neighborhood.

A good comparable for running a CMA for a property should include the following five considerations, which are listed in order of importance.

- **Area**—Where is the property located? If all of the comparables are in the same area they typically have a similar build.

- **Square Footage**—If one house is 800 square feet and another house is 8,000 square feet, you cannot make any adjustments. The difference is not only in size but also in quality.

- **Age**—A property built 200 years ago is not the same as one built last year.

- **Amenities**—An amenity is anything that adds value.

- **Terms of Sale**—This includes creative financing, time on market, or any other nuances.

To run a CMA on your computer:

1. Pull up the tax records for the area.
2. Pull up the CMA program on your MLS.
3. Run the CMA by subdivision, then run it by map area.

If you come up with more than 20 comparables, you need to enter more criteria to reduce that number. You can do this by limiting the square footage, the age, or maybe including a special amenity like a swimming pool if one is available. Do not limit too much to start or you might not get a good comparable base.

Once you have narrowed the comparables to 20 or so, stop and evaluate them. Look for the three best comparable properties using the above criteria. Once you have selected the three you will use, generate a full report on each of them, including the tax records.

A good, valuable comparable must be a property that sold within the last six months. Also, it should not be a distressed sale like a foreclosure. Many sellers believe that the seller and the real estate salesperson set the sale price of a property. This is not true; the marketplace sets the price. Again, you need at least three good sold comparables to for a worthy evaluation.

Outside factors, such as supply and demand, the local or national economy, and seasonal variations, also play a part in determining a listing price. Consider these factors along with the information you collected for the comparables. Through experience, you will develop skills to incorporate all the variables involved.

Questions for the Seller

When talking with a seller on the telephone, there are a few questions you should ask before you go on the listing appointment; doing so will aid you in completing a CMA.

KEY QUESTION: Do you have a second to tell me a little bit about your home?

1. How many bedrooms and bathrooms do you have?
2. How many living areas are in the house?
3. Is there a garage? If so, how many cars does it hold?

163

4. What kitchen equipment do you have?

5. Is your patio covered?

6. Is there a fence? What is it made from, metal or wood?

7. Does the house have a security system or an intercom?

8. Do you have a swimming pool or a spa?

9. Does the house have central heat and central air?

10. What type of flooring is used in the house?

11. Is there a fireplace or a wet bar in the house?

12. What else can you tell me about your home?

FINANCIAL QUESTIONS

1. How much do you want to sell your house for?

2. What is the amount remaining on your house note?

Appraisals Are Getting Tougher

Appraisals are getting tougher as demonstrated by the Federal Housing Administration's stringent property requirements, their review of completed appraisals, and the rapidly changing market values. Here are some hints about appraisals that will help you:

- Like = Like. The goal of any appraisal is to find comparable properties that are as much like the subject property as possible. If there are no similar properties, the appraiser must go to other sales and start adjusting for the values. It is better to use a similar property than adjust, because adjustment amounts are limited to no more than 10 percent of the value!

- Current sales are required. You can't use properties that were sold more than a year from the time of your listing. Six months is better. If there are no area sales in that time frame, explore other options. If the appraisal on a sale doesn't make the value of the sales price, rerun a current CMA to look at current sales. You have the right to question any mistakes you think the appraiser may have made.

- Be aware of economic and functional obsolescence. Economic obsolescence occurs when the market changes around a property (a house in the middle of an industrial district). Functional obsolescence occurs when the market demand makes features out of date (for example, a one-car garage vs. a two-car garage). These factors affect the approach the appraiser uses.

- Money has no time value. Just because you're seeing a rapid increase in prices in a neighborhood, you cannot project that rate of increase onto your listing. And, if inflation starts up again, you cannot use the rate of inflation on previous sales prices like you would if you had deposited the money in a bank earning interest.

- Property condition is critical, especially on FHA-priced properties. Some appraisers think that if they are doing an FHA appraisal, they must find defects in the property to be corrected. Otherwise, they are afraid the FHA will think they are too lenient. Be aware that the results of almost any FHA will require some repairs, so prepare your seller for that. Obviously, conventional appraisals are going to be somewhat easier. And, the more money a buyer puts down, the less closely a lender is going to look at the property. In any case, do not commit your buyer in a contract to make repairs. Keep in mind that lender-required repairs are always negotiable between buyer and seller.

- Do not be afraid to question how the appraiser got his or her figures and be prepared to share how you got your figures. Be nice, be open to suggestions, be reasonable, and you will find most appraisers will work with you.

Communicating the Results

When the time is right (one of the last steps in the listing procedure) you should communicate the results of the CMA. It is best to have the CMA on a typewritten spreadsheet. You can buy them for your computer relatively inexpensively or you can just create your own. A spreadsheet looks professional and official. If your handwriting is like mine it would take a code breaker to read it. I once had a seller look at my computer-generated CMA and comment that he did not agree with all the values given but it was done by a "computer" so it must be right. You would think he would know that *I* created all the values. But if it looks professional, people assume it is done by a professional.

Follow these steps while communicating the results of your CMA.

1. Explain how the CMA is organized.
2. Tell the sellers why each type of property in the CMA is important to the process.

3. Begin with recent sales, giving this section the most weight.
4. Describe each property thoroughly, comparing it to the sellers' homes.
5. Allow ample time for the sellers to digest the information.
6. Point out the range of values.
7. Present a net proceeds estimate based on the middle of your recommended range.
8. Remind sellers of their goals. Help the sellers to set the correct price.

Seller's Net Sheet

At this point in the presentation you should present a seller's net sheet, including the amount of money the seller will walk away with after all expenses have been paid.

Seller Presentation Manual

A seller presentation, also called a listing or marketing book, is a manual showing the seller the real estate salesperson's marketing plan for the seller's house. This manual sends a consistent message over and over again. Because it is consistent the manual keeps you from straying to areas that might be construed as violations of the Federal Fair Housing laws. (Hopefully this is not a problem but the manual helps prevent any errors.) The presentation manual serves two main purposes:

1. Provides a visual presentation of the services offered. A majority of people are visual in nature. This means clients may gain a greater understanding of the plan by seeing it all laid out rather than just being told about it. The presentation manual accomplishes this goal.

2. Provides a track for the real estate salesperson to follow. One of the biggest fears of a new real estate salesperson is the listing appointment. The salesperson just does not know what to do and what to say. The presentation manual overcomes this dilemma.

   My wife wanted to sell Mary Kay cosmetics. The company gave her a presentation manual to help sell their products. She was studying script trying her best to memorize the words. To help her, I was willing to show her the value of a marketing manual to keep her on track instead of learning the exact wording. Don't get me wrong, I believe in memorizing script, but that is not the purpose of a marketing manual. I took the manual and began a marketing presentation on Mary Kay cosmetics, which I knew nothing about. Each time I turned the page the heading gave me a hint of the concept I should cover. The manual works much like an outline does for a speaker. I did a great presentation with a subject I knew little about. Just think how good you could do if you knew the material.

Most real estate companies provide their real estate salespeople with some sort of seller listing manual. If you have one or need to develop one, here are some things that should be included:

- Questions to keep people involved.
- Pictures for variety.
- Bulleted statements, not complete sentences.
- A walk-through of each segment of the presentation.

Seller Listing Packet

A seller listing packet includes of all the documents needed to place a property on the market. Most real estate companies will make up listing packets for their salespeople. If the company does not do this, the real estate salesperson must. A complete listing packet should at least include all of the following items:

- Seller's Listing Agreement
- Buyer's Brokerage Agreement
- Seller's Property Disclosure Statement
- Agency Disclosure Form
- Multiple Listing Service Input Form
- Mortgage Information Letter
- Home Warranty Brochures
- Advertising Submission Form
- Yard Sign Call-Up Form
- Any additional forms required by law or your broker

Keep several of these packets in your briefcase and in your automobile. You never know when you might need a listing packet.

I say this because someday you will forget a listing packet when you arrive at a listing appointment. I was with a new real estate salesperson on one of his first listing appointments. He was doing great, so good in fact that when I looked at the sellers and said, "Will you put us to work for you?" the sellers agreed.

The salesperson began to talk about something else. I kind of nudged him for the listing packet. He gave me one of those looks like his hand was caught in the cookie jar. He had forgotten the listing packet. I turned to the sellers and said, "The next thing for us to do is to go to the office and input the data about your house and revise the Competitive Market Analysis. We can be back here in forty minutes, is that acceptable to you?" They looked confused but agreed.

Keep the listing packets with you to avoid the pressure and hassle.

Tools to Bring

Bring everything to a listing presentation. You never know what you might need to convince a seller to list with you and it's better to have too much than not enough. Keep what you're not expecting to need in your car. Here is a partial list:

- Listing packet
- Lock box
- Lock box key (if needed)
- Flashlight
- Note pads
- Writing utensils (more than one)
- Tape measure
- For Sale sign (if its size isn't a problem)
- Title insurance rate card

Arrival Time

Arrive on time to the listing appointment. Promptness shows the owner you will do what you say and it shows genuine care for the owner.

Do not be early either. My wife and I had made plans to meet an insurance salesperson at 7 p.m. At ten minutes until seven the doorbell rang. It was the salesperson. I was not ready and needless to say uncomfortable. By the way, the salesperson did not sell me insurance.

It's ideal to arrive about ten to fifteen minutes early, but do not go to the door. Instead, drive around the neighborhood and look for other houses for sale. This helps you look like the expert if the seller asks about any of the other sales in the area, and you might even pick up a For Sale By Owner. You want to be early just in case of mishaps, like getting lost.

Park on the street in front of the house, if possible. It is best if you do not park in the driveway because someone else might need to leave or park there. This way you won't have to get up from the presentation to move your car.

Another nice trick is to take an instant picture of the property. Place the photo in a folder with the property address and your name written on it. When the seller answers the door you hand them the picture and say, "Sometimes people do not have pictures of their home and I thought it would be nice if you had one." It's simple, but effective in breaking the ice. Digital cameras and computer technology can help.

Approach to the Door

When it is time for your appointment, either knock or ring the doorbell. Do something, don't just stand there, you might never get in. Which is better, knocking or ringing? Don't sweat the small stuff. Once somebody told me to give a hearty knock on the door. I hit the door so hard my knuckles started bleeding. The owner got to the door and I needed a towel to clean up the blood. Now, I ring the doorbell.

Once you ring the doorbell (or knock), you should take a step or two back allowing for a little space between you and the door. Look away to the left with your name badge on your right lapel so the owner can see it. You might want to whistle softly to show that you are calm.

Smile when the owner opens the door. Don't smile from ear-to-ear, which will make you look like a high-pressure salesperson. Again, something soft is appropriate. Then offer to shake the owner's hand. It's what we do in Texas. (Some studies in manners claim you should never offer your hand to a lady, but I say, do what is comfortable for you.) After you shake the owner's hand, introduce yourself and say, "We have an appointment for 7 p.m." Look at your watch, and say, "It is exactly 7 p.m." If this is comfortable it shows the owner you are prompt and you do what you say.

Entering the Home

Just as you enter the home be sure to wipe your feet every time. You do not ever want to track anything in the house. Also, look for shoes piled around the door. If you see this, offer to take your shoes off as it just may be their custom. Then pay the owner a compliment. Some tips for complimenting include:

- Never compliment the house. Doing so may drive up their price.
- Never compliment if it makes you sound like a high-pressure salesperson.
- Never compliment the spouse on how great he or she looks because someone else might take offense to that.

So what can you compliment? How about the children? This is the best line if it presents itself: "Mr. and Mrs. Seller, I just wanted to say how polite your children seem when I called here to set this appointment. That shows a great deal on how you are raising them." Now head for the kitchen table.

Meeting at the Kitchen Table

The first objective once you enter the sellers' house is to head to the kitchen table. This is where all domestic decisions are made. The living room is for entertaining and you are not there to entertain or to be entertained. The kitchen table provides the surface to spread your marketing materials out. It is the place where documents can be signed to start the marketing process. If you do not get to the kitchen table you are one major point down to get the listing.

170

The best way to get to the kitchen table is to lead. Once in the house and the compliment has been paid, head to the kitchen table. Don't hesitate. If the owner says the table is dirty, offer to help clean it off. No matter what, get to the kitchen table.

Once seated at the kitchen table, ask the seller for a glass of water. The hospitable thing for the seller to do is offer you something to drink. You are allowing the seller to be hospitable to you. Only take water, ice water if you prefer.

I arrived at one listing in the heat of the summer. It must have been 110 degrees in the shade. I was parched and asked the seller for some water. He held up a giant glass of iced tea and said, "My wife just freshly brewed some tea would you like that instead?" and the tea looked and sounded great, so I accepted a huge glass of and took a big gulp. It had to be the worst tasting tea in the world. It actually tasted like dirt. But I had to drink it all so as not to offend. If you do not drink bad tasting water no one is offended.

Wants and Needs Analysis

The next step in the listing process is to discuss the agenda for meeting. The sellers are curious about the events of the evening and will more likely wait to ask questions if they feel there is a process. The meeting should have the following track:

- **Ask Questions.** Find out the seller's motivation for selling and what his or her goals are. This is where I determine if I even want the listing. By the way, follow this approach for every listing appointment. Don't go into an appointment to get the listing, go in to see if you even want it. If you need a listing badly it will show. You will tend to take the property overpriced with the property in need of repair. If you go in to see if you even want the listing, you will be much stronger.
- **Inspect the Property.** Take a look at the property with the proper evaluation techniques.
- **Discuss My Abilities to Market the Property.** List the reasons for listing with you.
- **Discuss My Company's Abilities to Market the Property.** List the reasons for listing with your company.

- **Discuss My Personal Marketing Plan for the Property.** Discuss the services provided for selling the property.
- **Determine the Price that will Sell the Property.** Discuss the best price for the seller.
- **Discuss Working Together for the Benefit of Both Parties.**

Once you have gone over these items, ask the sellers if there is anything else they want to cover. They generally don't have questions, but if they do, be sure to take it seriously and write down the questions. No matter what the sellers say, if it is important enough for them to say it is important enough for you to write down.

Now ask the seller a series of questions. The questions should be written down and shown to the seller. Studies have proven that the salesperson who has a written list of questions is perceived as more organized and professional. These questions include:

1. Why are you moving?
2. When do you want or have to move?
3. How long have you lived in your present house?
4. What "major improvements" have you made to the house in the last year?
5. Who else are you talking with about the sale of your house?
6. Can you move without selling this house first?
7. Would you consider owner financing?
8. How did you arrive at your price?
9. Do you have any concerns about making a move?
10. Which of the following is most important to you: price, timing, or convenience?
11. What would it do to your plans if you just couldn't sell?
12. What would it take for you to list with me tonight?

These questions should be asked exactly as written as all of them, including the order in which you ask them, will make a difference. The questions put the sellers through a process of evaluating selling their house and the real estate salesperson has time to decide if he or she wants the listing. It is always better to walk away from a listing earlier than later. Let's analyze each question:

Why are you moving? This is a simple question, but the answer gives you insight into the seller's motivation. If the seller really does not need to move but would if he or she could get the desired price, that seller is not motivated. If the seller has a job transfer and must be in another state, that seller is motivated. A motivated seller will be more realistic in selling the house. You should already know the answer to this question if you have a "clear-cut" listing appointment, but you should ask it again. There is a big difference between what people tell you over the telephone and what they tell you in person. Facial expressions and body language reveal a lot. This question and the next one are a little tense for the sellers because they must now commit to a decision. Expect their hesitation.

When do you want or have to move? The answer to this simple question again gives insight into the seller's motivation. If the seller can move any-time within the next six years, he or she is not motivated. If the seller must move within the next 60 days, he or she is motivated.

How long have you lived in your present house? This question is designed to lighten the pressure the sellers may feel from the first two questions. The sellers know how long they have lived in their house, so they do not feel pressure anymore. The information value to the real estate salesperson is learning the seller's equity position. If the seller has recently purchased the house, he or she might not have enough equity in it to pay the closing costs. This may result in the seller demanding more for the house than it might be worth.

What "major improvements" have you made to the house in the last year? "Major improvements" is of importance with this question. Some sellers believe that changing a light bulb is an improvement. Write down every-thing and do not challenge anything now as this time is for information gathering, not for discussion, which will come later. This question will help identify any undisclosed features of the home you need to know about. This could make a difference in the value of the house. This question has very little pressure.

Who else are you talking with about the sale of your house? As a real estate professional, you need to know your competition, including their strengths and weaknesses. Do not disparage your competition, but if you offer a service your competition can't, be sure to emphasize that. If the seller is not talking to anyone else, that is also good to know. This question could generate a lot of pressure if the seller is telling you a secret. Some sellers believe they can play one real estate salesperson against another to receive a better deal.

Can you move without selling this house first? The answer to this question should smoke out any potential problems the seller may have, including not enough equity to sell. It also alerts you that these sellers might already be looking at other houses and you want to be the one to sell them their new home. If a seller does not need to sell first, ask about the buy side.

Would you consider owner financing? Owner financing is when the seller helps out the buyer with all or part of the financing for the house. If the seller is willing to help, it will open up this house to more potential buyers.

How did you arrive at your price? Pricing is usually one of the biggest objections a seller will have. Does it surprise anyone that the seller wants more than the house is worth? The answer to this question will help you determine how the seller got his or her price and whether or not is was based on fact or what just what the seller needs and/or wants.

Do you have any concerns about making a move? Some sellers may have a reason holding them back from moving. It would be very disappointing if you put effort into selling a property and received a good offer only to have the seller decline because he or she doesn't want to sell before the end of the school year or the construction on his or her home won't be finished for another three months.

Which of the following is most important to you: price, timing, or convenience? These are the big three when it comes to the motivation of the seller. Will the seller be motivated greater by the price received, the length of time it takes to sell the property, or the plain convenience of having the house sold so he or she can move on with life?

What would it do to your plans if you just couldn't sell? Some sellers don't believe they *have* to sell. This question makes them think ahead and maybe become a little more reasonable.

What would it take for you to list with me tonight? This is the most important question and it must be asked. It is a little intimidating to the real estate salesperson because it feels like high pressure. Don't mellow the question; ask it as it is written. The question is so important because you are asking for the seller's final objection to hiring you and you are asking it upfront. It is easier to ask now because it is not threatening to the seller at this point. If you wait until you begin closing, the seller might clam up. It also allows you plenty of time to overcome the seller's final objection, if any.

During my career, after I would ask this question and receive the seller's final objection, I would have the rest of my listing presentation time to come up with objection-handling techniques. The seller might say something like, "Well, we would list it with you if you can get us our price." But knowing the seller's price was too high for the area, I would spend the entire listing presentation making a case for a lower price.

Property Viewing

The next step in the listing process is taking a look at the property. You should only proceed if the seller answered the previous twelve questions to your satisfaction. Sometimes the seller is totally unrealistic on the price of his or her house. If you cannot overcome the objection and list the property at a reasonable price, DO NOT TAKE THE LISTING. This is not the time for price objections. If the seller is a little off on pricing, you should wait until it's time to discuss pricing. It is only when the seller is completely unreasonable that you would end the presentation.

If you find the sellers are worth spending more time with, you should involve them when you inspect the property. It will help them see the marketing of the property as a cooperative effort. During the tour you should make a note of all the seller's comments regarding the property. Again, if it is important enough for the seller to mention, it is important enough to write down. Discuss and list the items that don't stay with the property. Note the condition of the property and understand the difference between *maintenance* items and *improvement* items. Maintenance items are things around the house that should be taken care of before selling. Improvement items are the things the seller has added to the house, such as room additions, remodeling, and extensive landscaping. Some sellers believe the buyer should pay for a new light bulb. They shouldn't, as a new light bulb is considered a minor living expense. These types of expenses are maintenance items and should be ignored.

A real estate professional should be able to look at real property through the eyes of several other individuals. The first should be the appraiser's eyes. What would an appraiser look for? Will the property hold market value? The next set of eyes are those of a property inspector. What repairs should be done? Are there any hidden problems? The last sets of eyes are the eyes of a buyer. Is the property in show condition? Are there things the seller can do to impress the buyer more?

Your property inspection will undoubtedly reveal minor items in need of repair and necessary cosmetic changes. Your recommendations might include:

• Removing clutter or excess furniture so rooms will appear larger.

• Organizing closets and cabinets.

• Touching up paint.

• Landscaping.

• Removing family pictures.

During the walkthrough you should concentrate on building rapport with the seller. Make an effort to comment on situations that do not have to do with real estate. If you see golf clubs and you are a golfer, ask the seller about golfing. If you see a piece of embroidery in the making, ask about it. Do not "ooh" and "aah" about the house while walking through, which is common mistake made while trying to build rapport. We want to make the seller think we like the property, but we are not going to buy the property. A seller's most frequent objection is pricing. If you "ooh" and "aah" over the house, it will be difficult to tell the seller his or her price is too high. Every "ooh" and every "aah" raises the seller's expectations.

Laptop Presentations

If you have a laptop computer you can customize the presentation for the seller or you can use generic listing presentation software. The presentation can have incredible graphics, voiceovers, and music. Some sellers are technology sophisticated and expect a better presentation. You can make copies of the presentation on a CD and leave it with the seller to review. (Be careful never to leave anything with a seller that you don't want to end up in the hands of your competition. Weigh the pros and cons of leaving materials.)

But do not rely solely on technology. People need to feel they have a person to do business with and not some computer. Also, technology can fail, so always have a hard copy backup of your presentation manual in your car.

Discuss Personal Results

During this discussion you should share your personal results. These include the number of sales you have had in the last year, the clients you have helped to achieve their goals, and letters of recommendation. (If you don't have "letters of recommendation"—GET THEM!) Also discuss your personal successes, such as all of your real estate awards. Do not talk about your past career as your customers are only concerned about what you do now. If you are new to the business and don't have real estate successes, then spend your time talking about your company. You can use the word "we" because it is your company and your company's successes are also yours. Remember to "close" this section out by asking the seller if he or she has any questions up to this point.

Discuss Company Results

In this section of the listing presentation you should discuss the positive activities of your company. Use your listing manual at this point to make sure you stay on track. Discuss successes, including the number of sales and any recognition or awards. Form a list of a select group of house addresses and the lengths of time it took your company to sell them. The time should be 60 days or less. Use only the street name, not the street number, and avoid giving directions. All you want to do is impress the seller on the amount of houses your company has sold within 60 days.

During this time you should describe the team you have formed, including your broker, all the real estate salespeople in your office, and any affiliates such as appraisers, inspectors, mortgage officers, title officers, and structural engineers to name a few. This is a good time to promote anything your company does that the competition may not do. Think outside the box to develop this section to its fullest. Ask your broker and other salespeople in the office for their ideas.

During each section to follow you should be asking a series of questions to get your point across. I hate the word "presentation" because it means I talk and you listen. It's important to get the clients involved because we need their input and they feel better about us if we are concerned about their opinions. It has a much different effect when you ask, "What is most important to you?" instead of "This is the most important thing you should be concerned about."

I was once asked to view a new real estate salesperson's listing presentation because it was so good. I was excited to take notes on such a good presentation. We sat down as if I was a seller and the real estate salesperson began the presentation. Forty-five minutes later he was still going. I don't think he took a breath. He had no listing presentation manual, he never asked for my input, and I don't think he wanted me to talk at all. He spoke entirely on his past job. As a potential seller I was not only turned off by his arrogance, I was offended by his lack of caring. He lost me so bad that I disengaged and almost fell asleep. When he *finally* finished he said, "How was that?" I smiled, said "Great," and got up and left.

Now why did I not help him? When the student is ready the teacher will appear. If I had tried to help him he would have been offended. He did not want any criticism; he wanted praise. Too bad that praise will not make him any money. It is interesting to note that the seller will do the same thing to you, except you will hear the words, "We'll call you." They won't.

An involvement technique is to let the seller finish your sentences for you. Do not labor at this as it should be very natural. You have a sentence that is has an easily recognizable finish and instead of finishing it yourself, pause slightly to allow the seller to finish it for you. If the sellers do what they are supposed to do, congratulate them with, "Right" or "Exactly," and they will continue to do it.

Once you complete the discussion about company results, "close" this section out with the seller. Make sure to "close" every section to avoid objections from the seller later.

When I was a rookie real estate salesperson I was afraid of objections. What if I could not handle the objection? How silly would I look? Because of my fear and lack of presentation skills I received tons of objections and

178

was always stressed about listing appointments. I began "closing" each section by addressing questions as they came up, and I rarely received any objections late in the presentation. Try this:

> **Salesperson:** "Mr. and Mrs. Seller, do you have any questions about my company?"
>
> **Seller:** "No."
>
> **Salesperson:** "Do you believe my company can help you sell your house?"
>
> **Seller:** "Yes."

The key point here is that the seller must say yes. Do not settle for, "Well, I guess." Drive the point home by asking again.

Discuss Specific Marketing

A professional real estate salesperson should have two marketing presentations. The first one should be a standard marketing presentation for use in any situation. The second should be a marketing presentation directed specifically toward the current potential client.

Both presentations should follow the same format spelling out the step-by-step process for selling the property. Be sure to include each activity and a schedule for completion. This is a time some real estate salespeople fail. They do not mention the little things, such as:

- Entry into the MLS.
- Presentation to the office salespeople.
- Office tour.
- Advertising campaign.
- Marketing flyers.
- "For Sale" sign installation.
- Lock box installation.
- Presentation at the local Association of REALTORS®.

The presentation (marketing plan) should be updated as the marketing time progresses. Send it to the seller so that he or she knows you are working. Last but not least, "close" this section out.

Discuss Price

After the seller agrees to let you market the property, move to the last section of your presentation: pricing. This is last because pricing tends to be the seller's biggest objection. You can't fault the sellers, all they want is the most they can get for their property. As discussed in the "Clear-Cut Listing Appointment" section of this book, you should already know what price the seller is looking for. If this is in line with your Comparative Market Analysis (CMA), your pricing discussion should be as follows:

> **Salesperson:** "Mr. & Mrs. Seller, if I believe I can get the price you are asking for. Would you list with me right now?"

Right to the "close," I like it! Too many times we "professional" salespeople get so enamored with our presentation that we forget our purpose of getting the listing. Don't sell with LA–DE–DA when you can sell with LA. That simply means, don't oversell, don't talk too much, close early and often.

I went on an appointment with a new real estate salesperson to help out. He was doing great and the seller, a single woman, was buying into everything he was saying. It was going so well that I could sense it was time to close. When the salesperson failed to do it I stepped in and said, "Put us to work for you." The seller looked at us and said, "Yes."

Without hesitation I began to get out the paperwork for her to authorize. The other salesperson looked a bit shocked and continued his presentation. I looked at him with distress in my eyes and gave him the "finger across the throat" act to shut up. He did not. I assume he wanted to further impress the seller, his mentor, or himself.

Finally he said we could do an open house to get buyers in to see the property. Typical enough, most sellers like that. This lady said, "You would do an open house on my property?" The salesperson smiled brightly and exclaimed, "Oh, yes!" The seller stood up (bad sign, if you're at a meeting and the boss stands up) and asked us to leave. I am now reeling and say, "What is it about an open house that is a problem?" She said, "The last time I sold a house the real estate people had an open house and while it was going on someone stole a broach that was a family heirloom and that will never happen again. NOW GO!" I pride myself in handling objections but I had no chance here because the seller had become emotional. Do not oversell. Here are some words to live by:

Promise Less and Deliver More

Now back to pricing. If the seller's asking price is more than you think you can sell it for, begin the pricing process with the following questions:

Salesperson: "If the market won't give you the price you want, what will you do?"

Salesperson: "How did you arrive at that price?"

Salesperson: "If the property sells, what are your plans?"

Salesperson: "If you can't sell the property, how will that change your plans?"

Even though you might have asked a question before you might ask it again to see if sellers are consistent in their answer. Continue probing until you find a crack in the seller's armor. Typically a "motivated" seller will truly want to sell and if you find true motivation you can convince the seller of the correct price. One point here: I am making the assumption you are representing or will represent the seller. This is not meant to be manipulative because it *is* in the best interest of the seller to price a property correctly.

I have had unsuccessful real estate salespeople tell me that it is our duty to price the property at the price the seller wants and to do our best to sell it at that price. I disagree. We should meet the seller's goal and, in this case, that goal is to sell the house. And the only way to do that is to market the property at the correct price.

In my first two months in my real estate, I took 14 listings. That is very good. For some, it is a career and I did it in two months. Great, huh? I was invited to have breakfast in Dallas with the owner and founder of our company of 800 real estate salespeople. I felt good and thought, "This business is easy."

This business *is* easy, if you take listings at any price the seller wants (all overpriced). Out of the 14 overpriced listings I took, none were sold. Every day I got calls from sellers who were yelling at me, telling me I was worthless, and to release the listings. I started thinking of another career until I decided that I would rather make a seller upset now and happy when the property sells than happy now and upset when the property doesn't sell. I REFUSE TO TAKE OVERPRICED LISTINGS.

It is tempting at this point in the pricing section for the real estate salesperson to use the CMA to get the seller to understand what the price should be. Remember, the seller is acting emotionally and data (in this case the CMA) is logical information. Because of this I don't care how good the CMA is, the seller won't see it. Instead, keep asking questions. Eventually you can present the CMA, but again it is a tool, not a weapon. Don't beat the seller over the head with it.

Close for the Seller Listing Agreement

Once you and the seller agree on a price, ask the seller for the listing. Do not make this difficult. New real estate salespeople tend to be frightened about "closing" the seller. Most of the time if you have completed your presentation correctly the "close" is a logical outcome. My general final "close" is:

> **"Put me to work for you."**

Now did that really hurt? "Closing" does not need to hurt if you have done your job correctly. Many sales have been lost because we do not ask for the listing.

Types of Listings

Listing agreements obligate both brokers and sellers to perform. The five types of listing agreements include:

1. Open

The open listing allows anyone to sell the property. Only the broker that actually sells the property deserves to be paid. If the seller sells the property, no commission is paid. This type of listing is totally nonexclusive. The seller can list with multiple brokers at one time.

2. Exclusive Right to Sell (ERS)

With the Exclusive Right to Sell (ERS) listing, the broker that lists the property is the only broker to be paid. This type of listing is totally exclusive. Only one broker has the right to sell the property and all other brokers must work through the listing broker. The listing broker pays all other brokers who sell the property. If the seller finds a buyer, the listing broker is still due a commission. According to most ERS listings the seller does not even have the right to negotiate with buyers without the listing broker.

3. Exclusive agency

The exclusive agency listing is similar to the ERS listing except in an agency listing the seller could sell the property alone, without having to pay a commission.

4. Net

A net listing is a listing in which the seller wants a net amount of money including closing costs and the broker can have any amount over the net amount.

5. One-time

A one-time listing is a listing that is good for only one buyer for one period of time for one property.

Finalization

The last and best thing left to do is to ask for the listing. Once the sellers accept your offer, they must sign the papers in the listing packet. Be sure to get the seller to give you a key to the property, including keys that open gates, screen doors, outbuildings, and any other locked rooms. Also be sure to get the pass code to the security system if one is on the premises.

Here are some final points on listing presentations.

- Do not tell jokes during the presentations. What you think is funny may offend someone else.
- Do not talk to inattention. This simply means if the sellers are not listening, do not continue. I was on a listing presentation and a

neighbor knocked on the door. When the neighbor heard I was there he tried to excuse himself and the seller said, "No, come on in." Both the neighbor and seller sat in the living room, leaving me with his wife at the kitchen table. I asked the husband if he wanted to join us, and he said, "Just go on, I can hear you." That was not acceptable. I told them to call me when they were serious and I left.

- Film yourself. Get a video camera and have a friend film your presentation. As a young real estate salesperson, I struggled with listing properties. I could get the appointments, I just couldn't get the sellers to sign the listings. And nothing I did seemed to work. To find out why, I asked my dad to videotape my presentation. Oh my! After watching that video (which I immediately erased!) I wouldn't have listed with me either. I was trying to overcome my youth by acting professional and all I did was act cold. I had this serious look, a scowl actually. Because I could see myself on the tape, I was able to change my presentation for the better.

Postagreement Discussion

The postagreement discussion occurs after a listing is signed. During this discussion the real estate salesperson should mention the following:

- **Open houses**—The open house will occur only when needed and approved by the real estate salesperson. Discuss with the seller, who might feel the salesperson should do an open house every weekend. If the salesperson feels that this house is not conducive to an open house, the salesperson should tell the seller that. The salesperson should say: "Mr. & Mrs. Seller, we have discussed open houses. I feel that this house is not suited for an open house because it is located so far off the main traffic ways and it will not draw enough good buyers. Never fear, at open houses for other properties we will move buyers here. The good thing is that high traffic open houses draw a lot of people but those people tend to buy in more secluded areas such as this."

- **Pets**—Pets can be a problem as some people like cats and dogs, and some do not. Pets must be put up in a bathroom, utility room, or outside when the house is being shown. Too many pets are also a problem.

I was in a house once that had 62 fish tanks. Fish tanks were everywhere—in the living room, in the kitchen, in the bedrooms, and even in the bathrooms. All I remember about the house is the fish tanks and that the house was not salable until they were removed.

I was showing a couple a property. They seemed to like it. They wanted to go into the back yard but saw a sign on the door that said, "Beware of Dog." But we couldn't see a dog. I opened the door a crack and hollered, "No dog!" I opened the door wider and stepped onto the patio. Still no dog. The buyers then came out onto the patio—just about the time a huge Doberman Pincher came around from the side of the house, growling and baring his teeth. We all made it inside O.K., except for the wife, who took a shot to the back from my forearm as I ran over her to get inside. The couple never bought from me. A pet is not a real estate salesperson's friend.

- **Advertising**—Most real estate offices have an advertising policy to rotate listings, meaning a listing might only be advertised once a month. The seller expects it to be advertised every day. This is a snake and we need to kill it now. I will first talk about the realities of advertising and then tell you how you should describe this to the seller.

  Advertising's only purpose is to make the telephone at the real estate office ring with buyer and seller inquiries. It is not used to actually sell a property. Only approximately 2 percent of the advertising calls result in a related property selling.

  All of this is great except that the sellers just don't care. They want you to advertise their property all the time. To explain this to the seller, take a full-page real estate magazine advertisement with pictures and show it to the seller. Then ask the sellers to find their house. Of course their house is not in that ad. After a minute or so of them searching, point out another ad and say, "There is your house." They will immediately say, "That is not." Then point at another ad and say, "This is your house." Now the seller will look at you strangely because that is not their house either. Then say, "Do you understand why I'm pointing out all these ads and claiming they are your house?" The sellers will look blankly and shake their heads. Explain to them that when your office advertises one of its properties it is the same as advertising all of its properties. If call-in buyers do not like the house they call in on, the real estate salesperson will convert them to your seller's house. This is the advantage of real estate because every week their house is directly or indirectly advertised.

- **Security**—Explain to the sellers about not showing the property to any buyer who isn't accompanied by a real estate salesperson. This is a breach of security and should not happen. Leave the sellers a stack of business cards and tell them to call you if anyone like that wants to see the property.

- **Safety**—Look for things in the house that are not safe, such as exposed electrical wires, toys in walking paths, or dimly lit stairs.

- **Quick sale**—Prepare the sellers for a quick sale. This is another snake. If you do not prepare them for a quick sale and an offer comes in on their property the day after it is listed, they will believe their house is underpriced and they will resist the sale and you. Tell them that you will present all offers no matter what the price and terms and to be excited if they get an offer tomorrow.

- **Showing**—Tell the seller that you are paid as a marketing specialist. Your job is not to sell the house but to get the house sold. If the house is being shown, that is good. If you personally are not showing the house, that is good. The reason for that is that you are obviously marketing the house properly. Some sellers believe the listing salesperson should show the property. We will, but our first job is to get the property sold no matter who shows it.

Convince the seller to leave for showings. If this is impossible, then during the visit the seller must stay in one place and not wander around the house. The real estate salespeople let the buyers discover the house and say very little. The worst thing that can happen is a "talkie" seller. If a seller talks, the buyers cannot discover the home for themselves. Be sure you tell the seller to be invisible.

Prepare the seller that if a real estate salesperson is parked out front with a buyer (maybe they just happened by), they may want to see the house without notice. It should not happen often but the house still must be shown.

- **Odors**—Odors must be addressed. If you smell pet odors, cigarette odors, or other types of smells, it is best to just come right out with it and let the sellers deal with it.

- **Cleaning**—Tell the sellers if the house needs cleaning or is in need of repair. Create an itemized list of specific items that must be dealt with and give it to the sellers with a due date. Follow up to be sure it is done. No matter how much trouble, the house must be in show condition at all times.

- **Stuff**—If the seller has too much stuff, they need to get rid of it. I have had sellers take down pictures because potential buyers were spending too much time looking at pictures and not at the house.

Another time I set an appointment with an expired listing. The property was priced right but had not sold. When I entered the property I soon found out why. The seller had three complete sets of home furniture in the property, including sets from both the seller's dead mother and sister. We literally walked through two-foot paths separating the furniture. I thought the master bedroom was small until I looked into the back corner of the roof and noticed it was actually large. It appeared small because of the three beds in the room plus three dressers and end tables. Even if the seller is sentimental about something, it may have to be removed from the house. I finally convinced the seller to store all of the furniture. The property sold in less than two weeks.

- **Expensive items**—Have the seller remove from the house expensive items like breakable vases or jewelry. My dad always said that we lock our doors not because we believe people are evil but to keep from tempting the good ones. Same story here.

Also ask the sellers not to have money lying around. I had a new real estate salesperson call me and ask me to take a look at her new listing. She was concerned that the seller's house was vacant and they had left some baseball cards upstairs. I thought this new salesperson was overreacting but I went to see anyway. Upstairs I actually gasped for air. There were only two rooms, which adjacent to each other and about 400 square feet each. In each room there were baseball cards floor to ceiling on shelves. There were uncirculated, full sets of baseball cards from the 1940s to today. There were 6-inch binders full of individual players cards. I pulled one of the binders out on Nolan Ryan. Inside were rookie cards. I was literally frightened to be in the room. I called the seller directly and told her she had 48 hours to remove the cards. Can you imagine the liability on my part in showing such a property? I learned later that the seller's deceased husband had owned several card shops, although he collected more cards than he sold. The seller had no idea that the collection was valued at $3.2 million. Did you get that? Three million dollars in baseball cards in a vacant house worth $100,000!

- The seller should avoid answering too many questions. Remember, we are the professional negotiators, not the sellers. The seller could inadvertently cause liability for himself or herself.

- Tell the sellers you will call every week to give them an update.

- Ask the sellers to tell you anytime they are to be out of touch for any length of time. There is nothing more frustrating than a great offer that can't be presented because no one knows where the sellers are.

Seller Servicing

Seller servicing is taking care of the listing after the listing agreement has been signed. The number one seller complaint is that their real estate salesperson listed the house and never did anything else. Sellers basically want to know their money is not being wasted. Generally they are happy just hearing from their real estate salespeople.

Weekly Callbacks and Mail-Outs

Call the sellers weekly. They need assurance that you are still alive and actively marketing their properties. This is the most important aspect of seller servicing.

I had a listing that I had called on every week for almost 6 months. When I went to see the sellers, they relisted with me because they felt I had done everything possible to get their house sold. I sold it within a month from the time I relisted it.

In a different situation I failed to call the sellers for over a month because I was "busy." Sellers hate that. An offer on the property came in and I went to meet with the sellers. They accepted the offer but made sure that I knew their disappointment in me. They felt I had stolen their money because I had not done anything that deserved to be paid a commission. I had actually done a lot to sell their home but I did not convey that I was working. They called my broker, not to refuse to pay a commission but to make sure I didn't get any. Then they asked me not to show up at closing because they never wanted to see me again. Not good!

What is the difference? I did virtually the same for both sellers. The only difference is that the second seller never knew what I was doing.

You can mail the sellers information, but this should be in addition to the weekly calls. The timing of the calls should be the same time each week. If the seller has any questions, he or she should wait until the weekly time. This saves you from being interrupted by sellers calling for information midweek.

Open House

The open house can be a very good source of obtaining buyers and sellers. Notice, I said "and sellers" (more on this later). It is also a good opportunity to prospect in the neighborhood. The open house is used by a select group of successful real estate salespeople and for some it is their main source of prospective buyers and sellers. These salespeople can be called "open house experts" due to the special way they hold an open house.

Some real estate salespeople consider the open house a waste of time. There is no greater waste of time than sitting at an open house with no activity.

One important reason to hold a house open is to get the names, addresses, and telephone numbers of motivated buyers who are in the market and are looking for a home in that area. Another important reason to hold a house open is to locate those owners in the area who are thinking of selling their home in the near future to meet and get to know them, so that when the day to sell comes, they will remember you.

> Our main reason for holding open houses is to:
>
> **MEET PROSPECTIVE BUYERS WHO 98 PERCENT OF THE TIME PURCHASE SOME OTHER HOUSE**

The selection of properties for open house is very important. Your broker or manager can assist you in this selection and help you with procedures and recommendations to maximize the results of your open house.

The overall goal of an open house is to set a subsequent appointment.

The following procedures for open houses will help maximize your efforts.

The "Open House" Must Be Priced Right

It is a complete waste of time to hold open a house that has been priced at more than 4 percent above its true market value. To do so will make a sale more difficult and be harmful to your reputation. Your reputation is all you have in the long term. If you list a property for sale at $250,000 when it should be listed for $225,000 and then hold it open, several things happen. First any potential buyers who come by the open house will think less of you and do not want to work with you because you will show them other "overpriced houses." Second, you are wasting the sellers' time and yours. It is extremely difficult, if not impossible, to sell an overpriced property. The most important criterion for choosing an open house is to have that property priced at or below the market prices in the area.

Location Is Critical for the "Open House"

Hard-to-reach streets and/or dead-ends usually make poor open houses. The best open houses are the ones that are on high travel streets, although they are typically the most difficult to sell because of the high traffic.

Preferably a much-desired area, based on current and past activity, is the best for open houses. If no sales have occurred it might be a slow selling area and a waste of your time.

Advertising the Open House

Advertising is an important factor in preparing to hold an Open House. The newspaper ad must be a complete ad, never a "blind ad."

A "blind ad" is one in which some important detail has been omitted in the hope that the buyer, becoming interested in the rest of the ad, will be anxious to know that detail and will make a phone call to the office or come to the open house to find out.

Your ad should be all-inclusive, giving the street address and town, the size of the house, kind of architecture, number of bedrooms and baths, and the price. A person reading your ad will decide if the house is as good as you say it is and if he or she should take a look at it.

The enticement of open house viewing to average buyers is that they don't have to go to a broker's office. They can simply drive by the property and, if they like the appearance of the house and the price is within their means, they can go in. They don't feel obligated to one real estate salesperson. Again, you can see why the price must be right. If the buyers don't like the appearance of the house in relation to the price quoted in the ad, they will simply drive by.

Naturally, you want as many prospects to show up during the open house as you can possibly get through the door, and a good open house may bring in as many as ten or twelve prospects. But if it brings in only one it is worth the cost, for it is one more than you would have had without it.

Directional Signs Are Necessary

Another method of advertising an open house is by the use of directional signs. These should be placed at every corner leading from a main street to the open house. Always check with local authorities on the use of temporary directional signs.

Always ask for permission from the person who lives on the corner to place your directional sign. Explain that you will place it between the curb and lawn, so as not to injure the grass, and that it will be removed by six o'clock. Almost always, the owner will grant your request. In fact, he or she will probably chat with you about real estate, at which time you should invite him or her to visit the open house.

One excellent method of calling attention to a directional sign is to accent it with an Open House flags. These flags will draw attention to your directional sign from a distance five times farther away than will the directional sign by itself.

Always Schedule Two "Open Houses"

Every Tuesday the "open house expert" will select two market value priced homes to be held open the following Saturday and Sunday. The reason for selecting two homes is the possibility that between Tuesday and Saturday, a well-priced house will sell, wiping out any plans for an open house that weekend. If you select two and neither sells before the end of the week, you hold one open Saturday and the other on Sunday. If one is sold, you hold the other open both days.

The Owner Must Be Absent

Whenever possible, it is best to arrange to have the owners away during the open house period. This makes all the difference in the world. The buyers feel uncomfortable in the presence of the owners. They will not relax, ask questions, or raise objections. They will not make an offer, either. In selling residential property especially, you must make the buyers comfortable. They should be able to sit down, feel at home, and enjoy their surroundings. They cannot and will not do this if the owners are present.

With the owners away you can greet your buyers as they arrive by introducing yourself and remarking, "The owners have left for the day, won't you come in?" The buyer's reaction will be immediate. They will relax, inspect the premises, raise objections, mentally place their furniture, imagine living there, and get down to talking price and financing.

It is important, then, that the owners leave, preferably early in the day. The salesperson replies, "If I do not sell your property before this coming weekend, I intend to hold an open house on Saturday, or perhaps both Saturday and Sunday. I would appreciate your arranging to be away from the house on those days from 1:00 to 5:00 p.m."

It is not difficult to induce the sellers to be away for the open house if there is a definite plan and you have attitude behind your approach. Holding a house open for viewing is not a rushed, last minute arrangement but is, in the hands of an expert, a well thought-out plan.

Preparation for Open House

A. The day before the open house
   1. Deliver "Open House" invitations to neighbors and ask them and their friends to stop by.
   2. Drive by all listings in the immediate area and go see any you don't know.
   3. Check for recent area sales activity on the MLS.
   4. Inform the sellers of the open house and make sure they have plans to be away from the house.
   5. Go door-to-door around the area on the morning of the open house to remind neighbors.

    6. Have a backup person at the office who can relieve you from the open house in case you need to show a potential buyer another property.

B. Preparation of the property
    1. Pick up the yard, any old newspapers, trash, etc.
    2. Arrange patio furniture.
    3. Close garage door.
    4. Open drapes.
    5. Play soft music on the radio or bring your own C.D.
    6. Generally tidy up house. (You should have asked the seller to do this.)
    7. Start a fire in fireplace for warmth.
    8. Warm a few drops of vanilla in the oven to give a nice quality to the property.
    9. Turn on all the lights throughout the house.
    10. Have copies of the listing available for additional information and for any other brokers who have stopped by to show their buyers.
    11. Place directional signs and flags around the area so drivers can see them and have time to turn.

C. Closing the open house
    1. Turn out the lights.
    2. Close the drapes.
    3. Clean up from coffee, etc.
    4. Extinguish fire in fireplace.
    5. Turn off the oven.
    6. Lock up the house, including garage.
    7. Leave a thank-you note for sellers, including the day's results.

Buyers Who Are Sellers

Twenty-five to thirty percent of the people who inspect an open house are not buyers. Oh yes, they look like buyers, talk like buyers, act like buyers, and ask all the questions buyers ask, but they are not buyers. They are sellers and in most cases they are only potential sellers.

These sellers may have received one of your invitations or saw your house with the flags and signs reading, "Open House on Sunday." Now here is a house right in their own neighborhood. Wouldn't it be natural for them to go through the open house and act as a buyer to find out the asking price, make a comparison, and arrive at a tentative valuation of their own property? Such people are not buyer prospects, they are seller prospects.

At one time or another during a selling conversation a successful salesperson will ask the following questions of every person to whom he or she shows the open house:

Salesperson: "May I ask, Do you presently rent or do you own the home you're living in?"

Homeowner: "We own our home."

Salesperson: "Do you intend to sell your property before you purchase the home you are looking for?"

Homeowner: "Yes."

Salesperson: "Do you presently have your home up for sale?"

Homeowner: "No."

At this point the salesperson knows he or she has a seller instead of a buyer and should work toward a listing appointment. Consider using this script:

Salesperson: "Why don't I drop over to see your property this evening and talk over the situation? At that time I can do a market analysis and we can find out if you have sufficient equity established to do the things you are looking forward to doing."

If the seller already has his or her home on the market, follow this script:

Salesperson: "It is your house listed with a real estate broker?"

Homeowner: "No."

At this point the salesperson knows he or she has a FSBO instead of a buyer and should work toward a listing appointment. Consider using this script:

Salesperson: "I shall be happy to call on you this evening to inspect your property. There is an excellent chance that, among the buyers I contact daily, I will find a suitable prospect for your house. Do you mind if I cooperate with you while you are attempting to sell your own home?"

If the seller has already listed with a real estate broker, then help the homeowner as best as you can but do not try to interfere with another broker's listing.

Refreshments for the "Open House"

There are procedures for enhancing a homelike atmosphere. In the winter you can have coffee ready—freshly made, good, and hot. It is no chore to carry a little "open house" kit with you containing a coffee maker, coffee, little packages of sugar and cream, some disposable cups, and even some sugar cookies. Set this up in the kitchen and while you are talking with the buyers in the living room, you can offer them this extra bit of hospitality. It will have a mellowing effect, make them more responsive to your questions, and enable you to qualify them without seeming to be moving too fast.

In the summer you can vary the menu by serving lemonade or soda, perhaps outside on the patio or in the backyard if these are attractive areas. Though not as important as other items mentioned, such little hospitable touches will help the buyers relax, enjoy the scene, and experience the pleasure of living in the house. Be sure to clear the refreshments with the sellers.

Mail-Out "Invitation to an Open House" Cards and Door-to-Door Marketing

The Wednesday morning before the weekend of the open house, address 60 "Invitation to an Open House" cards (30 for each of the two locations) advertising the open house. Obtain the names and addresses from a cross directory or from a title company.

The cards are addressed on Wednesday so they will be delivered on Thursday or Friday, at the latest. The mailing of these 60 cards alone will produce little result, but as a basis for future personal meetings with these same neighbors it is extremely effective. Such meetings are brought about by professional door-to-door marketing just prior to the time scheduled for the opening of the house. Check with the local authorities for door-to-door marketing rules.

Door-to-door marketing plays a big part in the open house technique. The people the real estate salesperson calls on have received a card inviting them to the open house. Now the salesperson reinforces this contact with a personal invitation. In the process, the salesperson will persuade some of these people to accept the invitation and increase the sales potential for this house because neighbors sometimes buy "open houses." They may buy as an investment, if the price and payments are right, and rent it out. They may also have friends or relatives who might be interested. If they like the house they will call these friends and relatives and urge them to inspect it. Here is your script:

Salesperson: "Good afternoon, I am Dan Hamilton from Acme Real Estate. Did you get my card about the house we are holding open for inspection today?"

Homeowner: "Yes."

Salesperson: "I wanted to make sure it had been delivered and to add my personal invitation to visit. It is a beautiful, realistically priced home, and I am sure you would enjoy seeing it. The owners are away for the day so if you are free this afternoon, we would enjoy having you drop by. We'd also like to have your opinion on the price of this property in comparison with others in the neighborhood."

Bring the Following Items to Your Open House

1. An adequate number of open house signs and open house flags.

2. A hammer or mallet to help place the signs in hard soil. Be sure to check your local ordinances governing the use and placement of signs; if you aren't certain, check with your broker or manager.

3. A computer printout of the most recent sales in the neighborhood to use as a reference.

4. A legal pad or pad of scratch paper.

5. Your appointment book or PDA.

6. Your portfolio.

7. A calculator.

8. A blank Purchase Agreement. (It is rare for a house to sell at an open house, but it does happen.)

9. Several working pens.

10. Some work to do between visitors.

11. Your business cards.

12. A mortgage schedule.

13. Feature sheets and cards (special features specific to the home).

14. A guest register.

15. Buyer information and prequalifying worksheets.

Set up your laptop computer in a prominent location during the open house and have a virtual tour, complete with voice narration, running at all times. Have the volume up loud enough so that visitors can hear you narrating the tour.

Have alternative listings, including houses in other price ranges, ready to show. Showing them can salvage a prospect that is not interested in the home you're holding open. Such tours don't take long to put together and they can result in big commissions!

Have virtual tour presentations on disk ready to give away. Include area tours, a tour of the listing you're holding open, a tour of local schools, and tours for specific subdivisions and condo projects for visitors who are not interested in that particular home. Make sure the disks have nice labels that feature your photo.

Multiple Open Houses

If you have multiple listings in one area, hold them open all at the same time. I know of one real estate salesperson whose main focus is holding open houses. She makes close to a half-a-million dollars a year for herself with four or five open houses in a particular area every Sunday. In several rooms of each house she sets up huge framed boards on A-Frames with details and professional photographs of each of her other open houses. Each board also includes the price of the house and maps. If a buyer is in a house that is too expensive, for example, he or she looks on a board and notices a beautiful home in his or her price range that is open down the street. (Guess where they go?) She also has two real estate salespeople at every house and two "rovers" in place for security and to handle rushes. If a buyer wants to look at a different property, one of the salespeople on hand can leave the open house and show that buyer another property. If both salespeople need to leave, a rover will show up to supervise the open house. She never has trouble with finding willing salespeople because these open houses generate several qualified buyers.

If you don't have multiple listings in a certain area, you can form alliances with other real estate salespeople in your office. What about cooperating with competitive offices for the betterment of all?

Broker Open House

Broker open houses are for licensed real estate salespeople, not for the general public. They are designed to expose the property to real estate licensees, so they will be familiar with it in case they have a buyer who might be interested in this type of property. A broker open usually corresponds with area property tours and, like all open houses, the seller is not to be there.

While the listing salesperson should offer lunch during the broker open, some creative salespeople hold "progressive broker open houses." In the first house on the tour visitors have a salad; in the second house, they have a main course; and in the third house they have dessert. In each house the visitors receive coupons. And if there is a fourth house on the tour, visitors holding all four coupons are eligible to participate in a prize drawing. You can arrange this progressive open house with real estate salespeople from different real estate companies as long as the listings are in the same area.

The typical meal is deli sandwiches, cookies, and soft drinks. I have seen real estate salespeople do evening opens with alcohol served, but I don't think that is appropriate.

Broker opens can be expensive so don't hesitate to solicit the seller's help. I have had sellers offer to pay for everything and actually had it catered by a local barbeque restaurant. If you have talent for cooking, this might be your game. I knew a real estate salesperson who made the best chicken enchiladas. Real estate salespeople would drive thirty minutes just to go to her broker opens. It ended up being a great marketing tool for her.

Advertising

Advertising for the seller is one of the most requested things a seller expects his or her real estate salesperson to do. A real estate company usually advertises on a rotation basis. In a rotation, if the real estate company pays for a weekly advertisement that has twelve slots for listings and the company has forty-eight listings, your listing will be featured once a month. We will talk more about this in the advertising chapter of this book.

Office Tour (Caravan)

An office tour allows real estate salespeople in a real estate office go out to view (tour) the most recent listings the office has taken. Some refer to this as a jailbreak because the real estate salespeople almost run through the houses. The objective is to be familiar with the office inventory so if a buyer calls into the office you will be more helpful. Most sellers appreciate an office tour to show support for their sale. You should use feedback cards or a feedback sheet that has questions you feel are important about your listing. Some questions may include pricing, appearance, and whether the property is salable. Communicate the information to the seller immediately so he or she can make any necessary changes.

Some real estate brokers are trying virtual tours of their properties instead of walking tours. I will wait to see the results but I do not believe this will be considered an effective approach because the real estate salespeople won't remember as much from a movie as they will walking through.

Multiple Listing Service

The Multiple Listing Service (MLS) allows for worldwide property exposure. A buyer transferring from out of state can find houses that are currently for sale in the specific area he or she is moving to on the MLS. Some services are more protective and allow only real estate salespeople on the MLS site. A majority of the real estate sales stem from the MLS.

Internet

For real estate salespeople, the Internet is an advertising medium, and that is about it. Do not think it is a savior to all your prospecting needs. Some real estate salespeople pay thousands of dollars per month for Web sites that no one sees.

Yard "For Sale" Sign

There are basically two types of signs. The first is a post sign. It looks like a big upside down "L" with a sign panel hanging off the wood post. These are large signs and look very nice. The second is stake sign, which is usually made of metal and has stakes for putting it in the ground. If you install your own signs, be careful not to make a seller mad by damaging his or her sprinkler system.

Lock Box

A lock box is a security device that is placed on the seller's door. It has a key inside of it to allow access to the property. There are basically two types of lock boxes. The first is electronic and allows access through an electronic keypad. Without the proper codes the lock box is inaccessible. It records what keypad opened the lock box for security purposes. The second type of lock box is a dial-type combination lock that works like a padlock. It will open when the proper sequence of numbers is dialed into the lock box.

Some sellers are apprehensive to place a key outside their door. I had a seller who refused one lock box on his door. I went to my car and got out a lock box and brought it back inside with me. I handed it to the seller and told him if he could get the key out in less than a minute I would give him ten dollars. He struggled, pried, banged, and pounded the lock box for a while. I turned to his wife and causally asked her if she thought it would be faster just to break the window. She laughed and he accepted the lockbox.

Price Reductions

If a property is not selling it is sometimes necessary for a price adjustment. Some real estate salespeople believe they are in error if they told the seller to list it at one price and then later ask for a reduction. This may be true, but I know I am not perfect and I have listed property too high to sell. But making a mistake is not a problem if you learn from your mistake and correct it.

The best way to get a price reduction is to ask the seller. If the seller refuses or gives you grief, have your broker call the seller. The broker, as an authority figure, will be able to persuade the seller to drop the price. Over the years, whenever I allowed my broker to call for price reductions, the seller always came around.

While going through college my brother and I worked for a national pizza chain. I generally worked the front of the house and my brother worked the back. Neither of us were managers, but we were always left alone to run the restaurant. If there ever was an unhappy customer I went to get the acting "manager," my brother. He would walk up and you could see the customers change. They were no longer angry once they felt they were being heard. The same applies to real estate. Sometimes people just need to hear that, "Even the broker is involved."

Property Brochures

A property brochure provides details of the property. It is a minimum of four pages and is usually in color on high-quality paper. The cost of a property brochure usually prohibits the use except on fine homes and estates.

I know one real estate salesperson who only deals in elite executive homes. She publishes each property brochure with a blank page to hold her business card. She does this in an effort to encourage distribution to potential buyers.

Property Profile Sheets

Property profile sheets are also called property graphics. They are usually a single sheet of paper including details of the property and a picture of the property. The property profile sheet is much less expensive than property brochures and should be used on almost all your listings.

I printed up two kinds of property profile sheets exactly the same except the picture was in color on one set and black and white on the other set. Some of the color sets sat on the seller's kitchen table and the others were available for distribution at the real estate office. The set of black and white profile sheets was placed in an information tube or box attached to the real estate yard sign. The graphics sat in the box or tube for people that pass by to take. The reason these are black and white is that color is three times as expensive and you can go through a bunch of them on the sign. I have the printing company send the graphics directly to the seller and the seller's job was to fill the tube or box. No seller ever objects.

The property details on profile sheet include information about the number and sizes of rooms, all the best amenities, schools, taxes, and, most important, information about you and how to get in touch with you for a showing.

Staging the Property for Sale

Staging the property for sale is the setting up of the property to look its best. A listing's fiercest competition is new construction. Professionals decorate the interiors of model homes with the finest furniture and accessories. Your job is to compete with the model homes. The way to do this is room by room.

Walk through each room detailing the items to be removed, added, cleaned, or painted. Suggest things to do that will freshen the room. Add brighter light bulbs, and mow, edge, and landscape the yard.

These are the things the seller must do. Some sellers are hesitant to do anything while others are more than willing to do whatever it takes to sell. I guess Jerry Maguire was right when he said, "Help me help you!"

Residential Service Contract—Home Warranty

Home warranties are basic insurance policies that protect buyers for one year after the purchase of a home. The number one fear of any buyer is that he or she bought a lemon. The number one lawsuit is a result of a buyer feeling he or she was lied to about the property's condition. A home warranty can remove a lot of problems. It covers most mechanical items in the home. Check each policy for terms or better yet provide the buyer with several and let them choose the home warranty company.

Association of REALTORS®

The Association of REALTORS® is a great way to promote your listings. Every time they have meetings bring graphics on your properties and pass them out. One of the REALTORS® you talk to may have a waiting buyer and you make a sale.

Chapter Summary

With the many ways to market a property you could not possibly do all of them for each one of your listings. You should develop a marketing plan and checklist and work forward to market a property. Go prepared to your listing appointments. Get useful comparables in your CMA. Try to convince the sellers of the best market price for their homes, if necessary. Work open houses to the advantage of everyone. Always act professional, confident, and respectful.

Summary Questions

1. What or who covers mechanical breakdowns that might occur in heat/air, plumbing, electrical, and built-in appliances?
   A. Repair allowance
   B. Home warranty
   C. Hazard insurance
   D. Owner's title policy

2. What is the most critical factor in determining a good comparable for a CMA?
   A. Area or location
   B. Amenities in the home

   C. Square footage of the home

   D. Age of the home

3. A successful open house meets all of the following requirements except:

   A. It should be priced above market.

   B. It should be easily accessible.

   C. It should be in good condition.

   D. It should be fairly new to the market.

4. Which of the following is not a requirement in setting up an open house?

   A. Turn on every light in the house.

   B. Call friends over to increase the number of visitors.

   C. Create a pleasant smell throughout the house.

   D. Play soft music.

5. If an open house is slow you should:

   A. Take a nap.

   B. Use the seller's telephone to call friends long distance.

   C. Rummage through the fridge to see if there is anything to eat.

   D. Do client follow-up paperwork.

6. Which of the following is not a factor in setting up for a successful open house?

   A. Call the neighbors and invite them.

   B. Bring brochures about yourself.

   C. Put out one open house sign.

   D. Know all the properties for sale in the area.

7. What type of data should not be included on a CMA?

   A. Homes currently on the market.

   B. Homes whose listings expired.

   C. Homes that were foreclosed.

   D. Homes that were sold.

8. What is the minimum number of comparable sold properties that should be on a CMA?

   A. One

   B. Three

   C. Ten

   D. None

9. When should you arrive at the seller's front door for a listing appointment?
   A. On time.
   B. 10 minutes late so you look extremely busy.
   C. Early to look excited and enthused.
   D. Timing is not important, show up whenever.

10. What is the main goal for potential buyers at an open house?
    A. To provide them with your promotional materials.
    B. To schedule subsequent appointments.
    C. To establish rapport.
    D. To have them sign buyers agreements.

11. How often should agents communicate with their sellers?
    A. Twice a month
    B. Twice a week
    C. Daily
    D. Weekly

12. When generating a CMA, what must an agent remember to do?
    A. Use only active comparables.
    B. Highlight relocation features.
    C. Begin with comparables in the same area.
    D. Create an ad for each property.

13. What should the listing agent do to secure a price reduction?
    A. Get an agreement to reduce the price when the property is first listed.
    B. Market the property by spending twice as much on advertising as normal.
    C. Get the term of the listing in excess of two years to ensure the time to sell.
    D. Nothing. Don't ever take an overpriced listing.

14. What must a real estate salesperson remember to bring along when going to the client's home for the first time for a listing appointment?
    A. A new listing contract.
    B. A lock box.
    C. A CMA.
    D. Everything.

Chapter 9

Prospecting
for Buyers

Chapter Objectives

In this chapter you will learn how to answer the real estate telephone and convert the call into a buyer prospect. This chapter will delve into the types of buyers in real estate and how knowing the types of buyers can add value to your service. You will discover the best way to attract buyers through your specific efforts.

Key Words

Floor time: Real estate position of answering the company telephone for business.

Nonoccupant owner: One who has given up possession of a property but not ownership.

Objective: Uninfluenced by emotions or personal prejudices.

Technique: The way in which the fundamentals are handled with skill or command.

Introduction

Where do we find buyers? My response is always, where do we find sellers? It will work the same way. What works for the seller will work for the buyer.

There are several additional ways to generate buyers, including:

- Effectively selling the seller's property, now the sellers must buy.
- Wearing career apparel and a name badge.
- Asking for two leads at closing.
- Prospecting builders and their agents.
- Prospecting FSBOs as buyers.
- Prospecting other agents, other property managers, and apartment locators.

- Attending business luncheons and taking advantage of business networking opportunities.
- Conducting buyer seminars.
- Making hotel/motel and postal worker contacts.
- Contacting people that know people.
- Meeting new people.
- Prospecting your sphere of influence.
- Contacting past customers.
- Giving away your business cards.
- Displaying car signs and sign riders.

"FOR SALE" SIGNS

A large inventory of listings creates potential buyers.

ADVERTISING

Effective local ad campaigns can generate a great number of incoming calls for the office.

OPEN HOUSES

Properly conducted open houses generate numerous prospective buyers.

REFERRALS

Personal and company referrals give you current and future buyers.

COLD CALLS

Make cold calls to apartments to find first-time buyers.

Expand prospecting activities to include buyers.

Most productive salespeople quickly develop a pool of prospects from which to draw. Buyer leads can come from anywhere and everywhere. It's mostly a matter of being alert and curious.

Active

To be active in prospecting means that the real estate salesperson goes out and brings the business into the real estate company by direct action of the salesperson.

Telemarketing

Before we begin telemarketing for buyers we must know where potential buyers are located. We have listed several ways to find buyers. Let's now concentrate on renters that may desire to buy.

The best places to find renters are apartment complexes. These house multitudes of potential buyers in concentrated areas. Like all telemarketing you are randomly calling renters to determine if there is any interest in buying homes. As always, be aware of and abide by all national "do not call" laws. The best way to ensure getting a buyer client is to call until you get one who says, "Yes." Consider using the following basic script:

> **Salesperson:** "Mr. or Mrs. Renter?"
>
> **Renter:** "Yes."
>
> **Salesperson:** "My name is Dan Hamilton with Acme Real Estate Company. I am wondering if you have considered buying a home either now or in the near future."

Marketing Door-to-Door

Marketing door-to-door, which is more difficult than telemarketing, is actually knocking on doors in an area known for rental units. These will probably be single-family units, not apartment complexes. I say that because if you knock on doors of apartment complexes you can expect to be thrown out by security. They find it rude to make an effort to take their renters from them. This is one reason why telemarketing is easier.

Passive

Passive prospecting for buyers is making an effort and then expecting the client to come to you. Passive prospecting tends to be more expensive and takes a lot longer to receive results.

Nonoccupant Owners/Renters

One good way to find buyers is to examine the tax records and look for nonoccupant owners. A nonoccupant is a property owner who does not live in the home that is on the tax record. For example, if the property address is on Main St. and the owner's address is on Brittany Lane, the owner does not live at that property. When you find this situation you should send the renter at the property's address the following letter:

Dear Property Occupant:

Would you consider purchasing a home if the monthly payments were in line with what you are paying currently for rent? If you would like to learn more, please call me at:

Dan Hamilton
Acme Real Estate Company
P.O. Box 123
Dallas, TX. 77777
214-555-1212

Thanks,

This letter should be on standard 81/2" × 11" paper with no letterhead. The envelope should be plain white with a generic return address. In the body of the letter you must identify yourself as a licensed real estate salesperson.

Personal Marketing

Personal marketing is promoting yourself constantly. Do not be a secret agent. Secret agents are people who nobody knows are in real estate. They do not wear career apparel, they do not wear a name badge, and they never discuss real estate. They feel that would be uncouth. They also have no money.

Good personal marketers should have some of the following:

- **Personal brochure**—These brochures highlight the reason a person would and should do business with this real estate salesperson. The complexity and cost is only limited by the salesperson. There are companies that will create a brochure one for you at a price or you can create your own. Because of the cost, these should only be given to truly potential clients.

- **Professional business cards**—The business cards of the personal marketer set this person apart from the crowd. The card should be multicolored and include a picture of the salesperson. Limit the telephone numbers on the card to one or two as too many numbers are confusing and intimidating, and do not include your home number. If you do, you will soon have no family life and you put out the image that you are not professional. Do you have your attorney's home number?

- **Personal advertising**—Any advertising created by the personal marketer should promote the salesperson and not his or her real estate company. Local laws or office policies will dictate the need for the company name and size relative to the entire ad, but remember, you promote yourself and the company will promote the company.

- **Career apparel, name badge, car signs, and name riders**—The successful personal marketer always looks for ways to put his or her name in front of potential clients.

Floor Time (Opportunity Time)

Answering the phone while on floor time is a process. To prepare for floor time, you must:

- Know all the properties that are being advertised.
- Preview all the listings in the office inventory.
- Obtain a list of alternative properties.
- Be serious about answering the phone.
- Smile and smile BIG. Imagine the caller has a check made out in your name for $2,000, and all you have to do is get it. This should give you the incentive to pay attention.

Types of Buyers

Hot buyers—Hot buyers are ready, willing, and able to buy today. They have the money, they are motivated, and they have a specific time frame. A prime example of a hot buyer is one who just sold his or her house and has to move now.

Hot buyers can buy property today. They are being transferred from another state and are moving to your area. They want a home before the end of the month. They will be paying cash that they received from the sale of their previous home.

These buyers are HOT!!! Don't let them out of your sight. Pick them up at the airport when they arrive so they don't take a ride from a taxi driver who is a part-time real estate salesperson. Show them houses all day long, if necessary. Handcuff your ankles to theirs so they cannot look for houses in the middle of the night without you. Yes, I am that serious. I have said that you do not let real estate take time away from your family. The exception is when you're working with a hot buyer.

Warm buyers—Warm buyers are potential buyers who want to buy, but something is keeping them from it. You have a name and number, and you have met with them, but something is keeping them from buying today, such as:

- They have a house to sell.
- They are waiting for a credit problem to be cleared up.
- They are saving for a down payment.
- They are waiting for income tax refund.
- They just haven't found the right house yet.

Warm buyers may be very similar to the hot buyers, but they can eat your time up. Follow up with these buyers but don't waste too much time on them. They are not ready yet; maybe the time is not right.

Cold buyers—Cold buyers are potential buyers who have a specific need that can't be met at this time. You have a name and number but have not been able to get a face-to-face appointment. The best thing to do with these buyers is to refer them to real estate salespeople who have nothing to do but drive around cold buyers.

Cold buyers typically are in no hurry. They may be shopping and if the perfect house comes along, they'll make a move.

Focusing your time and energy on hot and warm buyers is more practical and makes economic sense. You can include buyers who are not ready to purchase in your client base to position yourself to work with them when the time is right.

Breakdown of property calls:

60% of calls are from cold buyers

35% of calls are from warm buyers

5% of calls are from hot buyers

Caller Objectives

One of the keys to determining a solid lead while answering an advertising call in the office identifying the caller's objective. Most real estate salespeople believe that the callers want to buy the advertised houses, so the salespeople try and sell them those houses. This is a critical mistake because buyers only buy houses they call in about less than 10 percent of the time; the rest of the time they buy different houses. Our job in the real estate industry is to sell the callers houses, whether or not they buy the houses they called in about. So what is the objective of the buyer if it is not to buy the advertised house?

The buyer's objective in responding to an ad is to eliminate the ad. The problem with that strategy is that when the buyer eliminates the ad he or she also eliminates the salesperson.

To prove my point, I wanted to buy a pick-up truck for hauling yard signs and other miscellaneous odd jobs that a car really cannot do. I did not need the pick-up to look good; however, it must run well as I do not work on autos of any sort. (Changing a tire could take me a week.) So I scoured the "Trucks for Sale" section of the newspaper. If read an ad that could be eliminated, I would eliminate it. For example, if the ad read, "Needs some work," I would eliminate the ad. If an ad read, "Could be a steal with a little work," I would eliminate it. If I found an ad I could not eliminate, I would call and ask, "How does it run?" If the person gave me any answer other than "Perfect!" I would make an excuse and hang up. Why? Because I do not want to buy a truck that needs work.

The same goes for real estate. You might eliminate yourself by telling too much or being too specific about a property in an ad. The things we think are important the buyer may not.

Salesperson's Objective
The real estate salesperson's objective is to get an appointment. It is not time to build rapport; that is for when you are face-to-face with a prospect. It is not time to describe a property, to overcome objections, or to sell you. It is only to get an appointment! And the only way to be sure you have a serious buyer is for that buyer to come into the office for the appointment.

Broker's Objective
The broker's objective is to make the telephones at the real estate office ring with buyers. It is not to appease an overpriced seller or make a real estate salesperson feel good because his or her name was in the newspaper. The only objective is to make the telephone ring.

Don't Forget the Seller
A large percentage of calls coming in to the real estate office are actually from people who need to sell their homes. They are calling to check out their competition. Finding out what other houses in the area are selling for and any additional information that will help them sell their homes faster are their primary goals. Always ask the question, "Do you live in the area?" If they say "Yes," change your mind-set to a seller call-in.

Telephone Techniques
Your broker spends thousands of dollars annually making the real estate office telephone ring. Your responsibility as a real estate salesperson is to maximize the dollar return on the broker's investment by converting

callers into prospective purchasers. Use the telephone to set appointments. Here are some key notes:

- Preview the properties being advertised.
- Have ad copy on hand.
- Prepare answers to possible questions.
- Ask questions (open-ended) to gain control of the conversation.
- Get the appointment to discuss home-buying needs and solutions.
- Have a positive attitude.
- Callers won't buy what they call in about.
- Callers don't call you back.
- Callers don't know what they want to buy.
- Callers have circled other ads besides yours.
- You can't sell a house over the phone.
- Have additional properties in the price range that might interest callers.
- The buyer is trying to eliminate the house they called about so don't try and sell it to them.
- The buyer will call other brokers if you do not eliminate those brokers.
- The only purpose for the phone is to set appointments.
- Buyers who call on ads usually can afford more.
- Buyers who call on signs usually can afford less.
- Answer a question with a question.
- Close early and often.
- Compliment callers.
- The sign caller is a more serious prospect than an ad caller because the caller already knows the area and what the house looks like from the outside.

One out of two ad or sign calls results in a sale. We take listings for inventory to advertise. That way people will call us and we can sell our listings. To do this we must get the buyer into the office.

Into the Office

If you are a professional and you believe in your company, then it will be easy to convince customers to come into the office. Getting the buyers into your office is your main goal and quite possibly your only goal. At the office you can conduct an interview with the buyer, which will give you a clear picture of the buyer's needs and wants. You can also determine the buyer's readiness, willingness, and ability to buy. The following are some reasons why you should meet prospective buyers at your office:

- Anyone who takes the time to meet you at your office is serious. Don't waste your time on people who are not serious.

- The offices provides security. I don't believe that real estate is a dangerous business. I also do not believe that it is ever the victim's fault. However, every case I have studied in real estate where a person was violated, it could have been avoided. A single real estate woman meets a "buyer" at a vacant house. It is not worth it and it is not limited to women. Be smart; meet them at your office. If someone wants to cause you harm, they won't be seen at your office. Meeting in the office also offers the buyer a greater sense of security.

- You have control. If you meet buyers at the property, they can leave anytime they feel like it. You cannot control the situation. You cannot look professional.

- Your broker or manager is available at the office to lend expertise if needed.

- You can make a presentation.

- You can financially qualify them.

- You can gather all the information you need.

- You do not lose business time. If they buyers are to meet you at your office and they don't show up, you can still be working. If you meet them at a property and they don't show up, you have wasted your time.

- It enables you to take advantage of the ready access to necessary files and other resources.

- It is easier and less threatening to the buyer.

- It allows you to build rapport. Experience shows that building rapport and uncovering the emotional issues involved helps build a foundation of trust and confidence.

The office has all the tools to get buyers the best house for the best price in the shortest amount of time. The process of handling an ad call is to first gain control by asking questions. Avoid questions about the property they called in about. Instead ask questions like:

Salesperson: "How long have you been looking?"

Salesperson: "How soon do you need a home?"

Salesperson: "Are you working with any other brokers?"

Then begin qualifying with questions like:

Salesperson: "How much are you willing to invest to buy your home?"

Use fair trades, such as:

Salesperson: "I will be glad to work for you; all you have to do is meet with me."

Finally, close for the appointment:

Salesperson: "I am at the office now or would this weekend be better?"

Property Knowledge

Before taking floor time you should have seen each of the properties that are currently advertised. This might be impossible, especially for the new real estate salesperson. However, you should make the effort to view property daily. This should not replace prospecting because nothing replaces prospecting. You should take a half of an hour or so to view three or four properties. This is possible if you do not drag your feet while at each property. You should also plan the viewing in an area where all of the previews are in a close proximity. Over time you will get to know the inventory.

Sphere of Influence (SOI)

One of the best sources of buyer leads is through your sphere of influence (SOI). Refer to Chapter 7 on seller prospecting and review the SOI section on page 135 and adapt that information for buyers.

World Wide Web

Refer to Chapter 7 on seller prospecting and review the World Wide Web section on page 147 and adapt that information for buyers.

Chapter Summary

The hope here is that you have learned more about buyers and how to find and deal with them. You should have also seen the differences and the similarities between buyers and sellers and to prospect for both of them.

Summary Questions

1. What is the best way to ensure that you get a buyer lead from calling apartments?
   A. Call one hundred renters per day.
   B. Call for two hours straight in midmorning.
   C. Call until a you get a buyer.
   D. Cold calling does not work.

2. Which of the following is true about buyers?
   A. More often than not, they have a house to sell first.
   B. They don't always feel loyal toward their real estate salespeople.
   C. They typically feel the best home for them is the one they have not seen.
   D. Each of the above statements is true about buyers.

3. Which of the following is not a good way to get buyers?
   A. Hold at least two open houses every weekend.
   B. Prospect the police officer as he puts you in jail.
   C. Wear your name tag everywhere.
   D. Call FSBOs offering relocation services.

4. Working with buyers does not include which of the following?
   A. Meeting them at the office first.
   B. Showing no more than five homes at one time.
   C. Allowing children to abuse the sellers' personal property.
   D. Watching the buyers for emotional reactions to the properties.

5. How can an agent convert an ad call into an appointment?
   A. Describe his or her background and success record.
   B. Ask the caller to come into the office.
   C. Give a detailed description of the property's features.
   D. Emphasize the property's price.

Chapter 10

Buyer Listing
Procedures

Chapter Objectives

Buyers are sometimes treated differently than sellers and they should not be. So I call this chapter buyer listing procedures just to upset the real estate veterans of the world because they believe that it should be buyer brokerage not buyer listing. The objectives of this chapter include the knowledge to set up a buyer meeting at the office and to complete that meeting for the benefit of both parties. The chapter explains the viewing of properties all the way to the purchase.

Key Words

Credibility: The quality, capability, or power to elicit belief.

Dominant buying motive: A guiding influence over the buying process.

Rapport: Relationship, especially one of mutual trust or emotional affinity.

Wants and needs analysis: Something required and the ability to determine that need.

Introduction

When asked your duties as a buyer broker, you should remember the duties are the same as they would be if you were representing a seller.

A few misconceptions about buyer brokerage include:

- It is the buyer broker's job to get the buyer the best deal. When you deal with a seller you know that full price is not always the best for the seller. Terms like "all cash," "delayed possession," or "seller financed" all make an impact on the seller's decision. The same applies to the buyer. The buyer might not need the best price if the seller finances the transaction. Also remember that the buyer buys emotionally, not logically, so do not assume your thinking is the best for the buyer.

- Buyers will not pay for a buyer broker. This thinking is based on cost, not value. If a buyer can understand the value given, the cost will not be the main factor. Also note that the buyer in reality will be paying the seller, who pays the listing broker, who pays the buyer broker.

- The buyer will not sign an exclusive buyer broker contract. This belief was held back in the 1930s, when all listings were open listings. At that time, real estate salespeople did not believe in their service. Eventually, the attitudes changed and real estate salespeople would only take exclusive listings. Today, you never see a property with multiple "For Sale" signs in the yard. The same thing will happen with buyer brokerage as soon as the real estate salespeople begin to believe in their service. I believe the key to dealing with any buyer is to treat that buyer just as though he or she were a seller. You would not throw the listing contract at the seller and demand they sign it. Do not do that with buyers either. Perform a buyer presentation to be given to all buyers you work with.

Preparing for the Appointment

To prepare for an appointment with a buyer, get your head straight. This simply means clearing your schedule. You don't want interruptions. Make all of the calls you need to make before your appointment. Behave in a professional manner. Mentally walk through the appointment before the appointment actually begins.

Buyer Representation Manual

One of the most important items you must develop is the "Buyer Representation Manual." The manual helps you and the buyer through the home buying process. It describes the services you offer and ends with an agreement to represent the buyer. ·

Buyer Representation Packet

The "Buyer Representation Packet" should include all the necessary paperwork to fully represent a buyer.

Tools to Have

To be prepared for any contingency you should have everything at your fingertips, such as a buyer representation agreement, a purchase contract, a calculator, and your buyer representation manual. This is a perfect reason to get the buyer to meet you at your office, because you should have access to everything you need at the office.

Appointment Time at Office

Working with buyers can be an emotionally satisfying experience. It can also easily become a frustrating time unless you first interview your prospects and then follow time-proven procedures on showing property and closing for buyers' agreement to purchase.

Your initial meeting should involve a balanced process of determining the buyer's readiness, willingness, and ability to complete a purchase; it's also an important time to establish rapport and build the trust and confidence necessary to earn the buyer's loyalty.

Meet at the Conference Table

Once the buyers arrive at your office, take them to the conference room. The conference room is where business decisions are made. Do not miss the power of a conference room. Taking them back to your desk is less professional, even if you have a nice work area. If your office does not have a conference room, you will have to make do. Avoid interruptions, forward your calls to another phone, and, if necessary, clean your desk of that cheeseburger from your lunch last week.

Discuss Agency Law

During your first interview with a buyer, a proper agency disclosure concerning your legal obligations to sellers may be required by state laws or local regulations.

Wants and Needs Analysis

A wants and needs analysis helps identify a potential client's buying and selling wants and needs. It helps you to match buyer's and seller's wants, needs, and motives to the specific properties available for purchase or sale.

The wants and needs analysis will give you an opportunity to "read" your clients better and paint a picture of their wants and needs.

The most effective way to "read" your clients is to listen. Spend more time listening and less time talking. When you do speak the best way is through probing questions or questions that have purpose.

In a wants and needs analysis, the rapport building step should take place in the first few minutes of each new, important contact with a person. From a psychological viewpoint, rapport is extremely vital to the outcome of the communications process. The significance of the rapport building step becomes apparent when we analyze it from a behavioral viewpoint. When individuals place trust in another or feel comfortable with another, they lower their defense mechanisms and become more open and agreeable to listening to ideas. The intensity of the defense barriers will vary with each individual and the specific situation.

It is your responsibility as a professional real estate salesperson to take action to reduce these defense barriers and relieve the tension that exists in all communication situations in the initial stages. It is important to recognize that this defensive reaction on the part of the other person is not a reaction to you personally. It is a reaction to the situation and is normal and natural. The specific techniques you utilize to lower defense barriers will vary depending upon your natural behavior and personality. The important point is that you should recognize that defense barriers do exist and develop your own techniques to lower them and establish rapport.

In addition to determining needs, an important by-product of wants and needs analysis is the establishment of a trusting relationship. The very fact that you are willing to take the time to listen is evidence that you are a concerned individual whose main desire is to help satisfy their needs. This trusting relationship will result in a close working environment in which you become a counselor to the person. "Ask For Action" Executive Consulting Services, Inc., 30700 Northwestern Highway, Farmington Hills, Michigan 48018.

When you begin questioning buyers about the specific things they are searching for in a home, the questions are naturally of a practical nature. That information will help you narrow the selection of properties to show.

However, the decision to buy a particular house is often more emotional than practical. Getting a sense of their lifestyle gives you a better insight into their emotional needs. Ask questions like:

- Will anyone else be living in your new home?
- How many bedrooms do you need?
- How will you use the third bedroom? Will it be a guest room or an office?
- Is a dining room important? Why?
- Are there any special features you must have in your home?
- How soon will you need possession?
- Must you sell your present home to buy another?
- Are you currently renting? If so, when does your lease expire?
- Are you familiar with today's procedures for buying a home?
- Have you seen any homes that you liked?
- Did you make any written offers?
- Are you working with any other real estate agents?
- Why are you moving?
- What do you like best about your present home?
- What do you like least about your present home?
- Do you have any special hobbies?

If you take your clients on more than three appointments and show them many houses with no strong possibilities, perhaps you should sit down and reevaluate their wants and needs.

Discuss Company Results

During this stage of the buyer interview you should discuss the results of your company. Have a detailed plan showing the features and benefits of doing business with you and your company. Include information on financial qualifying, client qualifying, product searches, market analyses, closing costs, and basic real estate buying information. Also include a great deal on past successes showing pictures of happy buyers, recommendation letters, and ancillary businesses that can help the buyer.

Discuss Personal Results

The personal results section of the interview can be tricky if you have not been in business long. If you do not have past successes with buyers, leave this section out and spend more time discussing your company. Do not talk about your past career, either, no matter what you did. The buyers expect you to be an expert in real estate. If all you talk about is your past career, they will quickly understand you are not an expert in real estate. You do not have to earn credibility; you are given it when the buyer first meets you. Your only job is to keep that credibility.

Discuss Financial Qualifying

Buyer financial qualifying is discussed in detail later in this book. It is addressed here only to show you the sequence of events.

After establishing rapport and talking in depth about the housing needs, begin to collect the financial information to determine their financial ability to buy. Information about the money available for a down payment, closing costs, and the affordable monthly payment helps you select the best properties to show. Explain the buying process and costs involved in buying a house to help set aside any apprehension buyers may have. Being well informed gives buyers the security to act when it's time for them to make a decision. The following are some questions you may want to ask:

- How much of your savings do you plan to invest?
- What is your present income?
- Do you have any other income?
- What are your current monthly expenses?
- Are you a veteran?
- Can you afford what you want?
- Is anyone else helping you with financing?

Most buyers expect to be qualified, so don't be shy. Remember to qualify all the time. Ask direct questions since you want and need clear answers.

Solve problems immediately. Problems do not solve themselves or merely go away. It is much easier to resolve them at the beginning of a transaction than later.

Always qualify buyers financially before showing them houses. If you don't, you may be wasting their time and yours.

Close for the Buyer Listing Agreement

After discussing your commitment to the buyer, you will be in a position to ask the buyer to allow you to be the initial contact for any property of interest. The following is a guideline of how your buyer appointment at the office should go:

1. Go to conference table. When the buyers arrive at the office, always take them to the conference room.

2. Pay a compliment. Say something nice to the buyers.

3. Show how you work. Bring out your buyer representation manual and begin your presentation.

4. Questions. Address a lot of questions to the buyers to elicit their involvement.

5. Financial qualifying. This is the time to find out if the buyers can actually buy what they want to buy.

6. Property qualifying. This is the time to do the wants and needs analysis, explained earlier.

7. Select 3–5 properties to view. Once you narrow the type of properties the buyers want, you search the MLS and find the matches to their wants and needs. Print out, in full page format, all the matches. Have them choose 3–5 to actually see.

8. Show properties. Once the buyers have selected the properties they want to go see, develop a tour of the best route and take them to see the properties.

9. After each property review, go over with the buyers the likes and dislikes of each home before proceeding to the next one.

10. After all properties close. You never know unless you ask, "Do you want to buy this property?"

11. Continue process until property selected. Once a property is selected, fill out the purchase agreement right there. Do not waste time taking the buyers back to the office. When they are ready, you should be too.

The following are some examples of both emotional and practical qualifying questions.

- "Mr. & Mrs. Client, how large is your family? What are the ages of your children?"
- "How long have you been looking for a home? Have you seen any homes that appeal to you? In which area is that home located? Tell me what you liked best about that home? Was there anything you disliked?"
- "What did you and your family like about your last home? Was there anything you disliked about your last home?"
- "How soon will you need to take possession of your new home?"
- "In which area do you prefer to live?"
- "What are your requirements for your next home?"
- "Do you own your present home or do you rent?"
- "Will you need to sell your present home before you buy?"
- "With whom are you associated, Mr. Client? Where do you work, Mrs. Client?"
- "Are you familiar with today's procedures in purchasing a home?"
- "Have you decided how you would like to finance your new home?"
- "Would you prefer a large down payment and smaller monthly payments or a small down payment and larger monthly payments?"

Working with buyers can be a rewarding experience. It is, however, more time consuming than working with sellers. Many sales associates rate buyers relative to their readiness, willingness, and ability to buy. If you have an abundance of listings, or listings that appeal to a certain type of buyer, you may want to direct your prospecting activities specifically toward:

- First-time buyers
  - o Do not have to sell a current home before purchasing
  - o Are often very motivated by the tax advantages
- Move up or down buyers
  - o Growing families
  - o Families with children approaching adolescence
  - o Upwardly mobile families

- o Empty nesters
- o People approaching retirement
- Investors
  - o Many people who recognize the value of having real estate in their portfolios buy residential real estate as an investment. This can be a lucrative source of business for you.

Property Viewing

Just before you leave on your showing appointment, you should explain to the buyers the protocol for viewing properties:

- Explain that you have officially set these viewing appointments and you must respect the sellers. This means that, if you pull up in front of a house and the buyers hate the outside, you must still go through the house. First, the sellers have spent time cleaning the interior. If they see you stop for a moment and then drive off they'll get mad and do their best to tell everyone they know. I once heard another real estate salesperson complaining that his seller was upset that another broker had pulled up and then left. He went on to say that the broker could not do anything about it because his buyers refused to view a property. I understood this to mean that this salesperson had no control over the buyers. You see, this is a snake and when do you kill a snake? Answer: Before the snake bites you.

- Agree with the buyers that they will stay together. The buyers need to stay together. If one person wants to stay in a room longer than the other, discuss the fact that they should still stay together. The reason you want them to stay is to watch their behavior. Are they giving buying signs? (discussed later)

- When going to view property you should drive together. Do not let the buyers drive their own car no matter what their reason. You need to hear what they are saying about the houses you're visiting and what they are saying about you. You cannot listen from a car behind. The way to handle buyers is to act assertive. If all else fails ride in their car with them.

- Be prepared to accommodate infants and children. Discuss with the buyers that the children won't be able to play with toys while they are in the house.

- Reinforce your accessibility to any listing for showing.

Upon Arrival

If you have properly educated the buyers, the showing will go smoothly. Here are some principles for showing houses:

- Make your showing appointments for an approximate time. Arrange for sellers to be absent or inconspicuous.
- Start with homes at the lower end of the buyer's range, moving up in value as you go.
- Do not show more than five properties without taking a break for review. Some buyers want to see every house on the market. If they did they would be too tired to enjoy the property and they could not possibly remember details of any single property. Stop at a fast food restaurant and buy them a drink. (Some agents offer to pay for lunch.) Review each property you have seen and eliminate all but one. Then ask them to buy that home. If they want to see more properties, fine, but now they only have one property to compare all the new properties to. The others they have seen can be forgotten.
- Make sure you have all the necessary keys, if applicable.
- Have information about each property readily available.
- Be flexible.
- Use traveling time to learn more about the buyers and prepare them for the next showing.
- Point out neighborhood features, especially those the buyers have identified are important.
- Park across the street to provide a full view of the property. This will also ensure you don't block anyone else from using the driveway.
- Enter through the front door, even if it is not the most frequently used entrance. You enter first and have the buyers follow.
- Briefly introduce buyers to sellers if the sellers remain in the house. Then tell the sellers if you need them you will find them.
- Lead the buyers through the house. Turn on and off lights as you go. Unlock and lock each door.
- Watch for the buyers' responses, verbal and nonverbal.
- Show their "hot buttons" first and return to them before leaving. "Hot buttons" are the things the buyers mentioned during the wants

and needs analysis as their wants. Such things as, "We really want a swimming pool, but it is not mandatory."

- Stay in each room until the buyers are ready to leave. Allow time and quiet for "psychological ownership."

- Stand close to the wall to enhance room size.

- Ask questions to help the buyers visualize their furniture in the house.

- Don't sell the home, just reinforce positive comments.

- Advise the buyers to make notes about each property after inspecting it.

- Point to any defects you know about, but point out a positive feature at the same time. For instance, "There is a crack in the wall but the listing sales associate told me the sellers have had it inspected by a qualified engineer and are having it repaired. If this is the right house, we can get the documentation as part of the offer."

- When you are driving to a property, you may want to forewarn buyers about a particular problem or even overplay it so the problem doesn't seem as bad when they see it for themselves. Be sure to discuss problems when you are away from the sellers.

- Allow the buyers to discover the property. Point out only those features they might miss.

- Explain features as benefits.

- Listen to the buyers' comments, both positive and negative. Ask additional questions to clarify needs.

- Make sure the home is secure before leaving.

Buyer Signs
While viewing the properties, you also should be aware of buyer signs or cues that indicate an interest in the property. Do this by listening to verbal signs, by watching nonverbal signs, and by asking questions.

Verbal buyer signs include:

- Specific questions.

- Presenting minor concerns.

- Asking about personal property.

- Wanting to show to a friend or relative.

Nonverbal signs include:

* Lingering.
* Nervousness.
* Imagining furniture in rooms.
* Touching each other.
* Touching things in the house.

After Viewing the Property

Ask questions to refine the list of properties you'll show later. Some questions that will give you good insight include:

> **Salesperson:** "What did you like best about this house?"
>
> **Salesperson:** "Would you consider this house as your next home?"
>
> **Salesperson:** "Why did you like the second house better than the first?"

Buyers don't always want what they think they want. Sometimes you need to stop, regroup, and clarify. If you've shown several homes and sense that nothing is clicking, probe beyond the buyers' stated likes and dislikes. Try to uncover additional information that will give you insight into their emotional and psychological needs.

Remember to complete a competitive market analysis to show the buyers what the market indicates the price should be. The buyer cost sheet indicates the amount the buyer will be charged at closing to buy a property. The process to figure a buyer cost sheet is the same as figuring the seller's cost sheet.

Finalization

The buyers should make an offer the best they can. I have seen buyers try to steal a property by offering a low amount. This tends to set bad parameters for the transaction. The seller now believes the buyer is trying to take advantage and the buyer believes the seller is unreasonable. The third party real estate salesperson should help the buyer offer the best price the buyer can and let the seller respond to the best offer.

Chapter Summary

Working with buyers can be very rewarding. The most important factor to them is to know you care about them and that they are worthy enough of your attention. If you do not show them the attention they feel they deserve, they will find someone who does. Build rapport at the first appointment and then do a wants and needs analysis. Revisit their wants and needs over time, if necessary. Also, financially assess your buyers before showing them any properties.

Summary Questions

1. What is the maximum number of houses a real estate salesperson should show a buyer before taking a break?
   A. Three.
   B. Five.
   C. Ten.
   D. There is no maximum.

2. What are the two separate qualifications for a buyer?
   A. Needs and financial.
   B. RESPA and HUD.
   C. Price and terms.
   D. Timing and area.

3. What should you do if a qualified buyer hasn't bought a home after three showing appointments?
   A. Direct him or her to an area with like people.
   B. Increase the purchase price.
   C. Take him or her on more showing appointments. Your broker thinks you're working.
   D. Reanalyze the buyer's wants and needs.

Objection Handling Techniques

Chapter Objectives

The objectives of this chapter are to help you classify objections posed by your clients and to identify the differences among stalls, conditions, and objections. This chapter will enable you to use a multitude of closing techniques. It will give you the ability and confidence to deal with a wide variety of common objections. This chapter combines both theoretical and practical information and is based on the principle of overcoming the cause of the objection rather than dealing with the symptom.

Key Words

Benefit: Something that promotes or enhances well-being.

Condition: One that is indispensable to the occurrence of another.

Feature: A distinctive aspect, quality, or characteristic.

Objection: A ground, reason, or cause for expressing opposition.

Stall: To bring to a standstill.

Introduction

A lot of this chapter deals with making money. I say this because the real estate professionals who know how to handle objections and close the sale make more of the money. They know their clients and always acts in their clients' best interests. Professionals know their jobs are based on helping people make tough decisions. They must help the sellers price their houses right to get them sold. They do not want to overprice a house and jeopardize the sale even if the seller wants more money. The professional helps the buyer make a decision before taking a chance of losing the purchase.

Let me give you an example of a professional salesperson, my daughter at age four. Her name is Brittany, and at that time she could talk but reading had not come yet. We were driving down the road and she spotted an ice cream sign.

"Daddy, if you were to get an ice cream, would you get chocolate or vanilla?"

Now for you professional salespeople, you recognize this as an alternate of choice close. I cannot say the word "no." This technique will be discussed later.

I decided to find out what my little girl is made of so I said: "Well Brittany, if I were to get an ice cream I would get vanilla."

And without hesitation she said:

"So will I."

If you recognize this, it is an assumptive close.

Let's analyze. First, did she get the ice cream? Of course. How did she know what to say? When I ask this in sales classes assume that I taught her the technique. (I never discuss "techniques" around my house. Home is for family and business is for work; I try never to mix the two.) I believe the reason Brittany knew what to say is because she knows me better than anyone in the world. She knew that if she asked me to get her an ice cream I would have said "no," and she knew she could not argue with me once I said "no." So, in her little head, she said, "How would daddy respond best?"

Was Brittany's response manipulative? No, because she did me a favor. Notice how I said that? She did me a favor. What she did was allow me to make her happy and I would do anything to make her smile. That's professionalism! My only question is where did we, as adults, lose that ability to get to know people? We all could do it as kids. Now, as a father, I would not have it any other way.

If you are having trouble with getting the client to make a decision that is in his or her best interest, maybe you could spend more time getting to know the client and learning what works to help him or her.

New sales techniques, sales training, and selling methods are continually developing. Successful selling also requires that the real estate service is of suitable quality for its target market, and that the company takes good care of its customers. Service development, design and production, and the integrity of the selling company's service as well are crucial to successful selling but are generally outside the control of the salesperson. So the first rule for the salesperson is to work only for a professional, good organization.

Objection versus Rejection

It is important not to read the resistance in an objection as a personal rejection. All of us fear rejection to varying degrees and it is important to recognize that we may have a tendency to take an objection personally, especially if we've had a tough day. Begin thinking of objections as questions with emotional content. This will help you deal in a more positive way with the substance of the objection and the person objecting.

Whatever the case, don't worry. Most objections are not as serious or formidable as they seem. Often what appears to be an objection is merely a request for more information.

Objections can help you if they mean that your client:

- Is interested in what you are saying.
- Is listening attentively enough to have objections.
- Is thinking through your solution.
- Is trying to resolve foreseeable difficulties.
- Wants more information about your proposed solution.

Remember, too, that the *absence* of objections can be a warning that your client may not be interested, or is not listening.

Objection versus Question

The main distinction between an objection and a question is that a question requires only information. An objection has some emotional content and often indicates resistance to your proposal. In the latter case, you have to provide reassurance as well as information.

Types of Objections

All objections can be lumped into three categories—stalls, objections, and conditions. Of the three, you should be able to overcome all stalls and objections. If you run into a true condition, however, you cannot go forward. Important point here: you must believe there are no conditions. Most real estate people fail to close because they feel they have run into a condition. Again, you must believe there are no conditions.

It's often frustrating to hear objections, especially if you've heard them before and feel they are not justified. But it's important to remember that an objection is often a buying signal in disguise. Someone who offers an objection is reacting to your ideas or proposal and can be engaged in a conversation about them. The person who doesn't respond at all or just rejects an idea completely is probably not going to show any interest no matter what you do.

Definition of a Stall

A stall is what the prospects say when they want to hide, for whatever reason, the real reason they don't feel they should make a decision. Stalls sound legitimate, but make no mistake, they just feel nervous that they might have to make a decision. Do not believe the clients really will think about it. Here are some typical stalls:

- "We would like to think about it."
- "Can we call you tomorrow?"
- "If it is meant to be it is meant to be."
- "We never make a decision until the next day."
- "We need to pray about it."

Let's first take a look at what "might" happen if the client waits. The seller "might" lose a sale because the buyer might find another property. The buyer "might" lose a purchase because another buyer bought the property while your buyer waited. You might be saying that it is your client's decision. True, but you must help them make a decision, now, because in this business it is always your fault. If the seller waits and loses a buyer, the seller will blame you because you did not emphasize the need to act immediately. You are the professional third party negotiator and your client is willing to pay you a great deal of money to help them make the right decision.

One further note, if it is not in your clients' best interest to accept the transaction, you must stop them, but you should not wait.

The best way to handle a stall is to ask questions. These questions should be very directive and should be closed-ended.

1. Agree with the client.
2. Direct the client to his or her final objection by asking minor questions.
3. Now you know the client's final objection and you can handle a true objection. (discussed later)

The usual final objection is price for both the seller and buyer. So, direct them there by using closed-ended questions. For example:

> **Buyer:** "We would like to think it over first."
>
> **Salesperson:** "I understand that this is a difficult decision. Let me ask, are you thinking about the size of the home?"
>
> **Buyer:** "No, the size is fine."
>
> **Salesperson:** "Is it the area where the home is located?"
>
> **Buyer:** "No, we like the area."
>
> **Salesperson:** "Is it me, do you like and trust me?"
>
> **Buyer:** "Of course, we like you."

Big pause, then slowly . . .

> **Salesperson:** "Is it the price?"
>
> **Buyer:** "Well, you know, it is more than we wanted to spend."
>
> **Salesperson:** "I remember, but let me ask you, if we could agree upon a price, would you buy the property tonight?"
>
> **Buyer:** "Yes . . . yes, we would."

Notice the way the salesperson moved through a series of questions until the final objection and then closed on that objection.

Here is a last resort if the questions don't work. Tell the clients you will leave the room if you are at your office or you will go to the convenience store if you are at their house. This allows them time to discuss the situation with the knowledge that you will be back. Remember, this is a last resort.

Lastly, what if they say, "We want to pray about it." I don't know. I choose not to handle this one. I am very leery to challenge religious beliefs.

Definition of an Objection

An objection is the real reason clients don't believe they should make a decision today. However, if you are able to show them how their belief can change, they will proceed forward.

When I first began my career, I was so afraid of objection that it almost got the best of me. Now, I silently beg the client to give me an objection I cannot handle. What is the difference? Simply, I studied. Don't study while you should be prospecting. Study when you cannot be making money. Studying gave me knowledge and knowledge gave me confidence. Time will not give you knowledge; you must make an effort to learn.

To handle objections you must ask lots of questions. Sound familiar? It should. It is the same thing I said about handling stalls. When you become great at asking questions you will be great at handling objections. Your questions must have a purpose (we call these probing questions).

Here are seven steps for handling objections or addressing concerns that almost always work in your favor. These steps also work well in diffusing tense situations.

Step 1: Hear them out

When someone trusts you enough to tell you what's bothering him or her, be courteous and listen. Don't be quick to address every phrase they utter. Give them time; encourage them to tell you the whole story behind their concern. If you don't get the whole story, you won't know what to do or say to change their feelings. Don't interrupt either, because you may jump in and answer the wrong concern. Important point here: While listening to your clients take notes on everything they say. Doing so allows you time to analyze what they are saying and you have notes to reflect upon at a later time. But most importantly it shows you care about them.

Step 2: Feed it back

By rephrasing their concerns, you're in effect asking for even more information. Be certain the clients have aired it all so no other concerns crop up after you've handled this one. In doing this, you're asking them to trust you. Clarify the concern by probing to learn why they feel that way. People sometimes need help expressing their feelings. It helps all parties understand the true nature of the concern. Begin your probing questions as follows.

Salesperson: "If I understand . . .?"

Salesperson: "Are you saying . . .?"

Salesperson: "Will you tell me more . . .?"

Salesperson: "Will you explain further . . .?"

Salesperson: "What you are saying is . . .?"

When the concern is clear, move on to the next step.

Step 3: Question it

This step is where subtlety and tact come into play. If the clients object to your asking to put up a yard sign, don't say, "What's wrong with it?" Instead, gently ask, "A yard sign makes you uncomfortable?" If it does, they'll tell you why. Maybe they don't want their neighbors to know they're selling. If so, you have to build their confidence in the knowledge that the sign generates buyers.

Step 4: Dignify it

Dignify the concern by voicing genuine understanding of how the other person might feel the way he or she is feeling. Noting that many other people in the same situation have felt the same way warms the other person to your response.

Salesperson: "I can appreciate that. Other FSBOs have felt the same way . . ."

Salesperson: "I understand how you feel . . ."

Salesperson: "That's a reasonable point of view . . ."

Salesperson: "That's a good question . . ."

Step 5: Discuss it

Once you're confident you have the whole story behind a concern, you can discuss it by providing information that explains the advantages of your perspective and reassures the other party.

Salesperson: "We have a large inventory of buyers at this time . . ."

Salesperson: "Market data shows houses are selling in 90 days . . ."

Salesperson: "I could help you with . . ."

Step 6: Confirm your answer

Once you've answered the objection, it's important that you confirm that your clients heard and accepted your answer. If you don't complete this step, they are very likely to raise the same objection again. If they agree that your comment answered their concern, then you're one step closer to persuading them. If they are not satisfied with your answer, now is the time to know, not later when you're trying to get their final approval to go ahead. Confirm that the concern has been successfully addressed. Ask the clients if they believe the information you have just presented could make a difference in the situation at hand. Ask if they see the benefits. (Make sure it is no longer a concern.)

Salesperson: "Will that be okay . . .?"

Salesperson: "Does that sound like a service you could use . . .?"

Salesperson: "Do you see the benefit of . . .?"

Step 7: Lead in

Lead into the next section. Don't just keep talking. Take a conscious, purposeful step back into your presentation. If it's appropriate, turn the page in your presentation binder or booklet. Point to something other than whatever generated the objection. Take some sort of action that signals to the other person that you're forging ahead.

These seven steps, if you learn them and apply them properly, will take you a long way toward achieving your goal of selling others even when they raise objections or concerns.

Definition of a Condition

A condition is the real reason clients don't want to make a decision today. There are very few true conditions. Too many real estate salespeople believe they are hearing a condition when in reality it is only an objection. Believe that there are *no* conditions and you will greatly improve your career. The best way to handle any stall, objection, or condition is to question it.

Reasons for Objections

Lack of Like or Trust—Your clients may see the value of your solution but still say no because of negative attitudes. They do not like you or trust you enough to make the decision. Negative attitude objections usually surface early in your conversations. That is one reason I emphasize building rapport from the start in any relationship. Rapport creates confidence in you and overcomes these kinds of doubts. These types of objections may come from:

- No Confidence: Your customer doubts what you say or questions your capability.
- Habit: Your customer is reluctant to change. He or she has been handling a situation one way for a long time like a FSBO. He or she might not be entirely satisfied, but the prospect of change is not appealing. (Your job is to assure the individual that change is easier than it might seem and will bring immediate benefits.)
- Fear: The customer is apprehensive about trying out a new way of doing something.

No Perceived Need—Although your customer might have needs, he or she might not be aware of them or might not sense how important they are. I have had sellers tell me they are in no hurry to sell and then say they have to be in Montana in six months. These sellers need you to tell them it may take six months and the time to list is now. Someone in this situation might say no to you because he or she doesn't see a reason to take action. You have to prove there is a need.

No Perceived Solution—Your customer lacks confidence in your solution or simply is not impressed with your proposal. There is the possibility that the client thinks that someone else might offer a better solution. The client wants to interview other brokers.

No Clear Answers—This may be a problem of confusion or misunderstanding, or it may be some kind of emotional resistance. You must ask questions to draw these objections out.

No Money—The customer may object to your solution because he or she cannot afford what you are proposing. A renter paying $850 per month in an apartment may not feel he or she can afford a home. Your job is to get the customer to a mortgage officer for prequalification.

Questioning Techniques

Why do we ask questions?

- To gain control.
- To isolate areas of interest.
- To get minor agreements.
- To arouse emotions.
- To isolate objections.
- To answer objections.

Questions can be placed in two major categories: the open-ended question and the closed-ended question.

The open-ended question solicits a discussion on the part of the receiver. The receiver can talk forever because of your question. The best open-ended questions paint a picture and the receiver finishes that picture for you. Some examples include:

Salesperson: "If money was no object, what would your dream home look like?"

Salesperson: "What are your concerns about selling your house?"

Salesperson: "Think back to your parents' home, what are some of those things you want in your home?"

The closed-ended question is meant to solicit a "yes" or "no" answer. It is used to direct the client, preventing the client from expanding on an answer. Some examples of closed-ended questions include:

Salesperson: "Do you want to buy this home?"

Salesperson: "Can you make a decision today?"

There's another reason to discipline ourselves to ask questions instead of immediately responding with our own answers: a question engages the other person and helps create a more meaningful exchange and a better relationship. It shows we are interested in what that person has to say. You can't move forward in real estate sales with a reluctant prospect unless and until you manage to create a climate in which that person is talking with you, not just listening to you.

Objection Handling Worksheets

Objection handling worksheets are used to prepare for all anticipated objections during a sales presentation. Realize that while all objections cannot be overcome, good sales presentations help buyers and sellers move closer to problem resolution. The main key to handling objections successfully is identifying the specific nature of the objection, which can only be given by the buyer. Remember that any time an objection is resolved, the opportunity exists to move the buyer closer to purchase or problem resolution.

Here are the basic steps in writing an objection handling worksheet:

1. List all potential objections you can anticipate for someone to buy your service.
2. List all the potential causes of those objections.
3. List potential questions to identify the cause for the individual's objection. You will need more than one question to match the style of the interaction. Phrase these in actual question format.
4. List objection handling techniques for each cause. Phrase these using your actual wording.

If you complete these objection handling worksheets you will find that you are prepared to handle almost any objection. Note the objections you struggle with on a worksheet.

Features and Benefits

Professional salespeople know the difference between features and benefits. The features are the aspects of the service. The benefits fulfill a need or satisfy a preference. I have known many real estate salespeople who never figure out the difference between features and benefits. They go through their real estate career trying to sell the features of their service only to have the clients reply, "So what?"

I believe that selling is an art form. My family and I went to DisneyWorld. While there we were offered free tickets if we listened to a presentation on time-shares in Orlando. My wife was not thrilled, but I love to get in front of salespeople. I find that I learn from the good ones and I also learn from the bad ones.

When we arrived, a young salesman greeted us. He shook my hand, introduced himself to my wife, and then bent down and smiled real big at our daughter, Brittany. He then spent time making friends with Brittany. I bring that up because, if you want to score points with me you can do it by becoming friends with Brittany. If Brittany likes you, I like you. Selling is an art form and it is beautiful to watch.

We sat down and the salesman began asking us a lot of questions. Did you hear that? He asked questions. I wonder where I have heard that before? He found out a great deal about us that he would need later.

We then went to look at a time-share unit. Of course, it was immaculate. It overlooked DisneyWorld and two full-sized swimming pools. The interior was perfect, with fine dinnerware on the tables, designer comforters on the beds, and beautiful furniture, none of which would be there when we got there. I could see through the show because I was a professional salesperson myself, but I think I started losing my wife. She remembered our cramped hotel room for several hundred dollars a night and now she was looking at plush accommodations. Selling is an art form and this guy had it down.

We went back to the conference room. The salesperson began asking more questions. You mean you can ask MORE questions? Yes, you can! This is how he set me up. Remember, I am not interested and I am a professional salesperson myself. By the way, did he know I was in sales? Of course, he questioned my occupation.

> **Salesperson:** "Dan, (I gave him permission to call me that, otherwise it would have been, Mr. Hamilton) do you and Kimberly have money set aside for Brittany's college?"
>
> **Dan:** "Yes we do, we have a mutual fund." (He wasn't going to catch me not taking care of Brittany.)
>
> **Salesperson:** "Dan, do you and Kimberly have money set aside for your retirement?"
>
> **Dan:** "Yes we do, it also is in a mutual fund." (He wasn't going to catch me not providing for my family.)
>
> Long pause
>
> **Salesperson:** "Dan, do you have money set aside for time with your family?"

How good is that? He drew me in like a fish on a line. He asked questions; he even knew how I would answer. Then BAM, he hooked me. What could I say? I knew where he was going but I could do nothing but stammer. I was not angry: I was flat-out amazed. Selling is an art form and artists ask the right questions to get interest and will never alienate their clients by making them mad.

I was not done yet. I had objections. Do you think he already knew what they were? A professional salesperson always knows the clients' objections before they even ask them. I am amazed when I see a so-called professional salesperson look bewildered when I have an objection. How could they not be more prepared?

> **Dan:** "Sure, it sounds great, but what if we can't come down here the same time each year?"
>
> **Salesperson:** "Dan, that is an excellent question. If I could show you how you can come here anytime would you buy today?"
>
> **Dan:** "Uh, no, but explain what you mean."
>
> **Salesperson:** "I would be happy to. Here at Acme Time-shares we believe in you and care about you. We actually do not sell fifteen

> units and keep them set aside for you whenever you want.
> Just call us a week in advance and we will have one set
> aside for you and your family. Isn't that a great feature? Can
> you see how that benefits you?"

Oops, he took care of my first objection well. Notice his questions. Notice his words. Selling is like an art form.

      Dan: "Yeah, that is nice. But what if I get bored with Orlando?
               Have I just wasted my money?"
Salesperson: "Dan, take a look at this."

He brings out this book. In this book is all the destinations around the world that are part of a time-share network. Within this network you can trade with and you go to a chosen destination and they take your spot in Orlando. Notice, he changed his delivery. You cannot use the same techniques every time. A sales artist is always changing.

Closing Techniques

When I meet a person, my first goal is to get him or her to like me and trust me. If you tell me something, I have a tendency to doubt you. Work on not telling, but asking. The following are techniques used either by you or on you. Some of them are manipulative. To be manipulative the technique benefits only you, not your client. Be sure your interest is always directed toward your client. If you choose not to use them at least you will recognize them when they are used on you. These techniques are in no specific order.

Trial Close

The trial close is used to take the temperature of a buyer or seller. A trial close asks a question and if the clients agree, they are interested. If their answer is negative, the clients are not ready to make a decision. The best trial closes are "tie-downs" and "if-then" closes.

The following is an example of a trial close: "When do you want to take possession of the house?" If the clients like the house they will answer. If not, they will protest. Now you know whether or not to move to the final close.

The Tie-Down Close

A tie-down is a question at the end of a sentence that demands a "yes" response. It is used to affirm a positive the client shows an interest in. A trial close is used to see if the client has any interest. If the client responds with a "yes," he or she might be interested. If the client is apathetic to your "tie-down," then this is not right for the client and you must move on. For example:

Salesperson: "A reputation for professionalism is important, *isn't it*?"

Salesperson: "It would be convenient to move as a family, *wouldn't it*?"

Salesperson: "Double moves are expensive, *aren't they*?"

Salesperson: "As a specialist in this area, I can better serve you, *can't I*?"

Salesperson: "You are interested in the home having complete exposure, *aren't you*?"

The question is not necessarily used to get an answer; just a nod of the head will do. Use the tie-down in the beginning of the sentence and in the middle if you so desire.

Salesperson: "*Wouldn't you agree* this a peaceful neighborhood?"

Salesperson: "A big back yard, *isn't it* exciting the activities that can be done there?"

Like all the techniques, this one can be overused, so be careful.

Alternate of Choice Close

An alternate of choice is a question with only two answers. Both are minor agreements leading toward major decisions. For example:

Salesperson: "I have an opening now, or would later today be more convenient?"

Salesperson: "I can be available at 2:00 p.m. or 4:00 p.m. Which time would better suit schedule?"

Salesperson: "I can clear my schedule for you on Saturday or Sunday. Which would you prefer?"

Salesperson: "If everything goes according to your plan, about how soon would you like to move, 60 or 90 days?"

Assumptive Close

An assumptive close is a question clients have to ask themselves after they've given someone the listing. They must stop you or you are moving forward. For example:

Salesperson: "Mary, what personal property do you want to leave?"

Salesperson: "We have our preview of new property on Friday. Will you be home or shall I bring a key?"

Feedback Question Close

The feedback question close is taking a minor objection and warmly feeding it back in the form of a question. For example:

Seller: "I don't want to give out a key."

Salesperson: "You don't want to give out a key? Will you elaborate on that?"

Seller: "We don't want to tie the property up with a listing."

Salesperson: "Oh, you don't want to tie the property up with a listing? Will you elaborate?"

Seller: "Can you have the home sold in 60 days?"

Salesperson: "Does 60 days suit your time schedule best?"

Seller: "Will you put a sign on the property?"

Salesperson: "Did you want a sign on the property?"

Seller: "Will you call before coming over to show the home?"

Salesperson: "Would you prefer that we call for an appointment before showing the home?"

Similar Situation Close

Relating a story (must be true) about someone else who was in the same situation that your seller is in is a similar situation close. For example: "They were so hesitant they went ahead with the listing, and today they're moved and so happy."

Seller: "We can always rent this home. We don't have to sell it."

Salesperson: "That certainly is true. Renting a home is a good investment; however, it's a proven fact that few tenants take the pride in ownership that an owner does. In fact, it's feasible that any appreciation in value could be offset by what we call deferred maintenance. Have you ever rented or managed a home before? It can be a rude awakening. In fact, the other day I was listening to a tape program in which the instructor decided to rent his home. Unfortunately, he rented to people we call 'professional tenants.' He said that after receiving no rent for six months, he finally went through eviction proceedings. He also said that it cost him over $4,000 to repair and refurbish the home. This is the type of thing that bothers me about renting the home and I would hate to see the same situation happen to you."

Reduce to the Ridiculous Close

There are all kinds of ways of describing the price of something. If you went to the Boeing Aircraft Company and asked them what it costs to fly a 747 from coast to coast, nobody would tell you it is $50,000. They would tell you it is eleven cents per passenger mile.

You are working with a buyer who truly wants to buy a certain house but doesn't want to pay the extra $5,000 the seller wants. Consider using the following script:

Salesperson: "I know $5,000 seems like a lot of money, but tell me, how long do you plan on living in the home?"

Seller: "The rest of our lives."

Salesperson: "Well I appreciate that, but let's say you live there only for the duration of the loan. The loan is for 30 years. If you break down that $5,000 per year you're only looking at (punch your calculator, since you carry one with you) $167 a year. If you look at that from the big picture, you get the home you want with the whirlpool tub in the master bedroom for the price of a hotel room. Let's see what that works out to be (punch the calculator) less than $14 per month. That's lunch money! Could the two of you miss one lunch during an entire month, because if you could, you could get the home you really want.

We looked at several houses and this is the only one that . allows you room to put in that garden you always wanted. I wonder what that is per day. (Punch the calculator) Forty-six cents per day! That is less than you would pay for a cup of coffee.

Let's get serious, you want this house. We are sure the seller will accept the offer if you raise your offer by $5,000. As a matter of fact (rummage through your pocket for two quarters and toss them on the table), let me pay for your first day. All I need you to do is authorize this paperwork and I will do my best to get you into this home." (Hand the buyer your pen.)

Some explanation is necessary. First, not all techniques work all the time, but all of them work some of the time. Also note that the buyer wants this house. If you are pushing the buyer into a decision just to make a commission, you are being manipulative. We are professionals, not high-pressure salespeople. To use this technique properly, start big at an annual figure and work your way down to the daily amount.

I used this technique on an accountant once. After I finished the accountant said, "Your numbers are all wrong. Financing $5,000 is a lot different, plus there are tax consequences and the time value of money to consider. But we want the house so we will pay the $5,000. Now, I am not sure what happened, but the buyers got the house they wanted. Sometimes the buyers just need a moment to reflect.

Puppy Dog Close

This close is just like it sounds and it came from pet shop owners. A family might walk into the pet shop and look at a cute puppy dog. The kids fall in love with the puppy and the wife falls in love with the puppy. The husband also falls in love with the puppy but is hesitant to buy the puppy. The pet shop owner says, "It's Friday, take the puppy home with you over the weekend and, if on Monday you don't want it, just bring it on back." What happens? Of course the family never brings the puppy back.

This is a favorite technique of auto dealers. They offer to let you take the car for a test drive, hoping you will fall in love with it and won't be able to give it up.

So how can we use this in real estate?

This happened to me. I had a couple of "those" buyers. You know, the kind of couple that can't agree on the same house. He likes one house and she likes another. I was willing to stay with them because I knew they would buy and use me. We finally went through a house and neither of them had anything negative to say. Still, they were not ready to make a decision. So I asked them to sit down in the living room. After about 20 minutes of silence, one of them said, "What do you think?" And the other replied, "Yeah, we should buy this one."

Good Guy–Bad Guy Close

The famous police integration: One bad cop beats up and threatens a perp until it gets out of hand and the good cop steps in and removes the bad cop. "Come on Joe, go get yourself some coffee." Joe steps out saying, "O.K., but I am not done with you yet!" The good cop says, "Man, you had better tell me what I want to hear before Joe gets back, 'cause I have never seen him that mad."

I have never attempted this close, but some friends of mine worked this one to perfection. They are a husband and wife real estate sales team. He is the bad guy and she is the good guy. He takes over the listing appointment and "tells" the sellers what is needed to get the house sold, including price. His information is correct and some sellers agree and sign up. Other sellers hesitate and he pounces on them. He begins to raise his voice and his gestures become forceful. Just about the time the sellers throw him out, his wife steps in and says, "Honey, stop, go to the car." To the sellers she says, "I am sorry for his behavior, but his point is valid. . . ." They sellers list with her at the correct price and terms.

The team has learned that some sellers need the real aggressive type while others prefer a softer approach. The team literally covers all territory.

Take Away Close

The take away close is most famously used by car salespeople. They ask you for your best offer and whatever you say they reply, "What? I can't do that; I guess you will have to find another less expensive car. Could I show you the. . . .?" But no other car will do for you so you pay the greater amount.

My dad worked this technique against the same car dealers and he is the most-mild mannered man you will ever meet. He never studied these techniques, he just knows them. I wanted a new car for college and I found my dream: a brand new Ford Mustang. It was a beautiful car, I was in love. I am glad my dad was there because I would have paid anything to get that car. (Salespeople are the easiest to sell). My dad made an offer; the salesperson refused and took the car away. I was hysterical but my dad calmly said, "O.K. Bye."

The salesperson said, "Wait a minute, let me check with my manager." He came back a few minutes later and said, "Can't you give a little more?"

My dad said no and got to the door of the office before the salesperson said, "Hold on, take a seat. Maybe we could do this. . . ."

After a while my dad said no and was up again. This time we made it to the front door of the dealership. The next time we made it to the car, and the last time dad was in his car driving down the street. The salesman was running after us screaming, "You've got your deal! You've got your deal!"

Later on I asked my dad how he knew he could get that price. His calm words were, "They made more than one Mustang, whatever they claimed was their best deal I knew we could go elsewhere and get the same deal." What a concept! There's the advantage of a third party negotiator.

You can use this technique in real estate, but be very careful. This one is highly touchy. Sellers can and will feel you are manipulating them if you use this technique more than once. I went to a listing appointment that had been expired in an area of town that had been declining for about five years. Prices were dropping so much that people owed more on their houses than they could sell them for. I wasn't real thrilled to go to this listing appointment because the sellers were probably upside down and I could not help them. The house had been priced at $64,000, so I figured (CMA) it should sell for about $60,000. At the appointment I asked these questions:

Salesperson: "So how do you feel about the price?"
Seller: "I don't agree with it."

(Great, I thought, now let's see if he lowers it by $4,000.)

Seller: "We want to raise the price to $75,000!"

Salesperson: "What? It did not sell at $64,000, what makes you think it will sell at $75,000?"

Seller: "It's worth it and we will wait till we get our price."

Salesperson: "And I don't blame you." (I begin to gather my books and things together.)

Salesperson: "I have just one question for you. What is the market doing in this area? Is it going up? Or is it going down?"

Notice I did not judge the area, I just asked a simple question. I continued packing my things. About this time the wife looked to her husband and said:

Seller (wife): "I won't be here in a year." (Notice who she didn't invite?)

Seller (husband): "But honey, we can't give the house away."

Seller (wife): "I won't be here in a year."

Seller (husband): "What will it take to sell?" (Husband now looking at me.)

Salesperson: "After looking at the CMA, I believe. . . ." (Wife interrupts me.)

Seller (wife): "Put it on the market for $48,000!"

Seller (husband): "But. . . ." (Wife interrupted with just a look and it was over. I listed the house at $48,000 and it sold in 10 days. The take away close worked so well here because I was prepared to leave. Don't try to fake this one, you will be caught. I later found out that the couple's son was being beat up every day at school and parents will do whatever is necessary to protect their children.)

Appeal to the Higher Authority

When a real estate salesperson is asked to do something that he or she does not want to do, he or she is tempted to blame it on someone else. For example, a seller ask us to cut our commission and the standard reply is, "My broker won't let me." Don't you hate somebody telling you, "I'm sorry we cannot do that because it is against company policy"? That is an example of appealing to the higher authority. The real estate salesperson must be thought of as the higher authority in a transaction. Never use the words, "I have to ask my broker." Or "It is against the law for me to do that." Both are reckless uses of "appeal to the higher authority."

If–Then

The "if–then" close is one of my favorites. It is the perfect trial close. For example:

> **Buyer:** "Will the sellers leave the refrigerator?"

Most real estate salespeople respond with:

> **Salesperson:** "They probably will."
> Or
> **Salesperson:** "We can ask."

There just isn't anything there. No talent, no skill. The buyer is interested because he or she asked a question about the house. Let me rephrase the buyer's question:

> **Buyer:** "We really like this house. We want to buy it if you can close us. If not we *will buy* it through another real estate salesperson. Oh by the way, if we could get the refrigerator that would be great!"

Does that phrasing help? In my book that is what the buyer is saying. If buyers want the house that bad I am going to get it for them. If I were to close them right here we will see how motivated they really are.

> **Salesperson:** "Mr. & Mrs. Buyer, if I get the sellers to leave the refrigerator, then would you buy this house?"

However the buyers respond, I now know a whole lot more than I did ten seconds before I asked the question. Don't miss the opportunity to use a great close if it is handed to you. This is the difference between a professional real estate salesperson and "just another" salesperson. As with all techniques, don't overuse this one.

Chapter Summary

The ability to handle objections will give you confidence in a sales situation and that, in turn, should make you more money. The fear of objections is a huge problem in the real estate industry. It will freeze potentially successful real estate salespersons into inaction, and that will lead them out of the business. Study this chapter over and over and make it a part of you.

Summary Questions

1. An objection is a question that should be answered.
   A. True
   B. False

2. In what type of close do you ask, "When do you want to take possession of this home?"
   A. "If–then"
   B. "Questioning"
   C. "Trial"
   D. "Puppy Dog"

3. What must an agent do to handle an objection?
   A. Give lots of reasons.
   B. Ask a lot of questions.
   C. Ignore the all objections.
   D. Take a lot of notes.

4. A "benefit" to a seller always answers what question?
   A. Will I make more money?
   B. Will it sell faster?
   C. So what?
   D. Will it be more convenient?

5. While listening to your clients, what is the most important thing for you to be doing?
   A. Smoking a cigarette.
   B. Thinking of how to close them.
   C. Watching their body language.
   D. Taking notes on everything they say.

Chapter 12

Client
Follow-Up

Chapter Objectives

The objectives of this chapter are to help you learn about the clients and their needs. You should learn that the sale only begins with the "close." Moving forward, you will learn to keep in touch with past clients and turn them into future prospects.

Key Words

Event: A social gathering or activity.

Internet: A wide area network that connects thousands of separate networks and provides global communication.

Introduction

You must develop tracking techniques for your business. The best way to do this is with computer and client management software.

If you do not have a computer, you can use a simple card file with dividers separating daily and monthly sections. If a contact should be called in a week, put them in the daily section four days out. For contacts that don't need follow-up for a year, put them in the six-month section of your file. Whatever the time frame clients give you for following up, divide the time by two and call them then. For example, if a client tells you he plans to put his house on the market in six months, follow up with him in three months You do not want to make a follow-up call to client who listed with another salesperson just last week.

Tracking Techniques

Track your entire current buyer and seller leads in the manner discussed above. Tracking all of your current business includes active listings, pending listings, and any buyers working on financing. Do not let this information slip through your fingers. You should have people to call back every day.

Software

Client management software not only records your client base but also notifies you when they should be called, tracks when special dates (birthdays) occur, and monitors your expenses for tax purposes. There are several good software products on the market.

Internet

One inexpensive way to follow up with clients is to use the Internet. With little to no money and a touch of a button, you can send mass e-mail messages to all of your past clients updating them on area market data. This is why you want to get the e-mail addresses from all of your leads. You can have a Web page that your past clients can always tap into if they want information about real estate or want to leave you a message. The Internet is also the fastest way to stay in touch. (Why do you think people call mail from the post office "snail mail"?) Be sure to get permission from your client before sending them e-mail. Be sure to follow the national anti-spam laws. And include a good subject message so your clients won't mistake your e-mail for unwanted advertising or spam. Also, be sure to check your e-mail at least twice a day.

E-Newsletters

Sending out an e-newsletter is an easy way to keep in touch with your past and present clients. With the click of a button, your message is sent to as many people as you like. And, like e-mail, the cost of sending out an e-newsletter is almost nil. You can even work from an e-newsletter design template so you're not faced with coming up with a new design each time you want to send the newsletter. When you do this, all you have to come up with are the words that you want to communicate. Again, it is so important to obtain e-mail addresses from all of your contacts.

When you host an open house, have your notebook open to your e-newsletter. As your guests sign in, offer to e-mail your monthly newsletter to them. You can also customize it with local market information so your clients know they are getting something that they can't get anywhere else. It's a great follow-up tool to capture uncommitted buyers.

Closing Gifts

Offer a closing gift to clients you want to remember you long after the closing. The gift should not be too expensive, but not cheap either. Avoid gifts that can be used up, such as gift baskets fill with fruit or, tickets to the opera, or anything else that will be forgotten when used up. Instead, gifts should be long-lasting. For example:

- A brass door knocker with the owner's name and your name as "Presented by Dan Hamilton with Acme Real Estate." This will last for as long as the owners are in the home. Every time they enter the home through the front door they will see your name. When it comes time to sell they will remember you. You might consider offering to put it up for them; otherwise they may never get around to mounting it.

- A six-inch binder with sleeves to hold all of their important house documents. You can put this together easily for a few bucks. The sleeves should include things like:
  - Closing papers
  - Survey
  - Appraisal
  - Deed
  - Tax records
  - Purchase agreement
  - Insurance papers
  - HOA documents
  - Information on you

  The exterior can be as fancy or as simple as you wish. Each involves cost. Some companies provide these already made up for you for a price. The owners will keep this book for as long as they own the house. They will refer to it when they need any of this information and they will know how to contact you if their plans change.

- Offer to take digital photographs of the contents of their house for insurance purposes once the owners get settled. Put the photos on two compact disks (CD)—one for the owners and one for yourself (with their permission of course) in case theirs is destroyed. The CD case and disk face should include your contact information for future use by them. This is a thoughtful gift and it is very inexpensive.

Whatever you do, do something. Don't let these buyer's become real estate waifs.

Events

One way to thank your past clients is to have a year-end party. This is also a great time to see old faces and remind them you are still in the real estate business. You should invite ALL of your past clients because time heals all wounds. If the transaction went great, then they love you. If the transaction went bad, then they have forgiven you. The party can be expensive; however, it is well worth the money. Here are some suggestions:

- Have the party at a movie theater on a Saturday morning. It is relatively inexpensive and fun.
- Host a chili cook-off. This inexpensive for you, considering the cooks bring the food and allows loads of time for building rapport.
- Offer some take-aways to remind them of you after the party.
- Provide snacks.

This is for fun; do not make it an advertisement. These people already know you; all you want is for them to remember you.

Chapter Summary

Whatever method you choose for follow up with your past clients does not matter as much as the actual contact. Do not let your past clients become some other real estate salesperson's waif.

Summary Questions

1. What is probably the best and least expensive way to follow up on past clients?
   A. Let them call you when they are ready.
   B. Using the Internet.
   C. Direct mail weekly contact.
   D. Area billboards.

2. How often should you check your e-mail?
   A. Weekly.
   B. Hourly.
   C. Daily.
   D. Twice a day.

3. What is a good closing gift?
   A. A plant or tree.
   B. Theatre tickets.
   C. One-month membership to a health club.
   D. A monogrammed door knocker.

4. What skill must a real estate salesperson employ when learning to read a potential buyer?
   A. Listening.
   B. Speaking.
   C. Writing.
   D. Organizing.

Chapter 13

Contract Writing

Chapter Objectives

In this chapter you will study the elements that make up a valid contract. You will learn the most effective ways to write a contract on real estate and understand the laws involved in contract writing.

Key Words

Addendum: Something added, especially a supplement to a contract.

Common law: The system of laws originated and developed in England and based on court decisions, on the doctrines implicit in those decisions, and on customs and usages rather than on codified written laws.

Competent: Legally qualified to perform an act.

Consideration: Payment given for a service rendered.

Contract: An agreement between two or more parties, especially one that is written and enforceable by law.

Valid: Having legal force.

Introduction

The law of contracts is one of the most complex areas of common law to study. We will not address contracts with that complexity. It is expected you have been or will be introduced to contract law in other courses. We will discuss writing contracts in a manner that will give you a professional appearance.

Contracts normally used in real estate include listing agreements, earnest money contracts, leases, deeds, mortgages, liens, and partnership agreements. In this chapter, the discussions of contract law will be centered on the creation and construction of contracts.

Purchase Agreements

It is important that some of the fundamental elements of contracts be generally understood before discussing the specific requirements of real estate contracts. A contract can most simply be defined as an agreement between one or more parties with the following four requirements:

competent parties, legal subject matter, consideration for the promises contained in the contract, and mutual assent.

Competent parties are those individuals who have the mental capacity to understand the agreement they are involved. Competent parties must be of legal age. For most states that is at least eighteen years old. If a party is not competent, the contract could be held as voidable by the incompetent party or by that parties guardian.

The contract must be legal. Any contract for an illegal purpose is considered void, as if the contract had never happened. A real estate salesperson I knew listed a house with the "seller." The next day a different man called her and asked about the sign she had put in "HIS" yard. Come to find out the renter was trying to sell the property without the knowledge or consent of the actual owner. That contract would be held void because the contract was not legal.

Consideration is something in exchange for something. There are two types of consideration: valuable and good. Valuable consideration is something of value. Generally this is hard currency (cash). It can be interest in a car, boat, or other things of value. Good consideration, on the other hand, is for "love and affection." Good consideration is when a father gives his daughter a house for her wedding present. Even though no valuable consideration changed hands, the courts would still consider it a valid contract because of the good consideration that was exchanged.

- Mutual assent is an "agreement of the minds." It is when all parties to a contract agree to all the terms in that contract. A purchase agreement (a contract) is the written form of mutual assent. The Statute of Frauds states that any agreement for the sale of real property must be in writing to be enforceable.

Contract Writing Hints

The following are a few hints on writing contracts:

1. Keep the contract neat. If you don't have neat and legible writing, use a typewriter or word processor computer forms. I have seen contracts so sloppy that it put the real estate salesperson in

jeopardy. If you have to handwrite a contract or significant changes have been made and you feel to be clear it needs to be rewritten, rewrite it, and get signatures on the new contract. With contracts, neatness counts. Always keep all versions of the contract on file.

2. Do not leave blanks in a contract if you think something is unimportant. There's probably no risk in doing so, but completing the entire contract makes you look so much more professional. Use "N/A" (Not Applicable) as needed.

3. Use blue ink on originals to differentiate from copies.

4. Use full names. Ask the parties for their full names when filling out a contract. This makes the contract clearer and helps the people at the title company with their research. Do not use Latin in describing a person (such as: et ux, et vir, et al, femme sole, baron sole, and the like).

5. Always double-check all the numbers and figures.

6. Always double-check that all the dates match and that you are not closing on unattainable dates (weekends, holidays).

7. Be sure to collect all personal checks necessary (earnest money, option).

8. Be sure your clients initial all pages and changes and sign the back.

9. Be sure your clients receive copies of everything they sign and as soon as possible provide them with the original.

10. Be sure all addendums necessary to the contract are with the contract.

11. Always double-check the legal description to be sure you wrote it correctly.

12. Explain the contract to your clients but do not make stuff up. I have heard real estate salespeople create answers to their clients' questions because they think they should know the correct answers. If you don't have an answer, say so, and then find the correct answer. Do not assume the way something has always been done is the right way. Verify all of your information through some other reliable source. Start asking yourself these questions: "Is this correct? How do I know?"

13. Do not promise these contracts do anything except put the desires of the parties to sell real property in writing.

14. Do not get creative in writing contracts. "Creative" in this context means "practicing law." Only licensed attorneys may practice law.

15. Do not use the term "as-is." Instead use the term "no repairs."

16. Never use the word "sue"; you are not a judge.

17. If the contract has a "$" symbol before the blank, use a dollar amount. Do not get creative here and use a percentage even if you are trying to avoid changes on counteroffers.

18. Do not accept poorly written contracts from other real estate salespeople. Doing so may put you at risk also. Instead, rewrite the incorrect portions with the approval of your client.

Addendums

An addendum is a document that is "added to" a contract. Addendums typically add information that is needed to clarify the contact itself. For example: an addendum is usually needed for financing because the paragraphs in the standard form need more information to be clear. Addendums are also known as riders or attachments.

Chapter Summary

As a real estate person, you do not have the authority to write contracts from scratch. You may only complete or fill in an approved contract by your state real estate commission through the direction of the parties involved. In this chapter you learned some effective ways to write contracts to be completely legal.

Summary Question

1. Which of the following is not an essential element of contract writing?
   A. Good handwriting.
   B. Completing all blanks.
   C. Including the clients' full names.
   D. Including the clients' weight.

Chapter 14

Negotiating
and
Closing

Chapter Objectives

The objective of this chapter is to provide you with information about mortgage and title companies. You will learn to differentiate between mortgage brokers and mortgage bankers. Finally, we will take you through the closing process.

This chapter will provide you with a basic knowledge of negotiation. You will learn certain words and how they sound to your clients. You will learn negotiating strategies, how to use them, and how they are used on you.

Key Words

Mortgage: A pledge of property to secure the repayment of a debt.

Negotiate: To confer with another in order to reach an agreement

Premium: The amount paid or payable, often in installments, for an insurance policy.

Strategy: The skill of using stratagems in endeavors in business

Underwriting: To support or agree to something.

Negotiating

Introduction

Negotiating is an art. The best artists are paid the best money. Negotiating does not mean one side wins and the other side loses. It does mean coming together to a reasonable conclusion. The best negotiating is accomplished when all sides feel they have achieved their goals.

Communication

An important part of negotiation is communication. If during a negotiation the other party does not understand your meaning, you may end up with the wrong solution or no solution at all.

Nonverbal Communication

Non-verbal communication is all of the communication two or more persons send and receive without the use of words. It is the way you hold your face. It is the way you hold your hands. It is the way you sit, are all types of nonverbal communication. Paying close attention to the nonverbal communication of your clients can give you insight to their wants and needs. If they tap their feet and stare off into the distance, you are probably losing their attention. Be careful of overanalyzing a person. Not everyone who scratches his or her nose is lying; maybe he or she just had an itch. The real estate salesperson needs to recognize and understand these nonverbal cues.

According to psychologist Albert Mehrabian, 93 percent of communication is nonverbal (1971).

Verbal Communication

The basis of communication is the verbal interaction between people. For real estate people communication is the key to the business. If you cannot communicate effectively with clients, you may want to find another career or learn how to communicate. Some clients have a hard time to articulate their wants and needs. Our job is to communicate with them by asking a series of questions to clarify their desires.

Listening

Many people assume that to be good in real estate sales you need to talk constantly. This couldn't be further from the truth. In fact, the most successful real estate salespeople are those who are active listeners. The best skill employed in learning "to read" a potential client is listening. By listening you not only become more likable, you are also better able to hear the wants, needs, and objections of your potential clients. The problem is, too many times we focus in on what we want to say without really hearing what the potential client really wants. To persuade, influence, and motivate others to buy and sell real estate through us and earn more money is to become an active listener.

The Five Rules of Active Listening

1. **Limit your own talking.**

    You have two ears and one mouth. The more you listen, the more opportunity you'll have to find out what the customer really wants. Spend half as much time talking and twice the time listening. Practice this when you are in a group. Don't talk; just listen. You will find that everyone likes you better and you will find out a lot more information.

    Too many times we are so concerned about what we want to say that we don't hear the other person. By not paying total attention to our clients, we "sell" them on what we think is important and not what they really want. This frustrates the potential client and in many cases we lose the sale. You will hear the phrase, "We want to think about it." Which means that you were not listening to your client. Check out the wants and needs analysis section of this book to find out more on determining what the client really wants.

2. **Don't interrupt.**

    By interrupting the client, sensitivity, rapport, and commitment are all destroyed. If you continually interrupt your clients, you will eventually shut them down and you will not receive any more important information. Although at times it seems expedient to interrupt, this perceived lack of respect for the prospect helps to deteriorate the relationship and makes it harder to close the sale.

3. **Notice nonverbal communication.**

    If you're talking to prospects and they start doing things such as crossing their arms, crossing their legs away from you, yawning, leaning back, looking bored, or avoiding eye contact, you need to "listen" to their body language as well as their words. If their body language is telling you to change your delivery—change it. Remember, this is for them not you.

4. **Use an appropriate setting.**

   To get others to listen to us and have them focus on the substance of our message, distractions must be minimized. Is your office too hot or cold? Is the telephone ringing all the time? Are you doing two things at once? Are there other people around? Do you have distracting habits like pen-tapping? Are you making direct eye contact or are your eyes wandering around? Just ask yourself, do you like it when a "customer service representative" is talking to someone on the telephone when they are supposedly helping you? To make sure active listening takes place, you must alleviate all distractions and pay total attention to your client.

5. **Use lots of questions.**

   Instead of talking, spend more time asking questions. Questions clear up what the client is thinking. It is also important to repeat what the client has told you so you can be sure he or she understands and you are proceeding in the right direction. The amount of information you can gather by just asking questions is amazing. The only trick is to not get sucked into the conversation and begin talking about yourself. Stay focused on the client and you will do well.

To close more sales we must determine the wants and needs of our clients first, and then work backward to determine the best services for them. The best way to do that is to start with listening intently.

Words Mean Things

Before negotiating strategies we should learn that words mean things and we need to be aware of what we say. We have all heard of buyer's remorse, which occurs, for example, when a buyer puts in an offer on a property and then backs out because he or she becomes afraid or regrets the decision. I believe some of that fear and doubt comes from the real estate salesperson. Be careful with the following words:

Dangerous Words	Better Words
Contract	Paperwork, Agreement
Sign	Authorize, O.K.
Down payment	Initial payment
Monthly payment	Monthly investment
Sales price	Total investment
Terminates	Ends
Commission	Fee for service
"As-is"	"No repairs"
Et ux	And wife
Home if buyer	House if seller

Negotiating Strategies

Negotiating is used throughout your real estate career. Here we will primarily concentrate on the presentation of an offer because this is the most concentrated time for negotiating. I have seen transaction after transaction fail because the real estate salesperson did not negotiate properly.

The first thing you need to do before presenting an offer is prepare. Do not take this lightly. Preparation is necessary whether you're preparing for a listing presentation or an offer to purchase presentation. Doing so will give that extra ingredient for a successful presentation. Here are some basic steps to follow:

Step 1—Do not discuss any aspect of the offer over the telephone. You are representing your seller's best interest and you cannot do a fair job explaining the offer unless you are face to face where you can see the seller's face for approval or disapproval. Furthermore, the seller must sign the contract, so there's no sense in wasting your time and theirs talking on the telephone. I know there will always be circumstances where you must present an offer over the telephone (the seller lives out of state), but do your best to avoid it.

Most real estate commissions state that you must present all offers to the seller. I will take it further. You should present all offers no matter what the circumstances. I did not say "how" you are to present those offers. The understanding here is that you feel this offer is unreasonable. If the seller's property is worth $180,000 and someone offers $60,000, go ahead and present that offer over the telephone. "Mr. or Mrs. Seller, you have received an offer for $60,000 and I think you should reject it, what do you want to do?"

The following two suggestions offer some help setting up a meeting with the seller without discussing the aspects of the offer over the telephone.

a. Have your broker or another salesperson call to make the appointment. Be careful on this one; if you normally call and now someone else calls it might raise red flags with the seller. If you normally have an assistant call, there should not be any problem.

b. Politely say you don't have the offer in your hands and close for the appointment without pause. By the way, it can be in front of you; just don't have it in your hands.

Step 2—Review the facts about the listing including number of showings, days on the market, and feedback.

Step 3—Update the comparable sales in the area for any changes that may have occurred.

Step 4—Make up a new seller's net sheet.

Seller's Net Sheet

A seller's net sheet is a document that allows the seller to examine all the possible costs associated with selling a property. Typical sellers are more interested in what they walk away with in their pocket than what the property actually sells for.

To effectively prepare an estimate, you will need the following information from the seller:

- Principal balance of the loan.
- Monthly payment amount.

- Yearly taxes.
- Yearly hazard insurance premium.
- The type of financing on the loan.
- Closing costs they will pay on the buyer's behalf.
- Any secondary liens on the property (swimming pool).

The following sources are available for this information:

- Seller's verbal estimate or answer.
- Seller's monthly statement from the mortgage company.
- Returned Mortgage Information Letter (MIL) from the mortgage company.
- Tax records (MLS) or the actual taxing authorities (tax info only).

Preparing an estimate before going on the listing presentation can be accomplished easily if you get the information before you meet with the sellers. They will rely on your expertise to estimate what the house will sell for, what type of financing will be used, and how fast it will sell. As more information becomes available to you, you will need to adjust your estimate. For example, the seller told you he owed about $85,000. You receive the MIL from the lender and it shows that the seller owes $88,000. When you receive a physical offer, you will need to prepare another estimate based on the terms of the offer. If anything changes between the time the contract is executed and the closing date, you will need to adjust the numbers again. Remember, the seller is holding you accountable.

Figuring a Seller Net Sheet

Use the following data to construct a seller's net sheet.

The sale price of a property is $100,000. The owner's title insurance policy is $992, which is given on a title insurance rate card. (Generally these rates are set by the state for all title insurance companies.) The escrow fee for the seller is of $250. Recording fees are $50. The deed preparation fee is $75. The home warranty is $495. The real estate commission totals 7 percent of the sales price. There is a first mortgage payoff of $70,000. There is no second mortgage payoff. There will be a miscellaneous fee of $200 to cover any possible overages but there should not be any additional expenses. These fees will be explained in later chapters. Notice that all the fees are added together to get the seller's total cost of sale, which is then subtracted from the sales price to find the seller's net amount.

Description	Cost	Receives Fee
Sale price	**$100,000**	Seller
First mortgage payoff	$70,000	Previous lender
Second mortgage payoff	$0	Previous lender
Owner's Policy of Title Insurance	$992	Title company
Prepayment penalty	$0	Previous lender
Escrow fee	$250	Title company
Title attorney fee	$0	Title attorney
Lender attorney fee	$0	Lender attorney
Filing/recording fees	$50	County
Restrictions	N/A	Lender
Deed preparation	$75	Title company
Loan discount points paid by seller	$0	Lender
Underwriting fee	$0	Lender
Home warranty	$495	Warranty company
Photos/amortization schedules	N/A	Lender
Tax certificate	N/A	Title Company
Tax service fee	N/A	Title Company
Wood Insect Inspection (POC)	N/A	Inspector
Buyer costs paid by seller	$0	
Real Estate Commission	$7,000	Real estate broker
Courier/overnight delivery	N/A	Title and/or lender
Miscellaneous fees and expenses	$200	
Other expenses	$0	
Seller's settlement costs	**$79,062**	
Prorated interest (0–30 days)	N/A	Previous lender
Prorated taxes	$900	Tax authority
Other prorations	$0	
Prorations for seller	**$900**	Seller
Total cost to seller	**$79,962**	Seller
Estimated net to seller	**$20,038**	Seller

Calculating Sellers Estimated Charges

Use the following data to construct a seller's net sheet.

THE TERMS OF SALE

Sales price: $150,000

Title insurance: $1,306

Financing: Conventional

Home warranty: $360

Taxes: $3756 yearly

Insurance: $1116 yearly

Monthly payment: $1,085

Principal balance: $97,650

Closing: May 15th

Commission: 6.5%

Use the normal costs associated with all other expenses listed above.

The seller has owned the home for three years and has a conventional loan.

Step 5—What are the benefits of this offer?
  a. Closing date?
  b. Possession date?
  c. Terms?
  d. Qualified buyer?

Step 6—What are the possible objections?
  a. Price?
  b. Closing costs?

Presenting offers is a very challenging aspect of our business. The success you achieve can be attributed to the following procedures:

1. **Humanize the Buyer:** The sellers want to feel that the buyers will take care of their "home." Some sellers have lived in their home for years and have raised their families there. It is curious how important a "wholesome" buyer is to the seller. Your job here is to talk favorably about the buyers. However, if the buyers are a risk you must tell the seller.

2. Present Terms and Conditions of the Agreement:
    a. Agree on minor items before getting to major items.
    b. Show the features of the contract, but sell the benefits.
    c. Continuously interject the seller's motivation for selling.

3. **Present the Net Sheet:** Remember the net sheet (like the CMA) is a tool, not a weapon.

4. **Overcome the Objections:** Ask lots of questions.

5. Ask for the Seller's Approval:
    a. Acceptance
    b. Rejection

Notice I only listed "acceptance or rejection" as the seller's options. The reason for this is because a majority of real estate salespeople will tell the seller they can "accept, reject or counter." The only thing the seller will hear to do is to counter. Don't suggest it, at least at first. By the way, a counteroffer is actually a rejection of the first offer and putting forth a new one. So a counter is a rejection.

Getting your offer accepted by the seller is not always possible or recommended (if the offer is not in the best interest of the seller). Negotiating a counteroffer can save the sale if you follow these steps.

Step 1—If the seller doesn't take the buyer's offer, start by reducing the net difference. Subtract all possible expenses the seller might incur if he or she waits for another offer. Always counter the sales price, not the terms of the contract. The reason for this is because if the buyer needs the seller to pay for a portion of the closing costs and the seller refuses, the buyer probably cannot buy the house. However, if the seller asks for more on the sales price the buyer could do that because he or she is financing the purchase as long as the house will appraise for the additional price.

Step 2—Confirm that the seller's objection is the only thing standing in the way of the sale. This is isolating the objection. If you do not do this, the seller will keep coming up with new objections.

Step 3—Negotiate a counteroffer from the seller. What does the seller believe is a good offer?

Presenting a counteroffer to your buyer requires some additional negotiating skills. The following are recommended procedures:

1. Go directly to the buyer.
2. Discuss the seller's concessions.
3. Present the seller's counteroffer.
4. Overcome any objections, including
   a. Selling price
   b. Down payment
   c. Monthly payments

Additional Negotiating Strategies

In the real estate business, negotiations between the actual buyers and sellers are rare because the communication is usually between the real estate salespeople. So let's take a look at it from that angle. The way you conduct yourself in a negotiation with another real estate salesperson can dramatically affect the outcome. Be sure that while negotiating you clearly know who you represent and never violate his or her negotiating position. Here are a few suggestions for better negotiating:

Get the Other Side to Commit First

Talented negotiators know that they're usually better off if they can get the other side to commit to a position first. Several reasons are obvious.

- The first offer may be much better than you expected. With real estate negotiation the seller has made the offer first by committing to a list price. From then on the negotiations move forward by the buyer (through his or her salesperson) making the next offer. If you are the listing agent, do not let a buyer's agent get you to budge from the list price without a formal written offer. Some buyer's agents might say, "My buyers feel the list price is too much. Will the sellers take less?" If you tell the buyer's agent the seller's lowest price, you are in violation of your agency duties to your seller. If a listing agent wants to know your buyer's lowest price, you (representing the buyer) cannot disclose the information.
- It enables you to bracket the proposal. If the listing agent states a price first, you can bracket the proposal. You have your list price (highest price) and you have the offer (lowest price).

Be Calm, Not a Know-it-all

When you are negotiating, you're better off acting as if you know less than everybody else does, not more.

The real estate salesperson who comes across as sharp and sophisticated commits to several things that work against him or her in a negotiation. These include the following:

- Someone who is a fast decision-maker doesn't need time to think things over.
- Someone who creates a defensive position from the other side.
- Someone who would not have to check with anyone else before going ahead.
- Someone who would never stoop to pleading for a concession.
- Someone who would never be overridden by a broker or manager.
- Someone who doesn't have to keep extensive notes about the progress of the negotiation and refer to them frequently.

The well-trained negotiator who understands the importance of acting calm retains these options:

- Requesting time to discuss the offer with his or her clients so that they can thoroughly think through the dangers of accepting or the opportunities that making additional demands might bring.
- Deferring a decision while he or she checks with the broker or manager.
- Asking for time to let legal experts review the proposal.
- Pleading for additional concessions.
- Taking time to think by reviewing notes about the negotiation.

Concentrate on the Issues

Professional real estate salespeople know they should always concentrate on the issues and not be distracted by the actions of the other salespeople. There was a world champion arm wrestler that would eat live crickets before each match just to freak out his competitors. He knew this would throw his competitors off their game giving him an edge. You wonder, "How in the world can anybody compete against somebody like that? It's such a game of concentration, it doesn't seem fair." The answer is that good athletes understand that the event is the only thing that matters. What the other athlete is doing doesn't affect the outcome of the match at all.

I have seen more real estate salespersons get so frustrated with the other salesperson that they lost their cool and hurt their client's negotiating position.

Former Secretary of State Warren Christopher said, "It's okay to get upset when you're negotiating, as long as you're in control, and you're doing it as a specific negotiating tactic." It's when you're upset and out of control that you always lose. To demonstrate how emotional negotiating can become let's take a look at a situation in which I was involved. I had a listing that the seller refused to accept a price less than $75,000. I agreed and we put the property on the market. A few weeks later we got an offer of $72,000.

The seller countered at $75,000; however because the buyer needed closing costs to be paid the seller's net was only $68,000. The buyer refused the offer. A couple of more weeks went by and I received an offer for $73,000, which netted the seller $70,000, which was more than the seller would have received from his first counter. Now I figured this was a slam-dunk, so I called him into my office. Once in the conference room, I handed him the contract and said, "Congratulations." He looked down at the contract and saw the price of $73,000. He stood up, picked up the contract, ripped it in half, and literally threw it in my face. He then shouted, "I told you I would not accept a dime less than full price!" Well, needless to say, I retaliated by yelling back and then I physically threw him out of the building and stormed back to my office. A short time later the manager of the office knocked at my door. I sheepishly opened the door. His only comment was that if he could get the offer through could he get half of the commission. My answer was, of course, 50 percent of something was better than 100 percent of nothing. He did get it through.

Now what did I do wrong? Easy, first I lost my temper, got too involved and acted unprofessional. Second, I did not prepare for the appointment. I just expected him to accept the offer and when he didn't I reacted. This cost me a thousand dollars—not smart! Be prepared.

Always Send a Thank You to the Other Real Estate Salesperson

When you're through negotiating, you should always congratulate the other side. The best way to do this is to simply send the other salesperson a thank you card in the mail. This not only keeps good feelings between you, it keeps the other side from being angry if you ever have to deal with them again.

The Closing

The closing is an action as well as a process. The action is when the buyer and seller sign the closing papers. You should try to avoid the buyer and seller getting together. Usually the buyer closes first.

Let me tell you about having the buyer and seller meet. While on a property tour once, we looked at a house that was typical except for the doghouse in the back yard. The seller obviously built the thing using left over brick from the main house. It was clear that he did not have a clue what he was doing; the bricks were not straight; you could see light between the bricks; the mortar was sloppy; and the roof of the doghouse was two pieces of plywood tacked together. Horrible! We all had a good laugh.

Several weeks later I happened to be at the title company and noticed the listing salesperson for the house we were looking at was there. I found out that the house sold and now the buyers were finishing up on their closing. As the buyers were leaving and the seller was arriving, the salesperson introduced the two couples. They started talking and the seller told the buyer how fortunate he was to get that great doghouse. The buyer laughed out loud and said, "That awful thing? I am going to tear it down with a sledge hammer!" Needless to say the seller was offended and claimed that he wouldn't sell his house to that particular buyer if he "were the last person on the earth!" The buyer shouted back, saying, "I wouldn't buy your stupid house, you @#$#$%!" They literally canceled the transaction. Now this does not happen every time, but we do like to avoid the buyer and seller getting together.

The closing process begins at the signing of the purchase agreement and goes through closing action. We will cover the basic process.

Mortgage Companies

Mortgage companies generally provide the funds to allow a buyer to purchase a property. The mortgage company takes a look at the buyer and determines the credit worthiness of that buyer. The mortgage company can provide the buyer with prequalification or preapproval. A prequalification is the least of the two. With a prequalification the lender asks the borrower some financial questions and usually runs a preliminary credit check. If the numbers work out the lender will give a prequalification in an amount the buyer should be able to buy for. The prequalification is not a guarantee of a loan. Several aspects of the buyer could prevent them from getting a loan. On the other hand, a preapproval is the lender's word that this buyer will be able to buy if the house they find meets the lender's approval. With a preapproval, the lender has run a full credit check, verified all work records, and checked previous residences for discrepancies. If a buyer has preapproval, he or she also has leverage with a seller because to the seller it is almost the same as cash.

Almost all real estate transactions require funds from third party lenders. Third party lenders are named that in the real estate business because of referring to the seller as the party of the first part and the buyer as the party of the second part and the lender as the third party to the transaction.

A mortgage company employs loan officers to contact real estate agents and/or builders to present them with the benefits of doing business with their company. The loan officer takes a buyer and works him or her through the loan process. They put all the paperwork together and handle all potential problems of the loan. These are the mortgage people with whom real estate salespeople generally deal.

Ultimately, the borrower will make the decision regarding the lender he or she will use, but real estate agents can have considerable influence in the selection.

The interest rate and loan charges are important in the selection of the lender. It is also important for the borrower to "like" the mortgage officer.

A loan processor works from the borrower's loan application papers to obtain verifications of employment, bank balances, charge accounts, and note balances.

Mortgage companies employ underwriters to make the final decision on each loan application the company is considering. The underwriter checks the work of the loan processor and the appraiser. The loan application is the initial meeting between the borrowers and the loan officer to complete the application and sign all disclosures statements.

Loan processing involves verification of employment, residence, and assets of the buyers. A full credit report will be obtained and an appraisal of the home will be made. All of the information necessary to meet the investor guidelines will be assembled and prepared for the underwriter's review.

The loan package is put together in a file and presented to the underwriter for review. The underwriter's job is to determine whether or not the loan package meets all investor guidelines. After the review process the approval is issued.

Upon loan approval, closing documents are prepared for closing. THE BUYERS MUST BRING A CERTIFIED CHECK to the closing made payable to the title company in the amount due. Do not forget to tell the buyers they must have certified funds because the title officer cannot close if they bring a personal check unless the check is for less than $1,500. During closing, the principals sign all of the closing documents (and there are a pile of documents), and then the title officer disburses all funds. This is where the real estate salesperson gets paid!

Mortgage Bankers

A mortgage banker is a lender who actually funds the loan at the time of closing. These companies are set up with underwriting, closing, funding, packaging, and selling of loans to the secondary market.

Mortgage Brokers

A mortgage broker is a company that originates and processes loans and delivers them to another lender for funding. There are many levels of service that mortgage brokers render to the consumer. Most brokerages are small operations that depend on the wholesale lender to help with processing, underwriting, and closing. Other mortgage brokers have good operations with adequate staff to give good service.

Title Companies

After the contract has been signed and the method of finance chosen, the title insurance company is retained to make sure that all the details come together and that the buyers receive insured title to their property.

The title company, working only from the contract and the lender's instructions, completes the entire transaction. Title insurers search and examine the title and inform the parties involved of title problems that may arise, such as liens or mortgages that were not properly satisfied. They also coordinate preparation of documents for the closing and secure a closing package from the mortgage company when a lender is involved. The services of a notary are included in the closing procedure, as well as recording the documents in the public records office and making sure all the expenses of the closing are paid.

A title company handles the funds for the closing or consummation of real estate transactions. A fee is charged for handling the funds and for the title insurance policy. The amount of premium paid is set by the State Board of Insurance and is dependent upon the price of the home. The title insurance policy protects the buyer from financial loss as a result of a title defect that existed when the property was purchased.

Closing Process

Once a loan has been approved, the mortgage company prepares a sheet of instructions for delivery to the title company, more specifically the title officer handling closing procedures. The closing instructions direct the title officer in how to handle the closing, what documents must be signed, and the correct legal name to be used. The instructions will include any special documents the mortgage company will need to finalize the loan and fund the transaction. Also, a truth-in-lending statement is prepared for the purchaser-borrower's signature at closing. The instruments and procedures may vary between title companies according to how their staff attorneys interpret state laws.

In most states, the closing is actually held at the title company. However, this is not a requirement. I have closed transactions at my real estate office, at the lender's office and at the seller's house. If one of the parties are at a different location, the documents will need to be sent by overnight courier and the closing could actually happen in different states.

At the actual closing the buyer and seller execute all of the required documents and the funds are distributed. The title company must pay all of the real estate fee to the correct persons. Here is a hint: If you want to be paid at closing, have your broker execute a "Commission Disbursement Authorization" form to the title company. This form gives permission to the title company to pay you at the closing table so you do not have to wait on your commission check. This is called table funding.

Chapter Summary

The type of information discussed in this chapter is covered throughout this book. Negotiating is a form of the objection-handling technique. It is used when dealing with clients. Review all the material in this book and you will find that negotiating is a thread that flows throughout. Remember to listen to verbal and nonverbal (body language) communication and to always keep your cool.

Generally real estate salespeople enjoy the closing action (usually when we are paid) but do not concentrate as much on the closing process. Real estate salespeople should track the closing process with the mortgage company and the title company to be sure the process is flowing properly.

Summary Questions

1. At the time of origination, a mortgage creates a lien on the mortgaged property in states that subscribe to which of the following theories?
    A. Lien theory.
    B. Title theory.

    C. Intermediate theory.

    D. Both A and B.

2. What do buyers need to bring to the closing?

    A. Driver's license.

    B. Verification of homeowner's insurance.

    C. Certified funds for closing costs.

    D. All of the above.

3. What is a better word than "contract"?

    A. Agreement.

    B. Form.

    C. Binding document.

    D. Legal document.

4. Which of the following offers should be presented?

    A. An offer that you know won't fly because the buyer is in bankruptcy.

    B. An offer for less than half of the sales price.

    C. An offer presented orally.

    D. All offers should be presented.

5. The listing agent has an offer to present to the sellers; how should they respond?

    A. Accept the offer.

    B. Reject the offer.

    C. Counter the offer.

    D. Any of the above.

Chapter 15

After Acceptance

Chapter Objectives

In this chapter you will learn what happen once an offer on a property is accepted—from the perspectives of both the seller's and the buyer's representatives.

Key Words

Appraisal: An expert or official valuation.

Radon: A colorless, radioactive, inert gaseous element formed by the radioactive decay of radium.

Survey: To determine boundaries or land or structures on the earth's surface by means of measuring angles and distances, using the technique of geometry and trigonometry.

Introduction

Just because we have a buyer and a seller who agree on a sale doesn't mean our job as professional real estate salespeople is over. We must now take care of all the details to ensure that a successful closing will take place. Do not forget to follow up with your clients because this is a critical time for them and you.

Listing/Buyer Status Changes

As soon as possible, the listing salesperson should change the status of the listing in the Multiple Listing Service to pending (or whatever is applicable). The listing person then turns a copy of the contract and the earnest money check over to the title company and receipts the earnest money. The listing person takes a file to the appropriate person within the company for processing.

The buyer's salesperson should get a copy of the contract (may require an original) to the mortgage company, to their own company, and to the title company.

Both principals need to have an original contract in their hands.

Appraisal

An appraisal is one person's opinion of value. An appraisal is generally required when a property is sold, especially if a loan will be originated. Ordering an appraisal is not typically handled directly by the real estate salesperson; however, the salesperson needs to make sure it is ordered.

If the appraiser undervalues (in your opinion) the property and you have additional comparable properties that might change the value given, most professional appraisers consider the new information and make a revision of the appraisal. It is totally up to the appraiser whether to change the value estimate to reflect the new information.

Inspections

Inspections of the house should be mandatory as they protect all parties involved in the transaction. There are many types of inspections. The inspections you use depends on the house and the buyer. Without exception, however, a general house inspection and a pest inspection should be performed.

House Inspection

A house inspection is a complete inspection of the house by a professional inspector. The inspector will look for signs of problems. For starters, the inspector should check all appliances, the electrical system, the plumbing system, the roof, the structure, the drainage, and the overall appearance of the house. The inspector is responsible for commenting on subjective things like carpet color or outdated fixtures. These things are based on personal preferences. The inspector will not generally make direct statements like, "The house has foundation problems." It is more likely he or she will say, "There are signs of cracking and I recommend a structural engineer report."

Some inspectors believe they should find something wrong with the house. I heard one inspector say that the toilet seat in the main bathroom was loose. It took longer to write that in the report than it did to tighten the wing nut under the seat. Here is a theory: Let the inspector find some stuff, and it will make them happy. What I mean here is don't have the seller fix everything before an inspector checks the house out. For example, don't fix a cracked window. That is easy for an inspector to find; they feel they have done their job. And it is not an issue for a buyer when looking at the property; they probably would not even see it.

The house inspection benefits the buyer, seller, and agents. You have house inspections to aid in disclosure of property defects. The number one lawsuit for real estate transactions is undisclosed property defects. The buyer should choose a licensed inspector.

The salesperson should not be the one to recommend an inspector, although if he or she provides a list of licensed inspectors the buyer could choose from that list. The buyer should also be at the inspection. The real estate salesperson may choose to attend as well. I believe new real estate salespersons should be there to experience the inspection. If you do go to an inspection, do not comment on anything because you could become liable.

Buyers sometimes want to save the expense of inspecting a property. Every reasonable effort should be made to convince the buyer to have the inspection. If the buyer refuses, a broker might consider asking the buyer to sign a waiver acknowledging that, against the broker's urging, the buyer chose not to have the inspection. The waiver also states that the broker is not a licensed inspector and has not made an inspection of the property.

Some purchase agreements give the buyer the right to have inspections and the option paragraph allows for negotiation between the buyer and the seller on repairs. A real estate salesperson should be aware that there are time constraints for the buyer to get inspections.

There is a difference between lender-required repairs and repairs on inspection reports. The lender-required repairs must be completed before closing or the lender will not make the loan. Any other repairs may be done or could have an allowance paid at closing if the lender agrees to allow it.

Pest Inspection

Pest inspections are designed to look for problems related to insect infestation. Mostly these inspections are concerned with termites and carpenter ants, both of which destroy wood. Be careful here because most mortgage companies want an original pest certificate before they will fund the money for the sale of the home to prove that pests are not present. This type of inspection is typically required by mortgage companies but is not a legal requirement. Make sure your buyer gets both the house inspection and the pest inspection. I told some buyers to get "inspections" and they called a house inspector. At the closing, the title officer asked the buyer for the pest report. The buyers did not have one and I was blamed for not being more specific. They were right. Most inspectors will do both; the inspector these buyers hired did not.

Septic System

Septic systems, for those "fortunate" to have them, can be a real problem. Most mortgage companies require a septic inspection to be sure they are working properly and have the needed capacity. Properties that typically have septics are more rural–where no public system is available.

Well Inspection

Like septic systems, wells are usually in rural properties and usually require an inspection. The inspector will test the water to be sure it is of the necessary standard.

Radon

Radon is a gas that seeps from the ground into a house. It comes from radioactive material underground, which is kind of scary. The proper inspector can check for high levels of radon gas in a house. Do not get a store-bought kit and measure the level yourself. By doing so, you assume liability.

Environmental Assessment

Environmental assessments are usually carried out on commercial properties or large tracts of land. These assessments test the soil for contaminates and other hazards. They are extremely expensive to conduct.

Structural Engineer's Report

A structural engineer's report comes from a structural engineer who looks at the structure, the soil conditions, the internal support system, and other aspects of a property to determine the viability of the structure. Reports written by engineers are extremely valuable because they are not biased. Reports that come from foundation companies find problems they can fix for a fee. Needless to say foundation companies almost always find problems.

Survey

A survey is a graphic look at the property boundaries. Usually on lightly colored paper, it is a drawing of the property's boundaries, easements, exterior of any improvements, and location of fences.

Repairs

If repairs are required by the purchase agreement, be sure they are completed according to the agreement. Take your time when describing the repair. I know of one real estate salesperson who wrote in the amendment regarding repairs that the tree limbs needed to be cut back six feet from the house. The seller cut the limbs back and left them on the ground. The seller refused to clean up the mess and claimed he had cut the limbs according to the amendment. Guess who cleaned up the three truckloads of limbs? The salesperson who wrote the amendment.

Repairs are generally required to be completed by licensed repair people. If the sellers want to do the repairs themselves, they need to be warned of the liability they will incur if a problem arises as a result.

If you are representing the buyer, provide the listing salesperson an itemized list of repairs to be completed. And remember to follow up to be sure the repairs have been made. The best way to do that is to allow the buyer the opportunity for a final walk-through.

Final Walk-Through

The final walk-through allows the buyer the right to observe the property just prior to the closing. The buyer should check for any damage to the property that occurred since the agreement was consummated. This is not the time for the buyer to ask for more repairs or remodeling. Tell your buyer that the purpose of the final walk-though is to check for damage, not to add to what was agreed.

Chapter Summary

The best way to remember all that is needed after acceptance of a contract is to have a checklist. Do not neglect your clients at this stage of the process because it is a great time to get referrals for business.

Summary Questions

1. What is a graphic look at the property's boundaries?
   A. Observation.
   B. Survey.
   C. Boundary analysis.
   D. Appraisal.

2. What is the colorless, radioactive, inert gaseous element formed by the radioactive decay of radium?
   A. Radiation.
   B. Gas of decadence.
   C. Radon.
   D. Inertia gas.

Chapter 16

Financing

Chapter Objectives

The objectives of this chapter are to introduce you to different types of financing and provide you with an understanding of the good faith estimate and qualification process. You should be able to use different creative financing options.

Key Words

Compensating: To offset; counterbalance

Creative: Characterized by originality and expressiveness, imaginative

Reserves: To keep back, as for future use or for a special purpose

Introduction

I once heard that "If a buyer wants to buy and a seller wants to sell, financing should not get in the way." I agree with that. The more we understand about financing, the more people we can help. If a buyer has two of the following three things, he or she should be able to finance a property:

1. Good credit.
2. Substantial, steady, and verifiable income for at least two years.
3. Large reserves of cash on hand.

Good credit will make up the basis as far as establishing someone worthy of a loan. But good credit must be matched up with one of the other two things to be adequate. With good credit and good income a person can buy a property with little or no cash. If someone has good income, and plenty of cash, but terrible credit, he or she also can get a loan. (The interest rate might be high but he or she can finance a property.) Last but not least, money talks and if the buyer has enough cash to put 25 percent or more down he or she can finance the rest of the cost with poor credit and no job history.

Now let's look more into the financing of real property.

Good Faith Estimate (GFE)

Within three business days of accepting a loan application, a lender is required to submit a good faith estimate (GFE) of settlement costs to the loan applicant. Settlement charges are estimated for each item anticipated, except for prepaid hazard insurance and cash reserves deposited with the lender. The estimate may be stated in either a dollar amount or as a range for each charge, and the information must be furnished in a clear and concise manner (no special form is required). It is basically the total amount of money needed to close the purchase of a home. The GFE includes fees that are paid for outside of the closing, fees paid for at the time of closing, and fees that are rolled into the note.

Here are several things to look for in a good faith estimate:

1. Loan fees, including:
    *   Loan origination fee
    *   Discount fee
    *   Buy-down fee
    *   Commitment fee

2. Non allowables. These are the fees charged by the lender/title company that the buyers are not allowed to pay when purchasing a home through Federal Housing Administration (FHA) or Veterans Administration (VA) financing. They are typically identified as a seller cost on the GFE. Look for two things:
    *   Are they identified?
    *   How much are they?

3. Title charges. Are they too high? Are they too low? Get to know what is normal and customary in your area. Compare estimated net sheets available to you from different title companies.

4. Taxes—Are they too high? Are they too low? How many months are being charged for escrow? Does the GFE estimate the aggregate adjustment?

5. Hazard insurance. How much is the premium? Is it too low? Is it too high?

6. Total cash out of pocket needed to close. Rule of thumb: FHA should be about 6 percent of the sales price with a minimum down; VA should be about 3 to $3\frac{1}{2}$ percent of the sales price with zero down. Conventional should be about 5 percent of the sales price plus a down payment.

Government Financing

The heading Government Financing is somewhat of a misnomer because the federal government does not finance real estate purchases. The federal government actually insures the lender against losses due to default. Lenders are concerned about risk—will they get their money back? If the government insures the loan, the lender feels certain about loaning you the money. You must qualify through the government entity that you are being insured by (FHA and VA are the most common).

Conventional Financing

Conventional financing is defined as any financing that is not government backed. Conventional financing is done through banks, mortgage companies, savings and loans, and any other primary lender. The lenders do not have the stringent guidelines any government insured loan normally has. Lenders are loaning their own money and will qualify a borrower using their own qualifications. Typically FHA financing is easier on the borrower and conventional financing is easier on the property. So if you had a borrower with credit problems, you might want to look to an FHA loan first. If the property is in disrepair, you might want to look at a conventional type loan. The point is that the VA is tough on the borrower and the property.

Creative Financing

Creative financing refers to sale of real estate with terms of financing that are different from those on new loans with terms established by current market forces.

Seller Financing

Some sellers want to finance their property for a buyer. The advantages include more potential buyers for the property, an income on the property, lower closing costs, and the seller will not have to pay capital gains taxes at the closing. The advantages to the buyer include lower closing costs, minimal qualifications, and faster closing. You will see seller financing on property that is difficult to sell like contracts for the sale of raw land.

Wrap-Around Loan

A wrap-around loan is a not an actual loan. This type of transaction usually involves a seller who has a current loan that does not have an alienation clause (an alienation clause gives the lender the right to call the note due and payable if the property is sold in anyway). The seller "wraps" an additional loan around the existing loan. For example, a seller has a current loan on a property for $60,000 and a buyer is willing to pay $100,000 for the property but cannot qualify through normal financing channels. The seller would "wrap" a note for $40,000 around the current loan of $60,000 for a total of $100,000. The borrower would make the payments directly to the seller and the seller would be responsible to the original lender to make the payments on the remaining $60,000. This type of financing should be done through attorneys who are familiar with wraps because of the unique way this transaction is formed.

Balloon Note

A balloon note is any note that the final payment is larger than any of the previous payments. The basis of this type of loan is to finance over a long term and get paid off in the short term. Let me explain. Say a seller would not mind financing a property for three years but not for thirty. The buyer could not afford the payments to amortize (equal payments until the loan is paid off) the loan in three years. You could construct a contract for the seller to finance the loan over 30 years and have a balloon payment for the remaining balance in three years. In three years the buyer could refinance and pay off the seller.

Lease/Purchase

A lease/purchase is a lease for a few months with a purchase at the end of the lease. The buyer must buy at the end of the lease. The lease/purchase is usually for a buyer who has some problems being approved for a loan. The time the buyer is leasing is the time he or she can clear up any outstanding problems with credit and be ready for a loan. The lease time is time for the buyer to save money for a down payment or a portion of the monthly rent payment can be used for the down payment later.

Assumable Loans

During the time in which all FHA and VA loans were assumable, some conventional loans lacked a due-on-sale clause, and the clause was found to be unenforceable in others (until 1982). The assumable loan is attached to the property, just like a physical characteristic such as a pool, fireplace, or garage. The sale price of a house should reflect the "value" of the assumable loan.

Buy-Down Mortgage

A buy-down mortgage is a fixed-rate mortgage in which the seller prepays some of the loan interest to "buy down" the interest rate for the buyer-borrower for some period. This type of financing becomes more popular in periods of high interest rates (such as the early 1980s). The seller is usually a builder seeking to promote home sales in a slow market. The buy-down allows the borrower to acquire cheaper financing in the early life of the loan. A typical buy-down would be: the prepaid interest buys down the borrower's interest rate by 300 basis points, 200 basis points, and 100 basis points over the first three years of loan life, respectively. Suppose the contract rate on the loan is 10 percent. This buy-down would give the borrower interest rates of 7 percent, 8 percent, and 9 percent, respectively, over the first three years. These lower rates would be reflected in a lower payment for the borrower. In the fourth year the payment reverts to normal since the contract rate is now being charged.

The good news with a buy-down is that the lower initial payments may allow the buyer/borrower to qualify for the loan when he or she otherwise might have problems. The bad news is that, as with other types of favorable financing, the seller will likely attempt to capture the value of the buy-down into the price of the property.

Buyer Qualification

A competent mortgage officer generally qualifies the buyer. We will touch on buyer qualification here just in case you do not have a mortgage officer on hand.

Buyer qualification refers to the process of determining the risk of loss on a residential loan. If a lender is willing to loan money for real property, the risk level for the lender must be tolerable. Qualification is used to determine the ability of the buyer to make mortgage payments from his or her current income and still have enough for family expenses.

Lenders use an income ratio and a debt ratio to measure a buyer's ability to pay back a loan. The income ratio is traditionally recognized to be of the buyer's monthly income. The debt ratio is the relationship between the buyer's long-term debt and the monthly income. For example:

How much can a buyer earning $3,600 per month afford to pay on a loan with an income ratio of 25 percent?

$3,600 × 25% (0.25) = $900 per month

Thus, the buyer can afford a $900 monthly payment.

Generally the debt ratio is greater than the income ratio to factor in for long-term debt. For example:

Using the above earnings, what could a buyer afford to pay if the lender allowed 36 percent for the debt ratio? The buyer has a long-term monthly car payment of $346 and a long-term monthly boat payment of $150.

$3,600 × 0.36 = $1,296

$346 + $150 = $496

$1,296 − $496 = $800

The debt ratio indicates the buyer could afford a monthly payment of $800. The lender will then look at the lower of the two ratios to determine the buyer's maximum payment allowed. Based on the examples, the buyer could afford only $800 per month as a payment.

Chapter Summary

Knowing how to finance real estate is key to your success in the real estate business. Knowing that one program or where to find a creative financing lender can be the difference in making the sale. It is not your job, though, to be a mortgage officer. You are paid to put a buyer and seller together, not to finance property. Keep your head clear on your goal.

Summary Questions

1. Dan and Kim wish to obtain a new loan. Their combined monthly income is $5,500. What is the monthly payment they can qualify for if the lender uses an income ratio of 28 percent?
    A. $1,450
    B. $5,500
    C. $1,540
    D. $2,800

2. Preston and Brittany have found a house that will have a monthly payment of $1,350. If the lender allows 27 percent to the income ratio, what is the required yearly income for the buyers?
    A. $36,450
    B. $60,000
    C. $13,500
    D. $64,800

Chapter 17

Referrals

Chapter Objectives

In this chapter you will learn to identify the two types of referrals and to find and obtain referral business. This chapter will also include the scripts that will help you obtain referrals.

Key Words

Incoming referral: Receiving a potential client from another salesperson for a real estate sale.

Outgoing referral: Sending a potential client to another salesperson for a real estate sale.

Referral: A buyer or seller of real estate who is sent from one broker to another.

Introduction

In addition to the business of listing and selling real estate, a sales associate has even more opportunities to make money by sending referrals to other real estate offices. As a source of both buyers and sellers, referrals are what every salesperson should seek, since a satisfied customer is an extension of you and your own sales effort.

Referrals are the most overlooked area to make money in real estate. Real estate salespeople tend to concentrate on other areas and neglect the referrals. I have had my own sellers move to other cities and I did not get the referral to that city because I forgot to ask.

There are two types of referrals: referrals sent (outgoing) and referrals received (incoming). "Referrals sent" means that the salesperson is referring a potential client to another salesperson for a real estate sale. The sending salesperson receives a portion of the commission back as a referral fee. The fees charged are negotiated between the brokers. "Referrals received" means that the salesperson is receiving a referral from another salesperson for a real estate sale.

Recognizing Referral Opportunities

To recognize a referral opportunity you must have referrals on the top of your mind. Some real estate salespeople never have any referrals to send out. The main reason for this is that they don't concentrate on referrals.

How to Cultivate Referrals

One of the most critical tools in the area of prospecting is referrals. New real estate salespeople are told over and over again to "get referrals, get referrals, get referrals." You make a sale and when it's completed you remember to "get referrals!" What do you do? Ask your clients if they know anybody else who is interested in buying or selling real estate. When they look at you blankly and say, "I can't think of anybody," it didn't work. After trying this three or four times you may decide that asking for referral business prospecting is no good. This not true; there is nothing wrong with referral business. What's wrong is that you did not know how to prospect for referrals.

Ask your clients the following questions: "Are you involved in any type of group participating sports activity? Do you golf, bowl, or belong to a club membership of any kind?"

If the client says, "Yeah, I golf," ask him if the last time was golfing, there anyone there who showed an interest in buying or selling real estate. You have given him something to visualize, which may help jar his memory. If he gives you a name, be sure to write it down.

You can break this prospecting into many areas, including church, parents, children your children play with.

Outgoing Referrals

Like listings, the outgoing referral is controllable and measurable. It gets your name out there and brings new business.

Send only qualified referrals:

- Customers who want to be referred.
- Prospects whom you have personally contacted.

- Prospects who are willing to buy or sell.
- Prospects who expect a contact from the receiving office.
- Prospects who are referred to a specific office.
- Prospects who have no prior commitment to another real estate company.

When real estate salespeople are asked, "How can Aunt Sally help you out if you are in Texas and she is in Montana?" the most frequent answer is, "If Aunt Sally moves to Texas." However, she can help you and never move. If she knows a person moving from one side of her city to the other side of her city, you can get a referral for the sell side and another referral for the buy side. We fail to communicate that information to Aunt Sally.

I remember being in real estate for a short period of time and going to my first year-end real estate awards banquet. I thought to myself how great it would be to go on stage and receive an award. The final top award went to the salesperson who had the most referrals sent over that year, which was eighteen. Interestingly, that's just over one per month; I thought, I can do that.

So now I had a goal to send more referrals than any other real estate salesperson. I asked around and learned that the referral business is based on luck. If you had the right seller, you might get a referral when the seller moves. You may get lucky on a call-in buyer, but that's about it. I also found out that real estate salespeople love referrals received (they will even get into confrontations over whose turn it is to receive a referral), but no one I found gave very many. I know of a company that spent hundreds of thousands of dollars to belong to a national referral service (they control corporate moves as well as individual moves and can give hundreds of referrals yearly). The company was under pressure to give more referrals to stay in the network. It is a sad fact that if a company isn't sending outbound referrals, their incoming referrals tend to decrease. The salespeople of the company loved to receive the referrals but none were giving any.

I, being new to the real estate business, had a different idea. If what everybody else is doing is not working, don't do that. Simple enough. I decided to go out and get referrals on my own. But how am I to do that? No one had an answer. I began to think of people moving and quickly came up with my answer: For Sale By Owners (FSBOs)! These people believe they can sell their houses themselves without using brokers. However, when they do sell, and some do, they still have to find another house.

I walked into my broker's office and asked to be the office relocation specialist. She granted my request, waved a magic wand through the air, and said, "You are the office relocation specialist." Now that I had my title I began calling FSBOs. Here is my script:

> **Salesperson:** "Hi, I am calling about the house for sale. Are you the owner?"
>
> **FSBO:** "Yes."
>
> **Salesperson:** "Well, my name is Dan Hamilton. I am the relocation specialist with Acme Realty. Now, I am not calling about helping you sell your home. I'm calling to see if I can help you after you sell it. Are you planning to stay in the area or are you moving out of the city?"

The answer didn't matter; I was getting a referral. I called for about an hour and got four referrals, which is twice what I have to do for my goal for the quarter. I did it in an hour. From then on, anytime I got bored I would call for referrals.

Once I was teaching a seminar in Lubbock, Texas. I was in my hotel room with nothing to do, so I picked up the local newspaper and began calling FSBOs. I ended up getting one FSBO who said she would be moving to Denver or some such place. I told her I would put her in touch with a real estate professional in Denver. She "Great, and one other thing, will you have someone from Lubbock help me sell our house here?" Notice, this is a good reason to call a FSBO and get listings in your area.

By the end of the year I had 38 referrals sent, over twice what was sent by the top referral person the year before, and I had not worked that hard.

There are several other sources for outgoing referrals, such as:

1. Listings.
2. Buyers.
3. Relatives.
4. Past clients.
5. Attorneys.
6. Spouse's company.
7. Floor duty.
8. Open house.
9. Anywhere.

Some questions you can ask include:

- On an ad call   Are you moving here from out of town?
  Is your home for sale now?
  May I have a real estate office give you a call?
- Buyers   Do you know of anyone else moving to town or
  being transferred?
- Sellers   Do you know of someone in your company or
  neighborhood who is moving out of town?

Offer to provide information about the new area at no cost or obligation.

Another great thing about referrals is that you do nothing but give them and then get money. If you are in some type of referral network, others in the network will follow the lead and make sure you get paid. You don't have to spend time tracking the progress of the transaction after you have made the referral. It is a great "fire and forget" weapon. I could be working in the office and my broker would come up and hand me a check of $200–$1,000 on a referral I had sent several months ago.

It's a good idea to track your referrals to make sure everything is being done to make the referral happy. This is not mandatory if you are dealing through a referral network, but it still is a good idea. There are at least five opportunities for you to stay in touch with an outbound referral:

1. Call the referred party the next day to make sure the receiving office made contact.
2. Call several days later to see if the referred buyer has received an information packet in the mail.
3. Call, if possible, during the buyer's home finding trip to check progress.
4. Communicate with the receiving sales associate to convey the transferee's wants.
5. Check back in several weeks (and periodically, thereafter) to make sure no problems have arisen. It's important for you to remain in control of the referral.

If you haven't gotten it yet, outgoing referrals are fun and easy!

Incoming Referrals

One of the first things you need to develop is a newcomer packet. This helps incoming referrals get to know you and the area. From there, treat referrals as buyers and expect follow-up from the referring broker.

Chapter Summary

Referrals should be a give and take; if you take a referral you should give a referral. If this would happen, a lot of real estate business would take place and all of us would make more money. Don't forget, referrals are probably the most overlooked and easiest part of the real estate industry.

Summary Question

1. What is the one of the most overlooked sources for making money in real estate?
    A. Buyer brokerage.
    B. Seller brokerage.
    C. Referral business.
    D. Door knocking.

Chapter 18

Deceptive Trade Practices Act and Consumer Protection Act

Chapter Objectives

In this chapter you will learn about the Deceptive Trade Practices Act and avoiding some pitfalls that can lead to trouble. You will discover the things to say, things to refrain from saying, and how to recognize and address problem areas.

Key Words

Deceptive: To cause to believe what is not true; mislead.

Fraud: A deception deliberately practiced in order to secure unfair or unlawful gain.

Misrepresentation: To give an incorrect or misleading representation of.

Punitive: Damages awarded by a court against a defendant as a deterrent or punishment to redress an egregious wrong perpetrated by the defendant.

Unconscionable: Not restrained by conscience; beyond prudence or reason; excessive.

Introduction

The Deceptive Trade Practices Act (DTPA) is probably the best protection for consumers in business transactions. Its provisions are believed by many to be unfair to real estate salespeople by making them responsible for things not always under their control. One DTPA case accused the salesperson of not disclosing the fact that the property had foundation problems because the floor sloped. How is the salesperson supposed to know that? The clients should expect professionalism, knowledge, integrity, and honesty from their real estate salespeople.

The primary purpose of the DTPA is to protect consumers against false, misleading, and deceptive business practices. The DTPA is sometimes used to bring a suit against a real estate salesperson when property defects are discovered by a buyer that the real estate salesperson failed to disclose to the buyer.

It is not unlawful to make representations in the real estate industry. However, if you make a representation you had better be right. My only question is: "How much are we paid for making representations?" The answer is nothing. So why do we make them? I believe we think the consumer expects us to know everything. The consumer only expects us to know how to find out an answer. For example, if the consumer wants to know the boundary line of a particular lot, the consumer does not expect us to actually know but he or she does expect us to find out.

The law provides for a consumer who prevails in a DTPA suit to receive actual damages. If it is found that the conduct of the defendant was committed knowingly (fraud), the award may be three times (treble) the amount of actual damages. These treble damages are called punitive (punishing) damages.

The DTPA applies to most business transactions, but our concern is involving the sale or rental of real estate, including the actions of real estate licensees engaging in the practice of real estate brokerage.

Punitive damages have been awarded even though the buyers would have discovered the misrepresentations had they exercised reasonable diligence. Reasonable diligence applies to the actions of the buyer. Suppose there is a crack in the plasterboard of a wall caused from foundation problems that the seller is aware of and with an ordinary inspection the buyer should have seen the crack. The buyer could still seek damages if not disclosed because the buyer is not required to inspect the property, the sellers (and their agents) are required to disclose problems.

A consumer may maintain an action for damages based on breach of an express or implied warranty or for any unconscionable action. An unconscionable action is defined as an action that takes advantage of the lack of knowledge, ability, experience, or capacity of a person to a grossly unfair degree or one in which there is a gross disparity between the value received and the consideration paid. Those are a lot of fancy words but it basically says that if you could do such a thing you must not have a conscience.

Misrepresentation

Misrepresentation is a false statement. Misrepresentation can occur by commission or omission. Commission refers to the making of a mistake or error and omission is the leaving out of information. Generally real estate salespeople have errors and omissions insurance to help protect them from these types of mistakes.

I once sold a town home whose owner knew there were monthly mandatory homeowners association dues. The listing broker knew there were monthly dues and I, the selling salesperson, knew of those dues. Guess whom I forgot to tell? The buyer. At closing the buyers monthly expenses went up by $120 because of the dues. I voluntarily took a commissionectomy of $120.00 × 12 to cover their first year. (A commissionectomy is surgery to remove all or part of your commission. It is a very painful operation and I suggest you avoid it.) Why did I take the commissionectomy? The answer is simple: I made a mistake and I should stand up and take responsibility. I do not believe in giving my money away but I do believe in doing what is right. I firmly believe the buyers would not have sued me and there was no fraud because I had no intent, which is necessary for fraud.

Misrepresentation can also involve fraud. Fraud is the intentional misleading of a person. No insurance will cover fraud. Certain factors must be in place for fraud, including:

1. **Reliance** on the information. The consumer must have relied on the information given. Would an ordinary person have believed the representation?

2. **Intent** to fraud. The person making the representation must have known the representation was incorrect and continued in the misrepresentation.

3. **Damage** to the individual. The individual must have incurred some type of damage caused by the misrepresentation.

They form the acronym RID.

A real estate professional is paid to put a buyer and seller together, not to make representations. I have seen more real estate salespeople in trouble because they will not shut their mouths. The buyer asks the real estate salesperson for the number of square feet is in the house, and for some reason the salesperson thinks he or she should answer that question. We have appraisers who answer that question. Please talk less and serve more.

Two Questions

DTPA virtually asks two questions:

1. Did you know there was a misrepresentation?
2. Should you have known there was a misrepresentation?

These questions are generally asked when determining if there has been an action for a DTPA violation. For example, after being sold by a real estate salesperson the buyer moves into the house and discovers foundation problems. Did the real estate salesperson know of the defect? If the answer is yes, meaning the salesperson did not disclose the defect, then he or she has violated the DTPA. If the answer is no, then should the salesperson have known of the defect? Again, how the salesperson spoke and acted would indicate if he or she should have known.

What should you as a real estate salesperson do to protect yourself from a DTPA lawsuit?

Three Defenses That Will "Probably" Work

The reason the word "probably" is inserted here is that most DTPA cases are settled without a ruling.

An investor was being sued for selling a house and when the buyers moved in they found a leak hidden behind the wall under the sink. They threatened a DTPA suit. The investor did not know of the leak and had no reason to know because the leak was only discovered after removing the wallboard. However, the buyer was threatening to sue for $250. The investor settled because it would have been ridiculous to go to court for $250.

These defenses should be used to protect you as much as possible:

1. Inspections by licensed inspectors. It is the job of licensed inspectors to find out what is potentially wrong with a property. Once they give their professional opinions on an inspection report, they are liable for their opinion.

If you or a buyer is unsure of the inspection report, consult the inspector. If you are at an inspection and your buyer looks at you and says, "What do you think?" you should smile and say, "Well, the inspector is here, let's ask him." Don't ever try and correct an inspector—inspections are the inspector's job, let them do it. Every time you open your mouth you assume more liability. If you can't resist speaking you should leave the premises or at least the room.

Recommending an inspector to your customers could create some liability. Instead, give the buyer a list of potential inspectors and let the buyer choose. You can develop a list from inspectors listed by the real estate commission and use their license numbers. This is not as dangerous as it used to be because most inspectors are licensed, bonded, and carry errors and omissions insurance if they make a mistake.

Inspectors tend not to say that the roof needs replacing. Generally, they will say there is evidence of roof damage and they may recommend a professional roof inspection. The buyer is now on notice of possible problems. This is disclosure to the buyer and it limits the buyer's right to sue if there is roof damage.

2. Written seller's disclosure statement. A seller's disclosure statement is a document that describes the property in detail. It allows the seller to note anything on the property and whether or not it is functioning properly. This helps the seller remember everything in the house and then whether or not it is working properly.

This statement is for the *SELLER*! The real estate salesperson should not be involved in any way. If a salesperson helps the seller complete the statement, then the salesperson could be held liable. To avoid the seller's questions about the form, I hand the statement to the seller and go and measure the rooms. Copies of this form should be left on the dining room table of the seller's house for any potential buyer to pick up.

The statement is not a mandated document. The law only requires that the seller disclose in writing. Some third party relocation companies use their own forms.

3. Information given by the government that you have no reason to believe is false. The government publishes such information as flood maps, zoning restrictions, and tax records, which usually include the year the house was built and square footage of a property. The real estate salesperson can generally rely on information to be correct. If he or she "knows" it is not accurate, the information cannot be used.

It is not necessary to verify that the government information is correct. Do not ever measure the area of a house; that job is for appraisers. Do not ever use square footage numbers if the seller gives them to you. I have had sellers measure the exterior walls of their house and claim the tax records were 400 square feet too little. After a few questions, I figured out that the seller had measured the garage, which is not considered a livable area and wasn't included in the tax record. If a seller is adamant that the records are in error, advise the seller to get an appraisal. Let the professionals tell you the area.

Notice, all the defenses puts the burden on someone else. We need to let the experts do their jobs and we need to put more effort in finding buyers and sellers. The word "misrepresentation" is interesting because, if you avoid making representations, you can avoid making misrepresentations.

Three Defenses That Will Not Work

The following three defenses under the DTPA will not work:

1. Waiver. You cannot waive your right to sue before the event happens. Suppose I went into a health club to try out the equipment. They would first have me sign a waiver giving up my right to sue if I get hurt on the premises. I sign it and then begin working out. One of the machines malfunctions due to negligence of the health club and crushes my foot. At the hospital I am upset that I signed one of those waivers because now I won't sue. The health club won because I believe I cannot sue. Well, my brother, the attorney, comes to see me in the hospital and asks what happened. I tell him and he says, "Lets go get 'em!" (His professionalism would not allow him to actually say that but this is just an example.) I tell him we can't because I signed a waiver. He just laughs because he knows the waiver will not work and the health club will settle.

I was told in a real estate class that a mother could not let her son ride the bus for a class trip if she would not sign a waiver. She asked me why the school made her sign a waiver if they don't work. My answer is simple: First it is not the school it is the school's insurance company that requires the waiver. And the insurance company knows that certain people do not know waivers don't work. Every time someone does not sue, the insurance company wins.

A man said his son was rear-ended by a car at a stoplight. The insurance company paid for the damages to the car and then sent him a check for $5,000 to settle any other claims. He said he cashed the check. He now has settled because this waiver will work. The event had already happened.

2. "As-Is." Similar to a waiver, this phrase means the buyer is stating that he or she will not sue the seller even though the buyer is not fully aware of the property and any problems the property could have. In the real estate industry we need to be sure to use the words "no repairs" if a seller refuses to do any work on the property. A crotchety seller retorts, "I'm selling that property as-is!" We need to agree and then correct his words with, "I understand you do not want to do any repairs." Then persuade the seller to disclose what is wrong with the property. The law says problems must be disclosed; it doesn't, however, require that you repair the problems.

I had a broker in class say he was involved in a nasty case where a seller was selling a lot with a torn-up shack on it. The buyer said he would pay cash to "tear down that old shack" and build a new building. All he wanted was the land. The seller sold the lot with the shack. After closing the buyer sued the seller, claiming that the seller failed to disclose that the house numerous problems, including the foundation and a leaky roof. The broker asked me what he should do and I suggested he settle. He then exclaimed that he was set up. I agreed, but that does not change the fact that the seller did not disclose. (The broker was involved because he should have advised his seller to disclose the problems or tear down the structure himself before offering it for sale.)

The "as-is" law does allow for certain types of transactions to use "as-is" and not be actionable. If you need further information of the exceptions, please seek an attorney. The better action is to disclose.

3. Caveat emptor (let the buyer beware). Under DTPA the buyer does not have to show due diligence. We must, therefore, disclose every material defect. The old times are gone. This does not work; do not try it.

Laundry List

The DTPA contains a "laundry list" of deceptive trade practices acts that are prohibited. There are several acts that violate the DTPA and for which consumers may sue. The following are some select acts that could apply to real estate:

1. **Passing off goods or services as those of another.**

   It is forbidden to claim that goods or services are of one company when they are not. Say a buyer insists on a home built by Hamilton Builders. They really like the house you are showing them, but it is built by Henderson Brothers Builders. When they ask you, you say, "Of course, this home is a Hamilton Built home." You have violated DTPA because you misrepresented the builder to earn a commission.

2. **Causing confusion or misunderstanding as to the source, sponsorship, approval, or certification of goods or services.**

   This section furthers section (1) by the words "causing confusion." It is a violation to say you are a certified appraiser when all you have is a real estate license.

3. **Causing confusion or misunderstanding as to affiliation, connection, or association with, or certification by, another.**

   This section would prohibit you from claiming yourself as a REALTOR® when you are not a member. (To be able to use the REALTOR® name you must be a member of the National Association of Realtors®.)

4. **Using deceptive representatives or designations of geographic origin in connection with goods or services.**

   This section prohibits a person from saying that the entryway tile is Italian Marble when it was mined at the pit up on Highway 7.

5. **Representing goods or services that claim to have sponsorship, approval, characteristics, ingredients, uses, benefits, or quantities but do not or a person claiming to have a sponsorship, approval, status, affiliation, or connection but does not.**

   This section is quite comprehensive. I own a property across a street from a very popular lake. My neighbors have a dock that is actually on the lake. If I was to tell a potential buyer they could use that dock, I would be representing that my property has benefits it does not have.

6. **Representing that goods are original or new if they are deteriorated, reconditioned, reclaimed, used, or second-hand.**

   This section prohibits a seller from claiming a roof is new when the roof is fifteen years old.

7. **Representing that goods or services are of a particular standard, quality, or grade, or that goods are of a particular style or model, if they are of another.**

   This section prohibits a seller from claiming appliances are of a designer name when they are not.

8. **Disparaging the goods, services, or business of another by false or misleading representations of facts.**

   This section prevents a real estate company from talking bad about a seller.

9. **Advertising goods or services with intent not to sell them as advertised.**

   I knew a real estate salesperson who needed one more house to fill out a full-page advertisement. He did not have any more listings so he put his brother's house in that slot. He said he would just tell any callers that that house is off the market. Problem, that is a direct violation of this section. Notice it is a variant of the ole "bait and switch."

10. **Advertising goods or services with intent not to supply a reasonable expectable public demand, unless the advertisement disclosed a limitation of quantity.**

    This section deals with the "rain check" you are offered at many retail stores. They advertise a television at an unbelievably low price but only have one in stock. This is illegal unless they offer the same price when their stock is replenished. The way this can be violated in real estate is to offer an apartment for lease at a low rate and when you get calls you only have one property at that lease price but you have several others at a higher price.

11. **Making false or misleading statements of fact concerning the reasons for, existence of, or amount of price reductions.**

   Some sellers try and mask the real reason for price reductions. The seller tells the buyer that the reason the price is so low is because they have been transferred and the truth is that the house has major foundation damage and the seller hasn't disclosed that.

Chapter Summary

The DTPA is designed to prevent the sellers of products or services from misrepresenting any aspect of their product or service. This chapter points to the need for such an act. DTPA is to protect, not punish, but if a violation occurs, the law can punish.

Summary Questions

1. The following are the three defenses that would probably work under the DTPA except
   A. Inspections by licensed inspectors.
   B. There was no intent.
   C. Written sellers disclosure notice.
   D. Any information given by the government.

2. Which of the following is not one of the three defenses that will not work under the DTPA?
   A. A written waiver.
   B. Agreement to an "as-is" contract.
   C. Caveat emptor.
   D. Did not know and should not have known.

3. What are punitive damages?
   A. Damages that are small in nature but big in principle.
   B. Damages that are punishing.
   C. Damages that were caused by a pun or joke.
   D. Damages that were faked or falsified.

4. What of the following is the nickname for the DTPA list of forbidden acts?
    A. Forbidden list
    B. Action list
    C. List of liolations
    D. Laundry list

5. What are the two main questions that are asked in reference to determining a violation of the DTPA?
    A. What is the damage? How much is the damage?
    B. Are you licensed? Did you act in accordance with a license?
    C. Did you know? Should you have known?
    D. Was there a signed agreement? Was an attorney representing you?

6. What are the two types of misrepresentation if fraud is not involved?
    A. Intent and reliance
    B. Commission and omission
    C. Remit and omit
    D. Remission and submission

7. A murder took place on a property you have listed. The sellers have insisted that you keep this information confidential. What is your duty to disclose?
    A. No duty to disclose; your duties lie with the seller.
    B. No duty to disclose; the murder does not physically affect the property.
    C. You must disclose; release the listing if the seller will not allow disclosure.
    D. You must disclose; but only if the buyer directly asks about the murder.

Appendix

Sales Communication Steps

Approach—

Need Determination—

Presentation—

Closing—

Objections—

Approach—The Process

Preapproach—

Collecting information prior to the approach.

Approach—

The first few minutes. Remove any barriers so the client's are willing to share. Sales role. People are automatically defensive.

Objectives:

1. Lower defense barriers
2. Establish rapport
3. Arouse interest

Lowerring Defence Barriers—

1. Use name
2. I care for you
3. Show genuine interest

"I'm not here to SELL you a house . . .
I'm here to guide you to finding the home for YOU."

Arousing Interest—

There is a difference between arousing your client's interest and getting their attention. Attention is only an event which causes a temporary change in focus. Interest is the answer to the question, "What is in it for me?" In selling we MUST get their interest!

Big Fat Claim— "Mrs. Jones, I'm confident that I can cut your house hunting in half."

Feedback—

Talk more

Relaxed

Body language

When to Bridge—

When they have shown an interest.

Bridge to Need Determination—

"Would you mind if I asked you a few questions?"

Need Determination—The Process

Concept/Importance—

Determines why you should sell the service.

75% of the entire sale.

Like taking an x-ray.

Like diagnosing the service needed.

Creates a trusting relationship by showing a concern for the client.

Asking Questions

Ask "open-ended" questions—(questions that require more than a "yes" or "no" answer)

Ask "wide-angle" questions

Information Needed—

What	Do they need, i.e. features
When	Timing
How	Ability to spend—$$$$ amount
	Seriousness of the buyer
	Are they ready to act . . . now?
Why	Are they buying
	Are they buying what they are buying
Where	Are they buying
Who	Is buying

Creativity—

Once you determine "Why" they want something—then you can adapt what is available to their needs.

Know the market!

Review Needs/Agreement—

Must review what we heard

1. Prioritization of wants/motivation
2. Attain—Dominant Buying Motive (DBM)/Dominant Selling Motive (DSM)

Note: Motivation is based on emotions!

Bridge to Presentation—

"I'm confident that we can satisfy your needs."

Need Determination

General Need vs. Specific/Motivational Need

General Need   Specific/Motivational Need

Buyer Client Questions

1. Why are you thinking of buying a home?

2. Are you currently renting or do you own a home?

3. How soon do you want\have to move?

4. Have you talked to a mortgage company yet?

5. Are you working with any other brokers?

6. Have you been through any other homes in the past 90 days? Why didn't you buy?

7. Describe your dream home if money was no object.

8. What things were in other homes that you liked, say your parent's home?

9. What things were in other homes that you would never have in your home, say a friend's home?

10. Do you have any special needs such as room for an RV or a boat? Do you need access for a wheel chair accessible. Would you like a sewing room?

11. What would it do to your plans if you cannot find a home you want to buy?

12. If we find the perfect home for you today, will you buy it?

Buyer Prequalification Worksheet

Date _____

Appointment Date _____   Time _____

Name _____

Family size (children) _____

Address _____

Phone Residence _____   Office _____

Husband's Employer _____
How Long _____   Income $ _____
Title or job duties _____

Wife's Employer _____
How Long _____   Income $ _____
Title or job duties _____

Expenses (contract debt 10 months or longer) $ _____

Why do you want to buy? _____

How soon do you want to move? _____

How much will your initial investment be? _____

What price home are you looking for? _____

What monthly payment would be comfortable? _____

Bedrooms _____   Baths _____   Age _____
Fireplace _____   Laundry _____   Lot Size _____
Style _____   Sq. ft. _____   Garage _____
Floor _____   Carpet _____   Built-ins _____
Drapes _____   Roof type _____   Den _____
Service Porch _____   Pool _____   Fence type _____
Patio _____   Schools _____   Handicap _____
A/C _____   Other _____   Special needs _____

Additional Buyer Questions

- Will anyone else be living in your new home?
- How many bedrooms do you need? How will you use the third bedroom?
- Is a dining room important? May I ask why?
- Are there any special features you must have in your home?
- How soon will you need possession?
- Must you sell your present home to buy another?
- Are you currently renting? When does your lease expire?
- Have you seen any homes that you liked?
- Which area is that home located in?
- Tell me what you liked best about that home?
- Was there anything you disliked?
- Did you make any written offers?
- Are you working with any other real estate agents?
- Why are you moving?
- What do you like best about your present home? What do you like least?
- Do you have any special hobbies?
- How much of your savings do you plan to invest?
- What is your present income? Do you have any other income?
- What are your current monthly expenses?
- Are you a veteran?
- Is anyone else helping you with financing?
- How large is your family? What are the ages of your children?
- How long have you been looking for a home?
- What did you and your family like about your last home?
- Are there any specific features you will require in your next home?
- With whom are you associated, Mr. Client? Where do you work, Mrs. Client?
- Are you familiar with today's procedures for purchasing a home?
- Have you decided how you would like to finance your new home?
- Would you prefer a large down payment and small monthly payments, or a small down payment with larger monthly payments?
- Can they afford what they want?

Closing Checklist

BUYER(S) NAME(S) _____

Home Address _____

Property Address _____

Telephone (H) _____ (W) _____ (Fax) _____

Selling Salesperson _____ Company Office _____

Company Address _____

Telephone (H) _____ (W) _____ (Fax) _____

SELLER(S) NAME(S) _____

Address _____

Telephone (H) _____ (W) _____ (Fax) _____

Listing Salesperson _____ Company Office _____

Company Address _____

Telephone (H) _____ (W) _____ (Fax) _____

Title Company _____ File Number _____

Representative _____ Assistant _____

Address _____

Telephone (H) _____ (W) _____ (Fax) _____

Lender _____

Representative _____ Assistant _____

Address _____

Telephone (H) _____ (W) _____ (Fax) _____

Loan Type _____ Loan Number _____

Down Payment _____ Points _____ Fee _____

Interest Rate _____ Term _____

Lock-in Date _____ Closing Date _____

PEST CONTROL _____ Telephone _____

HOME INSPECTION _____ Telephone _____

HOME INSURANCE AGENT _____ Telephone _____

Contracts for a for Sale by Owner

(2) Copies each of:

1. Assumption Earnest Money Contract
2. Cash/Owner Finance Earnest Money Contract
3. Conventional Earnest Money Contract
4. VA Earnest Money Contract
5. FHA Earnest Money Contract
6. Unimproved Land Earnest Money Contract
7. Deed
8. Deed of Trust
9. Note
10. Survey
11. Truth in Lending Statement (RESPA)
12. Tenancy Agreement
13. Rental Agreement
14. Lease/Option Contract
15. Unilateral Option Contract
16. Owner's Title Insurance Policy
17. Home Owner's Insurance Policy
18. Modification Agreement
19. Ways to Finance Property
20. Questions to Make Your *Home* Sell Faster
21. Home Warranty Certificate
22. Competitive Market Analysis
23. Mortgage Information Request Form
24. Intent to Prepay Letter
25. Quote Sheets From Mortgage Companies
26. Contract For Deed
27. Clause for Wrap Around Mortgage
28. Special Contract Clause
29. Contingency Clause
30. Qualification Form

31. Release of Earnest Money From Title Company Letter
32. Release of Earnest Money From a Seller Letter
33. Amendment for Repairs Form
34. Notification of Intent to Purchase Form
35. Seller's Disclosure Form
36. Bill of Sale
37. Meditation Agreement
38. Back-up\Second Contract Form
39. Sellers Net Proceeds Information Letter

Documentation Needed
At Loan Application

- Original Sales Contract
- Copy of Earnest Money Check
- W2s or 1099s for previous two years
- Pay Stubs
- Tax Returns
- Five-year history of past residences
- Bank statement from most recent two months checking and savings, all pages
- Credit references (current obligations), company names, addresses, account number's, balances
- Check for appraisal fee and credit report

The documentation is usually all that you will need to furnish at application.

Always keep in mind that you will probably have to provide additional documentation or you may have to write a letter for the file explaining some financial event or discrepancy. Remember that cooperation is paramount to a speedy closing.

Fair Trade Items (Seller)

1. MARKET ANALYSIS
2. ESTIMATE OF NET
3. TIPS ON MAKING THE HOUSE SALABLE
4. ADVICE ON TIMING OF SALE
5. METHODS OF NEW FINANCING
6. ESTIMATE OF REPAIRS
7. TIPS ON SHOWING A HOME
8. TIPS ON ADVERTISING
9. REASONS HOME DIDN'T SELL
10. AREA COMPETITION
11. SALABILITY CHECKLIST
12. COMPARISON FLOW CHART

Comparison of FSBO and Broker

Advantages of Selling "By Owner"

1. No commission.

Advantages of Selling through Real Estate Broker

1. Maximum exposure to the open market.
2. Warning before all showings.
3. Screening of potential buyers by professional real estate salespeople.
4. Feedback or reaction of prospective buyers.
5. Comparison data on other sold properties in the area (CMA).
6. Protection from professional buyers that know how to damage an unsuspecting seller.

7. Priced to sell to get the most money for the property in the least amount of time.

8. All legal forms supplied by the salesperson.

9. Best available financing methods are used with the buyers.

10. Appraisals will be handled by the real estate salesperson.

11. Escrow opened and all documents properly recorded by the title company.

12. Buyer qualified by a professional real estate mortgage officer.

13. Property not "tied-up" by unqualified buyer offers.

14. Salesperson looks after the seller's best interest.

15. Salesperson has access to show home even when seller is not at home; seller does not have to wait for customers.

16. Salesperson prequalifies potential buyers for security purposes.

17. The "For Sale By Owner" is obligated to let any one that comes to the door enter home.

18. Eliminates possibility of problems arising from housewife allowing stranger to enter home when she is home alone.

19. Salesperson furnishing advertising aids, signs, flags, newspaper ads, etc.

20. Seller can't afford eye-catching ads in newspaper.

21. Salesperson knows how to help potential buyers make up their minds and close the sale.

Hamilton's Rules of Real estate

1. The first offer is always the best offer.

2. If the buyer sees a personal item of the seller, the buyer wants it, no exceptions.

3. A seller is never in a hurry until the sign goes up.

4. A lease purchase is another name for no commission.

5. The real estate agent is always wrong. CORELLARY: the real estate agent is always at fault.

6. A real estate agent can choose his or her hours–it's just which 12 hours a day you choose.

7. A commission on a transaction can be $2,500 at closing (or $2.73 per hour).

8. If a transaction is full of problems it will close; if a transaction is smooth, it never closes. (Some agents are confused here because they have never had a smooth transaction!)

9. Always sell your own listings, it's the only way to assure a competent agent on the other side.

10. If all attorneys had real estate licenses, they could then mess up their own transactions.

11. If you go to closing nothing happens. If you miss a closing the entire transaction will fall apart over a minor problem you could have handled if you were there.

12. The more you use time-saving technologies and strategies, the less time you seem to have.

13. Doing something is always better than doing nothing.

14. We only get paid when we put buyers and sellers together. Everything else needs to be deleted, delayed to nonproductive times, or delegated.

Keys to a Smooth Closing

Communication between Real Estate Agent And Title Company Is Essential

Is the Contract Complete?

1. Have you chosen the right contract for the transaction? (Conventional, FHA, VA)

   Has the earnest money check been made out properly?

   Has the earnest money check been referenced on the contract properly?

2. Have you completed the "Option Fee" section correctly? If #1 has been chosen, has the fee been collected? Is the money to be credited to the Buyer at closing? (Did you check the right box?)

3. Have all parties signed the contract including Agents?

4. IMPORTANT! For Sellers, Buyers, Agents, and Lenders: Legible, complete addresses and phone numbers. In addition, for sellers: if available, fax number and forwarding addresses.

5. Have all parties initialed all changes?

6. Social Security numbers for Buyers and Sellers?

7. Is marital status of Buyers and Sellers shown?

8. Are full names of parties shown?

Information to Provide to Title Company

1. Single/Married/Divorced
   a. Marital status changes?
   b. Divorce involved? If so, is it pending or final? Where is the divorce filed?

2. Estate or Probate?
   a. When and where was the will probated?

3. Lender Information:
   a. Existing loan information in order to request payoff: names, addresses, phone numbers, loan numbers, OR Seller's current lender.
   b. Second lien information when applicable.
   c. New Buyer lender information (if more than one lender, include all).
   d. Don't forget to ask about pool or home improvement loans.

4. Assumption Transactions: (very rarely seen today)
   a. Homeowners/Hazard Insurance:
   Is the Seller's present insurance transferable?
   Is the Buyer securing new insurance?
   Need names and phone numbers of insurance agents.
   b. Important papers for seller to have available for quick reference:
   Payment Book, Insurance Policy, Survey, Seller's Title Policy, copy of Note, and Deed.

Getting Prepared for Closing

1. Is Power of Attorney to be used?
   a. Notify the Title Company and Lender Immediately. Both will need to approve the use of a POA and the form.

2. Will either party be out of town at the closing and need closing documents sent/faxed to them for signature?
   a. Notify Title Company immediately.
   b. Provide the Title Company with overnight delivery address (no P.O. boxes), telephone, and fax number.

3. Does Lender or the contract require repairs? Has the Title Company been given repair bills?

4. Are utilities involved? Does the Title Company have utility bills?

5. Escrow Agreements/Repairs
   a. Are any funds to be given to Buyer or escrowed for repairs?
   b. Obtain Lender approval of new loan involved and notify the Title Company immediately.

6. Is Pest Inspection required? Has the Title Company been given the invoice and the original inspection report for signature and submission to the Lender?

7. Does the Lender require a survey? Has it been ordered yet?

At the Closing Table

1. The "good funds" rule
   a. Has the Buyer/Seller been notified to bring funds to closing in the form of a cashier's check (or their bank can wire funds to the Title Company)?

2. Proof of identity
   a. The Buyer/Seller must bring photo ID to the closing.

3. Does the Buyer's Lender fund the day of closing? (table fund)
   a. If not, does the Seller know he/she won't be getting a check today?

4. Home Warranty
   a. Has home warranty already been ordered?
   b. Have you given the Title Company the invoice?

5. Termite Inspection
   a. Original report and invoice must be at the Title Company before closing.
   b. Are there conducive conditions or treatment required or shown on the report? If so, these probably need to be treated before closing, per Lender requirements. Usually the new Lender required a clear report before closing and funding.

Due to the RESPA Law, prior to closing, make sure the Title Company receives CDAs (Commission Disbursement Authorization).

21 Steps to Marketing Your House

1. Order nationally recognized yard sign (92 percent recognition rate).
2. Put listing in MLS Computer.
3. Notify ALL agents & brokers active in the area (Broker's Open House).
4. Set up and preview for all our Agents after weekly sales meeting.
5. Prepare professional Fact Sheet/Brochure with color picture.
6. Canvass neighborhood for possible purchaser (mail/hand out flyers to neighbors and follow-up with phone call).
7. Continue promoting to other agents and prospective buyers as the situations warrant (inquires on similar properties).
8. Advertise in local newspaper on rotational basis.
9. Advertise vigorously in real estate magazines.
10. Around-the-clock service from trained and professional office staff (open seven days).
11. Give weekly feedback on all showings and market conditions (Sunday evenings).
12. Set up, promote, and conduct professional open house (one every six weeks).

13. Reduce all purchase proposals to writing (prequalified buyers only).

14. Represent you and your interest when negotiating in a co-broker situation.

15. After contracts are signed see to it that deposit monies are collected at the designated time period.

16. Notify MLS of contracts signed.

17. Have the "SOLD" sign installed.

18. Get buyer's mortgage application started immediately (assist buyer through mortgage process).

19. Recommend three attorneys and, if necessary make yourself available to assist in transporting necessary paperwork.

20. Arrange for and be present at any engineering, termite, radon, appraisal inspections, certificate of occupancy, and any other meetings required to close escrow and title.

21. Hand deliver all documents if needed to speed up closing of title.

Net Proceeds to the Seller

Financing Type: _____   Yearly Taxes: _____

Date Prepared: _____   Commission Rate: _____

Estimated Closing Date: _____   County: _____

The following data is for informational purposes only and accuracy of the figures is not guaranteed. The actual costs with respect to each transaction will vary upon the circumstances.

Description	Cost
Sale Price	
First Mortgage Payoff	
Second Mortgage Payoff	
Owner's Policy of Title Insurance	
Prepayment Penalty	
Escrow Fee	
Recording Fees	
Deed Preparation	
Loan Discount Points Paid by Seller	
Home Warranty	
Buyer Costs Paid by Seller	
Real Estate Commission	
Miscellaneous	
Other Expenses	
Seller's Settlement Costs	
Prorated Taxes	
Prorated Insurance	
Other Prorations	
Prorations for Seller	
Total Cost to Seller	
Estimated Net to Seller	

Newcomer's Packet Requirements

A. General maps of the entire area.

B. Examples of listings (office listings).

C. Shopping information.

D. Tax information.

E. Preschool/secondary, schools/colleges/universities

F. Recreation information.

G. Transportation possibilities (buses, trains, carpools, airports, etc.).

H. Churches and synagogues.

I. Dentist, doctors, hospitals.

J. Utility information.

K. Demographics (if provided, be sure the information given does not violate fair housing laws).

L. Community profile (climate/community activities).

M. Area monthly magazine (listing weekend/monthly events).

N. Area personnel agencies.

O. Cover letter.

P. Information on you and your company.

Q. Local employment agencies.

R. Mortgage lenders.

S. Hotels.

T. Sports centers, attractions.

U. State information (contact state capital).

V. Relocation publications.

Any additional information specifically requested by the referral.

Open House

Trigger Card

1. May I show you through the home?
2. Do you presently live in the area?
3. Are you presently looking at property with another broker?
4. What would be the best time to show you property, weekdays or weekends?
5. Would _____ at _____ or _____ at _____ be better?
6. By the way, your name is?

Checklist for a Successful Open House

Be sure to call owner one week in advance for O.K.

SALES MEETINGS—One week in advance

1. Decide who will be there.
2. Newspaper ad written
3. Can it be run in conjunction with an Open extravaganza?

PHONE CANVAS THURSDAY—Prior to open house

1. Call at least 25 homes in neighborhood
2. Call at least 25 from your sphere of influence
3. Call *ALL* of your hot prospects

Put up "OPEN SATURDAY OR OPEN SUNDAY" rider

PERSONAL CANVASS FRIDAY of the 25 neighborhood calls

CHECK EQUIPMENT FRIDAY

1. Signs and sign riders

2. Flags

3. Open House Kit
    a. Business cards
    b. Contracts
    c. Prospect inquiry sheets and guest book
    d. Brochures
    e. Feature sheets (special features of this home)
    f. Feature 5 × 7's
    g. Brochures of other company open houses in area
    h. Real estate section of newspaper
    i. Corporate hand-outs
    j. Balloons

4. Call owner to remind him or her of ways to make home look better, and of *importance of leaving during open.*

Arrive at House 30 Minutes Before Open House

1. Plan schedule for putting up signs

2. Set up house
    a. Lights on
    b. Garbage out of sight
    c. Refreshments (with owners approval)
    d. Clean sinks
    e. Put up 5" × 7" cards highlighting special features of this home.
    f. Soft music
    g. Make sure enough ashtrays (owners *hate* ashtrays). Better yet, ask prospects not to smoke.

3. Be sure you have the following *memorized*
    a. Taxes
    b. Down payment needed and possible financing

    c. Monthly payments based on loan amount, including taxes and insurance

    d. Lot size

    e. Inclusions and exclusions

    f. Main room sizes

    g. School district

4. Clean up when through

5. Leave note and call owners Sunday night for end report activity

6. Post open house activities

HANDOUTS:

Brochures & Special Features

Area maps

Company information (Sold Brochures)

Coloring books & crayons

Mortgage schedules

Relocation

Brochures on similar homes

21 Questions that Help Your Property Sell Faster

(Answers to these questions help you get more cash for your property, in a shorter period of time, and with the greatest of ease.)

1. What is the buyer's first impression of the exterior of our house? What can I do to improve it?

2. Shall I reseed the lawn and get my landscaping in top shape?

3. Does the house or any part of the house need painting?

4. Should I replace the door mats with new ones that omit our family's name?

5. What about the screens? What about the windows?

6. I should give my sales associate a list of things my family likes about the house and the neighborhood.

7. What are buyers' first impressions as they step inside my house? What can I do to improve it?

8. Are pets under control at all times?

9. Does the carpet need cleaning or replacing?

10. Are all appliances in good working order?

11. Can I take items from kitchen cabinets to make them more spacious?

12. Do any cabinets need to be touched up or refinished?

13. Is there any furniture I could store or dispose of to make rooms appear larger?

14. Since a buyer will be looking in the closets, are they some clothes I can take out to make them look roomier?

15. Should I remove any item(s) that a buyer may want as part of the house?

16. Are the garage and storage areas as clean and neat as they can be?

17. Are the price and terms offered going to appeal to most of the buying public in my price range?

18. Before spending needless time and money, consult your salesperson.

Information Needed for a CMA

The following are samples of questions designed to get enough information to do a market analysis of the property and to get an idea of what the seller would like to net out.

- How many bedrooms are in your house?
- Is your house brick or wood frame?
- What style of house do you own?
- Tell me about the kitchen equipment you have.

- Do you have a family room?
- Do you have a wood-burning fireplace or a gas starter?
- How many baths do you have?
- Is your outdoor patio covered?
- Do you have a wood deck?
- What type of fence is on the property?
- Do you have a security system? An Intercom?
- Do you have a garage? Will it hold one or two cars? Do you have garage door openers?
- What type of heat do you have?
- Do you have a utility room?
- What is your lot size?
- Is your street paved?
- Do you have a septic system?
- Do you have a well?
- How much is owed on your house?
- What are your monthly payments?
- To whom do you make your monthly payments? (mortgage company, land contract, other)
- What do you think your home is worth?
- When was the house built?

Again, you want to find out as much information as you can. (Questions will vary depending on your area.)

Real Estate Services

- Multiple Listing Service (MLS)
- A push-in stake "For Sale" sign
- Post "For Sale" sign

- Present the property at the local Board of Realtors meeting for any of the attending Realtors and their buyers
- Color graphic picture of the house with descriptions to be left in the house
- Black and white graphic picture of the house designed as pass-out flyers with distribution to doors
- Install a graphics box on your yard sign
- Direct mail, fax, e-mail, or hand-deliver information to area residents
- Direct mail, fax, e-mail, or hand-deliver information to personnel directors of local companies
- Direct mail, fax, e-mail, or hand-deliver information to buyers currently in the market.
- Direct mail, fax, e-mail, or hand-deliver information to cooperating real estate offices
- Present the property at real estate office meeting for salespeople and their buyers
- Present the property at cooperating real estate office meetings
- Tour the home with office real estate salespeople to obtain their feedback
- Broker open for cooperating real estate offices
- Broker luncheon for cooperating real estate offices
- Public open house
- Provide necessary contracts
- Explanation of forms and contracts
- Helping buyers make a buying decision about your property
- Home warranty plan for your property
- Contract negotiation when an offer comes in on your property
- Showing your property to prospective buyers
- Property staging to arrange the property to make it show better
- Real estate advice
- Brokers Price Opinion, Competitive Market Analysis (CMA)
- Buyer qualification
- Seller's net proceeds from the sale estimated
- Meet buyer's inspector

- Meet property appraiser
- Verify insurance endorsement for buyer
- Meet buyer for final walk-through
- Follow up for removal of contingencies
- Register with relocation company
- Advertisement
    - Main newspaper
        - ♣ back page
        - ♣ real estate magazine
        - ♣ homes for sale section
    - Real estate weekly color magazine
    - Farm and ranch magazine
    - Additional papers
        - ♣ national
        - ♣ regional
        - ♣ local
    - Radio
        - ♣ national
        - ♣ local
    - Television
        - ♣ national
        - ♣ local
    - Billboard
    - Bus stop benches
- Internet listing
- Copies of keys
- Lockbox
    - electronic lock box
    - combination lock box
- Prepare property profile book
- Telemarketing
- Set buyer up for purchase loan
- Set property up for title work
- Deliver your check at closing

Scripts for all Occasions

I have found the following are scripts to be useful over the years. It's important, however, for you to feel good about the scripts you use, so modify them according to your personality and situation. If a script is not approved by your real estate commission, your broker, your manager or your association of REALTORS® please disregard it.

I use the terms "Mr. & Mrs." no matter who I'm talking to because so as not to show favoritism and direct my attention to only one person. If only one of your customers gave the objection you should address the script to that individual first and then the other.

I also used the word "salesperson" throughout instead of "real estate professional" since the two are interchangeable.

Scripts for Overcoming Seller's Objections over the Telephone

DON'T LIKE REAL ESTATE SALESPEOPLE

Seller: "We don't believe you can help."

Salesperson: "If I were to show you how you could save time and money and get your house sold, would you be interested?"

COMMISSION

Seller: "We don't want to pay the commission."

Salesperson: "And I would not want to pay a commission, either. I don't want to pay to get my taxes done, but I do. And what I have found out is that my accountant actually saves me money because he finds deductions I never would have known. Doesn't it make sense to have me out and at least see if I can sell your house and save you money while doing it?"

Seller: "What is the industry standard commission fee?" OR "What do you charge as a commission?" OR "Acme Realty said they would do it for less commission, will you?"

351

Salesperson: "What I charge for a commission is based on the difficulty of selling the house and I wouldn't know that until I have actually seen the house. Now, I am available at 2 p.m. or would 5 p.m. be better to stop by?"

PRICING

Seller: "What do you think my house is worth?"

Salesperson: "Well, I haven't seen your house but I am available now or will later this afternoon be better to evaluate your house?"

HAVE A FRIEND IN THE BUSINESS

Seller: "We will sell through a friend in the business."

Salesperson: "Great, let me ask you this, doesn't it make sense to see what is offered by more than one company so you can make the best decision possible for you and your family? If it is with the friend then, great, you haven't lost anything. Now, I am available at 4 p.m. or would 5 be better to show you our marketing concepts?"

TRY FSBO

Seller: "We are thinking of selling by ourselves for a while."

Salesperson: "Are you prepared for all of the obstacles that could occur?"

Seller: "Like what?"

Salesperson: "Tell you what, I can come by and share a little about marketing a house and while I am there show you some things to be prepared for if you do want to try selling it yourself. Do you see how this can help you?"

NO HURRY

Seller: "We are in no hurry to sell."

Salesperson: "Why are you selling?"

Seller: "Because I am being transferred to Seattle in four months."

Salesperson: "Did you know four months might not be enough time to sell the house?"

Seller: "What do you mean?"

Salesperson: "There is the marketing time, the processing time, and the closing time just to mention a few. I tell you what I can do. I can stop by and share with you a step-by-step walk-through of a real estate sale to give you an idea of timing. May I do that?"

Scripts for Overcoming Expired Seller's Objections over the Telephone

TRY FSBO

Seller: "We are going to sell it ourselves."

Salesperson: "Understood. Do you mind I stop by and give you some ideas to help make the selling process go more smoothly?"

MARKETING

Seller: "What makes you think you can sell it if the previous real estate salesperson couldn't?" OR "Why didn't you sell it while it was listed the last time?"

Salesperson: "I am sure I can show you what it will take to sell your property, but I haven't seen it yet. I can be available in about an hour or will 6 p.m. be better to view the property?"

Scripts for Overcoming FSBO Seller's Objections over the Telephone

DON'T NEED A BROKER

Seller: "I don't think you can help us. We're doing fine so far. We just put it on the market."

Salesperson: "Mr. Seller, it sounds like you're pretty definite about not using a real estate broker. Is that right?"

Seller: "Yes."

Salesperson: "Why is that, Mr. Seller?"

Seller: "Well, I think I can do it myself."

Salesperson: "So, in other words, you're not adverse to paying a commission. You just feel if I can do it myself, I'll do it? Or, is it the commission?"

Seller: "Well, we sold our last home by ourselves. I don't see any problem doing it again this time."

Salesperson: "So, let me see if I understand you right, are you saying you're not adverse to paying a commission if I had a buyer?"

Seller: "Not if you had a buyer."

Salesperson: "Why are you trying to sell it by yourself?"

Seller: "Well, a few years ago, when we sold our house, we originally had it listed with a Realtor® and they didn't do anything. They just left us out to dry. I swore then, that was the last time I was going to use a Realtor®. So, we put it on the market ourselves and it sold."

Salesperson: "How do you like selling your own house?"

Seller: "Well I'd sure rather be playing golf."

Salesperson: "We'll, let me ask you this: If I could help get you out on the golf course by doing three things, (1) getting you your money, (2) guaranteeing that, if you shake my hand, I'll get the job done, and (3) help you get into that new house in plenty of time, would you talk to me?"

Seller: "Yes, if you could do all those things, I'd talk to you."

Salesperson: "Well, let's do this: Find a time when I could stop over and take a look at your house. While I'm there, I'll do those three things for you, Mr. Seller. First of all, I'll show you that when we take a property we sell it, because of our marketing system. Number two, while I'm there, I'll show you how I can get you out with more money than you can get yourself. And, number three, I'll assure you that I can coordinate the sale from beginning to end, so that you can buy the new home. The end result is you're on the golf course, I'm doing all the work, and you get the money. That's what you want, isn't it? So, how would you like to make it 5:30 p.m., or would you like to make it even a little later for me to come see your property?"

Seller: "I've wasted six months listed with a real estate salesperson who did nothing. Not one offer. I can do a better job myself."

Salesperson: "From what you've told me, I don't think that your salesperson did very much to market the property. I can show you my comprehensive marketing plan for the property with deadlines of when I'll complete each phase. That will make a huge difference. I am available now or would tonight be better?"

LEASE IT

BUY IT

Seller: "Are you planning to buy it?"

Salesperson: "No, I'm not. But I may find a client who is looking in that area and price range. I may want to show it to them. Would 3:00 tomorrow be O.K. for me to drop by?"

Seller: "Why?"

Salesperson: "I try to be very professional and it's embarrassing to me to be driving by your home with a client and not be able to tell them all about your house. I want to know as much as I can about the areas I'm showing homes in. May I drop by tomorrow at 4:00 to see your home or would 6:30 be better?"

PRICING

Seller: "We are selling our home ourselves."

Salesperson: "I understand. I am not calling to list your home. I would like to offer you a service free of charge that may prove to be a benefit to you. When a buyer places an offer on your home, odds are great that they, too, will have a home to sell. As a service to you and your buyer, I will prepare a market analysis on your buyer's home which will show estimated market time and estimated net proceeds. This is information you would want, isn't it?"

Seller: "Yes, but why would you do that?"

Salesperson: "By providing this service, it is my hope that your buyer will give me the opportunity to compete for his or her business. May I come by and show you an example of a market analysis and estimated closing cost sheet that I have prepared on another property?"

Seller: "Yes."

CLOSE FOR AN APPOINTMENT

Seller: "No, just put it in the mail."

Salesperson: "I could do that; however, I would like to go over the market analysis form with you. Perhaps tomorrow at 4 p.m. or would 6 be more convenient?"

FRIEND IN BUSINESS

Seller: "If we list it, it will be with our friend."

Salesperson: "I'm glad you have an agent in mind; however, I show a lot of homes in your neighborhood and like to be familiar with all of them that are for sale. It's good business for both you and me, if, when I drive by your home with a client I can say, 'That home has three bedrooms, two baths, a lovely kitchen area. It is selling for $100,000.' My clients may wish to see your home. I can only do that if I have seen the home. Does that make sense?"

COMMISSION

Salesperson: "Why aren't you using a broker? I'm just curious."

Seller: "Well if we want to get in the other house, we have to get every penny we can out of this one. And, if we had to pay a commission, I'm not so sure we could even do it."

Salesperson: "So, it isn't a matter of you're being against using a broker. You just need all the extra money you can get. Am I hearing you right?"

Seller: "We don't have anything against Realtors®, no."

Salesperson: "In other words, if the money were the same, you'd use a broker?"

Seller: "I suppose if the money were the same, yes, I'd consider it."

Salesperson: "O.K. Then let's do this. Many times I find when I look at a property, for one reason or another, I'm able to get a seller more money than he or she can get selling it alone. And I have a dozen different ways of doing that. Why don't I find a time when I can stop and look at your home? While I'm there, I'll let you know what I think I can honestly get you out with. One of two things is going to happen: (1) It's not going to be enough money and you're going to ask me to leave, or (2) You're going to get as much as you can get for yourself and you'll ask me to handle the sale. Does that sound fair to you? Now, I couldn't make it over to look at your property until probably later this evening or I'm open tomorrow evening, too. Which would be best for you?"

Salesperson: "Selling your house yourself may seem like a money-saver, but surveys say that homes sold by real estate professionals gross dollars more than those sold by the owners. So even with my commission you'll do less work and probably come out with more money."

Scripts for Overcoming Seller's Objections at the Listing Appointment

OVERPRICING

Seller: "Another real estate salesperson will list it for a higher price."

Salesperson: "Why do you feel the other salesperson would do that? Maybe the other salesperson is trying to 'buy' your listing. Mr. and Mrs. Seller, do you know what I mean when I say 'buy' a listing? It is when a real estate salesperson tells the seller what the seller wants to hear so the seller will list with them. Then later the salesperson hammers the seller for a price reduction after it is too late. Mr. and Mrs. Seller, I would like to tell you what it will take to sell your house. Will you let me do that?"

Salesperson: "Mr. and Mrs. Seller, don't choose a broker based on price. Please do me and, more importantly, yourselves, a great big favor by not selecting a broker based on who comes in here with the highest price. Please remember that we're talking about your asking price, not our bid. A real estate salesperson coming in here with a price higher than the market will pull isn't offering to buy at that price. All of us have the same records; we're all Multiple Listing brokers. If you decide not to follow the market and price your house higher, I can do that too. And I'll back you 100 percent. I may not want to do it because I want to solve your problem. You have a need to sell here, so I may fight you a little bit on price. But please don't choose me based on pricing. Choose me for my professionalism, for my integrity, for my willingness to work, for my know-how, and for my honesty. The pricing we can work out."

Seller: "My home is worth more than you want to list it for."

Salesperson: "Mr. Seller, on what facts are you basing your price decision?"

Seller: Listen to what the seller has to say.

Salesperson: "Mr. Seller, let us look at our Market Analysis." [Emphasize the 'for sale' to show the competition and then the 'sold' to show the value. If the seller still feels their house is worth more, continue . . .]

Salesperson: "Mr. & Mrs. Seller, my job is to find a buyer who will pay top dollar for your house . . . perhaps you know something of which I am not aware. What information do you have that leads you to believe that a qualified buyer will pay that much for your house?"

Salesperson: "Mr. & Mrs. Seller, that is your decision to make, and I assure you that we will work very hard to get that amount for you. But I do want you to understand that no matter what you and I think your house is worth, the buyers are the ones that really decide the value of a house. You can't get any more for your house than a buyer is willing to pay. Someone looking at your house will view it in comparison to similar houses on the market. If we want to attract them to your house, we have to compete with the rest of the market."

Salesperson: "Before you do that, consider this, houses can get a reputation, usually within the first 30 days of their time on the market. After sales associates see an overpriced house in the Multiple Listing Service for two to three weeks, most will brand it negatively and won't show it. Even after the price is reduced, the notion persists that there is something wrong with the house. Let's not lose the impact of that first very important impression; it could make a lot of difference."

Seller: "Don't you think we could get just a little more for it?"

Salesperson: "Let me ask you this: Is that the only thing that's really bothering you at this point? That you want to get more for the house?"

Seller: "Yes, that's it."

Salesperson: "Remember when we discussed viewing your house as a product and how it's important that the product be priced competitively in order to sell?"

Seller: "Yes."

Salesperson: "I know that you need to be moved in four months. The figures I've shared with you about pricing are based on the prices of comparable houses in the neighborhood. If you price it too high, it won't sell. All it will do is generate a flow of buyers who will look at it and purchase other properties."

Seller: "Hmmm."

Salesperson: "I know we'd all like to get more for our house, but I think you'd agree that based on the facts of record, this really is the right range for you."

Salesperson: "I certainly want you to get as much for your house as possible. In fact, that is my job. But I don't want you to miss out on a buyer because of the listing price. It's true you can always come down later if your home doesn't move at $400,000, but there is also the danger that if you don't take advantage of the buyers presently waiting for a house like yours to come on the market, a later reduction won't solve the psychological stigma that will have surrounded your house."

Salesperson: "It is your decision to make, but my professional opinion that we should get as close as possible to your competitors' prices. How about putting, your house on the market at a price closer to the other properties currently available?"

Seller: "Another real estate firm said they could get me more for my home."

Salesperson: "Did that salesperson show you a detailed Comparative Market Analysis showing houses like yours, in this area, selling for that price recently? If you talk to enough people I'm sure you will find someone who will take your listing at most any price. There is probably no limit on how high you could go and still find someone who will take your listing."

Salesperson: "Sellers sometimes feel it is best to list with the real estate person who claims to be able to get the highest price. Actually the best way to get top price is to be the most competitively priced house in your market, thus attracting the largest number of buyers. It's exposure to the largest number of qualified buyers that brings top offers, not an inflated asking price."

Salesperson: "Mr. & Mrs. Seller, buyers determine how much you get for your house, not the real estate salespeople. All we can do is offer our opinions as to what buyers might be willing to pay. Sometimes salespeople will be overly optimistic about your house's value because of their desire to get your listing. I don't feel this is a service to you and I don't think you do either. The Competitive Market Analysis on your house shows us what buyers have been paying for similar houses, doesn't it? Taking this into consideration, what do you feel your house will honestly bring?"

Salesperson: "Let's try reversing positions, Mr. & Mrs. Seller, and look at your property from the standpoint of the buyer. We will pretend that you are that buyer and, for purposes of comparison, let us say there are six or seven other properties on the market of equal value to yours and just as desirable. Assume that I have shown you five of these: You like them all and it is difficult to decide which one to select. However, one is priced at $275,000, another at $270,000, a third at $262,500, the fourth at $260,000, and the last at $252,500. All things being equal, which house would you choose?" Obviously, the seller would have to admit that his best choice would be the one priced at $252,500.

Salesperson: "Mr. & Mrs. Seller, they can all be purchased for $250,000. The house priced closest to the market value will sell first in every case. Now, you say you want to sell, not have your property used as a comparison to sell others, so why don't we start at $252,500?" *If the seller remains adamant, refusing to lower the price, repeat how the Multiple Listing Service works and how you propose to induce other real estate salespeople to become interested in the sale of his property. Reopening your listing binder you say:*

Salesperson: "Mr. & Mrs. Seller, almost all of my listings sell quickly because I work harder than most salespeople to make them do so. Every Tuesday morning I am at our weekly office meeting, along with many other top salespeople from my office. The average salesperson doesn't make an effort to attend these meetings. Next Tuesday I intend to place extra emphasis on the salability of your property when I talk about it. There are some hundreds of other properties listed on the Multiple Listing Service and I have found that I must make an extra effort to encourage other salespeople to look at and show my particular listing, rather than any other. I have excellent rapport and a good reputation with these other top salespeople and they know when I talk about a listing, it will be one that is worth looking in to. These top salespeople will jot down your address and possibly come by to see your property. The point is this, Mr. & Mrs. Seller, I cannot talk about an overpriced listing. If I do, those other salespeople will soon know that my offerings are unrealistic and they will not bother even to write down the address, much less look at and show the property. Further, every salesperson knows that when I place a property on the office tour it is a salable listing. Mr. & Mrs. Seller, please don't frustrate my attempt to put your property before every possible buyer. Give me the flexibility to talk about it with enthusiasm and get these other people to work on it with the same enthusiasm, as I am sure they will, if it is priced right. Let's set the listing at $250,000, or at the highest $252,500."

Seller: "Let's price it higher at first and we can come down on the price later."

Salesperson: "I realize, Mr. & Mrs. Seller, that that approach to the problem does sound reasonable at first, but the difficulty is that this practice tends to discourage those buyers who are now in the market for a home like yours. If you will remember our previous discussion a high percentage of the properties we sell are sold during the first week of the exposure period. The mistake most homeowners make is to overprice the property at the beginning. When your home first comes on the market it will be seen by many salespeople and if they feel the property is priced right for their prospective buyers, they will hasten to show it. Now, if either the salesperson or their prospects are discouraged by the price, no offers will be presented. Once we exhaust these buyers who are immediately available and interested in purchasing, we must start the long drawn-out process of advertising and looking for possible new buyers. This is what happens to most listings taken by salespeople who do not know what they are doing. A listing, which stays on the market for a long time, becomes shop worn just like the merchandise in a store when it has been picked over by many shoppers. The greatest opportunity for the sale of your home is when it first comes on the market and for this reason I strongly recommend it being listed at a price of no more than $250,000." *Now is the opportune time to talk about the amount of cash to be derived from the sale of the property at $250,000. If this amount is sufficient to meet the seller's needs in the purchase of another home, then you have taken his attention away from something he dislikes and focused it on something acceptable.*

Salesperson: "Mr. & Mrs. Seller, if I were interested only in getting a listing and tying up your property for 180 days, I would write it up at $275,000 or even $300,000, but let me explain what would happen if I did so. Our Multiple Listing Service keeps very accurate statistics on properties sold. Those statistics show that when a property is listed above its market value there is only slim chance that it will sell within a 90-day period. Now the point is this: No matter which price between the high of $300,000 and the low of $250,000 the property is listed, it will sell eventually for no more than $250,000. Mr. & Mrs. Seller, there are no foolish buyers in the market. It may be that, if you list at the figure I suggest, a buyer who considers him- or herself a 'smart operator' will try you out with a lesser offer, but he will buy at $250,000. You say you want to sell—then I propose that we go after 100% of all buyers immediately with a $250,000 price, or at most— $252,500." *By concentrating on each property individually in comparison with the seller's house, you will eventually arrive at a figure very close to the true market value of his home as shown on the competitive market analysis which should be $250,000. You can now quote this directly to the owner, at the same time drawing comparisons of speculative price and term price in relation to market value, somewhat in this manner:*

Salesperson: "Based on these figures, Mr. & Mrs. Seller, I would say that your property should sell for right around $250,000, if we have an average buyer with an average down payment." *If the seller has been convinced and answers your question directly, then your job of appraising is complete. If, on the other hand, they don't answer directly by saying, "Well, we still want more," then you still have a selling job on your hands. At this point continue to ask questions and look for a break in the sellers armor that you might come to an agreement on price.*

COMPANY TOO LARGE (SMALL)

Seller: "We don't like large companies, they are too impersonal."

Salesperson: "Yes, Mr. & Mrs. Seller, I understand how you feel. It's not a comfortable feeling to imagine yourself to be just a number, is it? But wouldn't it be really great to do business with a locally owned company with salespeople who are all your neighbors and still get the same national exposure that the largest corporations get?"

Salesperson: "I understand. It seems what you're concerned with is whether my company can effectively market your home, correct? Let's review the marketing plan. Please stop me at any part that you don't understand."

BETTER SERVICES\MORE SERVICES

Seller: "Acme Real Estate Company has better advertising than you do."

Salesperson: "Mr. & Mrs. Seller, did you know that advertising only gets your home sold approximately two percent of the time? We offer a 21-point marketing plan to get your house sold. Let's take a look at it."

Salesperson: "My office orchestrates a comprehensive marketing campaign designed to prompt potential buyers to call our office, This flow of buyers through the office can mean more potential buyers for your property and a greater chance of getting the right price for your property."

Salesperson: "Mr. or Mrs. Seller, our company spends a great deal of money each year on national advertising. How does that benefit you? We have the ability to have the strongest marketing campaign in the real estate industry, which in turn has provided us the ability to capture interested buyers in the properties we market. What do those buyers do when they decide to buy? They call our office. Don't you think it would be prudent to have your property listed with our office getting all of those buyer calls?"

Seller: "Acme Real Estate Company has more services than you do."

Salesperson: "Really? What did they offer you that I failed to mention?"

Virtually every service the seller was offered you can do too.

Seller: "Will you advertise our property in the local newspaper every week?"

Salesperson: "We have an ongoing advertising program and your house will certainly be part of that marketing campaign until it sells. What we use in our office is. . . . . ." *Describe some specific things your office does like advertise in the newspaper, home guides, on television, etc.*

Seller: "Will you hold our house open every weekend?"

Salesperson: "Open houses can generate a flow of buyers, but rarely do those buyers purchase the specific house they saw open. Why don't we give my marketing campaign 30 days to produce results? Then if it doesn't, we can consider an open house."

Seller: "We want you present at all showings."

Salesperson: "What we have done in the real estate industry is cooperate. This means that a licensed real estate professional salesperson will escort each and every buyer that wants to view your property. This protects your house from the wrong people. This also allows me the time to actively market your house to get more people through."

Seller: "We don't want a lock box because it will be inconvenient."

Salesperson: "I understand your concern, but remember, it's important to be competitive. And being competitive means not only pricing the property properly and getting it ready to show, but also making it accessible to salespeople who may be working with the best buyer. How about if we use a lock box and at times when you are there and don't want to be disturbed, you use your deadbolt or chain lock. Are you comfortable with that?"

Seller: "We don't want a lock box because we were once robbed."

Salesperson: "Considering the problem you had with the robbery, it seems like there's really only a couple of alternatives. Either I can keep a key in the office and only give it out to licensed real estate salespeople who will show your property or you will need to make arrangements to be here with a 10-minute notice anytime the property is going to be shown. Which will work best for you?"

Seller: "We don't want a sign in our yard."

Salesperson: "This is the most widely recognized yard sign in the real estate business. Buyers know it without ever being close enough to read it. This can mean more potential buyers for you. This is important since the largest number of potential buyers do come from yard signs."

Seller: "We don't want a sign in our yard."

Salesperson: "Is that the only thing we need to address?"

Seller: "Yes."

Salesperson: "I'm sure you have a very good reason. May I ask why?"

Seller: "Because we don't want the neighbors to know we're moving. What would be the benefit to the neighbors knowing?"

Salesperson: "In other words your neighbors will know your house is for sale, is that right?"

Seller: "Right."

Salesperson: "I understand how you feel and you don't want them to know. However, they may be a major source of buyers for us. Your neighbors will want someone to move in that will be a good neighbor and they might know of someone interested right now. Since the neighbors can actually help us sell your home, let's put the yard sign up and enlist their help from day one."

Seller: "We don't want a sign in our yard because we don't want our neighbors to know we have to sell."

Salesperson: "I can understand why you want to keep your move from some of your neighbors. But you know, last year a great deal of the buyer inquiries into my office were generated by 'For Sale' signs, it's one of our most powerful tools for finding your best buyer. Without the sign, you limit your exposure in the marketplace which means fewer potential buyers and ultimately, a longer time to sell. Buyers sometimes look in neighborhoods for houses and if a for sale sign is not up, they could pass it up and besides real estate salespeople need to be able to find the house easily when they are showing property."

Seller: "We don't want a sign in front of our house because we are nervous about security."

Salesperson: "I understand your concern about the sign. Security is not to be taken lightly, but the biggest producers of potential buyers that we have are from 'For Sale' signs, I wonder if we can find another way to work with the sign. I can certainly distribute flyers about your house. We can also use bulletin boards in the community to give it exposure. I wonder, though, would you willing to have a portable sign that you just put out when you're home and take down when you go away? Would that make you feel more comfortable?"

FRIEND IN BUSINESS

Seller: "We have a friend in the business."

Salesperson: "Mr. & Mrs. Seller, if you were convinced that another real estate professional could actually get you more money in the time frame that is best for you, with the least inconvenience, would you still be committed to giving the listing to your friend?"

Salesperson: "Tell me, do you feel an obligation because of the friendship or because you believe your friend will actually be able to get you the most money in the time frame you desire with the least inconvenience?"

Salesperson: "Mr. & Mrs. Seller, you owe me nothing, but you owe yourself the very best. In the real estate industry, 80 percent of the property is sold by 20 percent of the salespeople. You have a tough decision to make, no matter who you hire to protect the equity you have built up in your home. One of us will be disappointed. Be sure you're not disappointed too."

Salesperson: "Most sellers believe a house will sell for X amount of dollars, regardless of who sells it. That is not so. Statistically, real estate professionals can get more money for property than private sellers can, and some real estate people consistently get more for homes than other real estate people. Look at my record in the area."

Salesperson: "I know just how you feel. Friendships are certainly valuable. Think a minute about your friend. We all know the old adage about not doing business with friends or relatives. By asking your friend to market your property you put him in a delicate position. As your friend, he would be hesitant to give suggestions that might improve the marketing conditions of your property because be doesn't want to take a chance on hurting your feelings. It's very difficult to be objective when we are emotionally involved with an obligation of friendship. Actually, your friend might be relieved to have you list the home with someone more objective and not be placed into the position of being your employee. Your home is an important investment and you certainly want to protect that investment by putting it the hands of an objective professional. Listing, on the basis of friendship only sometimes proves costly in the sale and in the friendship as well. Certainly, it is something you should consider very carefully."

Seller: "If we do list we've got a friend in the real estate business."

Salesperson: "Sure, When were you planning on listing?"

Seller: "Probably in another couple of months."

Salesperson: "If I could show you how I could perhaps do the same good job for you, but put more money in your pocket than your friend could, would you be interested in considering do business with a *new* friend?"

THINKING OF GOING FSBO

Seller: "I can sell my home without using a real estate professional."

Salesperson: "Mr. & Mrs. Seller, at any given time there are a certain number of people in the market for a home who are well qualified and serious about buying a home. Do you agree? They look in the newspaper and discover that 91 percent of the homes for sale are in the hands of real estate professionals and only nine percent are for sale through private sellers. Tell me Mr. Seller, if real estate professionals have over 90 percent of the houses for sale, where do the serious, qualified buyers have to go? That leaves the private seller with bargain hunters, unqualified buyers, and weekend hobby lookers. That is the reason our company has sold so many homes in this market. We can expose your property to the greatest number of qualified buyers. Do you see how by attracting the largest number of serious, qualified buyers to look at your home we can help you net top dollar?"

Salesperson: "Mr. & Mrs. Seller, tell me, what is the number one advantage you hope to gain in selling your home directly to a private buyer? Save the real estate fee for service, is that right? Mr. & Mrs. Seller, put yourself in the buyer's shoes, what is the number one advantage to you as a buyer in buying direct from an owner? The number one advantage is to save the same commission you hope to save as a seller, isn't that so? Mr. & Mrs. Seller, can you see any possible difficulties you may have in trying to save the real estate service fee? Research shows private sellers can net four to six percent less by selling their home 'By Owner' than by selling through a real estate professional and paying a fee for service."

Salesperson: "Mr. & Mrs. Seller, there are serious buyers, qualified buyers, and potential buyers. A potential buyer is anyone who might buy. A qualified buyer can buy. A serious buyer wants to buy. There are qualified buyers who are not serious and serious buyers who are not qualified. So the only kind of buyer that counts is a serious, qualified buyer. We in the real estate industry have well over 90 percent of the inventory of the homes for sale. Where do you suppose the serious, qualified buyers are likely to go to find a home? They will go to the professionals in real estate. Isn't that right?"

Seller: "I don't want to list, but I will pay you a commission if you bring me a contract."

Salesperson: "I understand how you feel. However, our company doesn't consider that fair to you. You are willing to pay us for doing less than our best for you. Everybody's business is nobody's business. If we accept an Open Listing from you, you will be expecting action from us that we just can't give. When we accept the responsibility of finding the right buyer for your property, we are licensed and trained to accept the full responsibility of acting as your agent and using all our contacts and professional marketing tools to do that job. We have an obligation to all the owners who list their property in the Multiple Listing System to give exposure to their properties. We would violate the best interest of those owners to try to find a buyer for your unlisted property over theirs."

Seller: "We have several people who are interested in the property and we want to give them the time to make up their minds."

Salesperson: "I understand how you feel. It seems there are often people who are interested in a property who are simply not qualified to buy it. Of course, it is difficult for you to find out about their financial capability, especially if they are friends. Yet, you must be careful not to limit your chances for a sale by keeping the property off the market for people who are not financially qualified to pay the top value. Mr. & Mrs. Seller, I suggest that you call the prospects and tell them the property is listed and if they are sincere prospects and they are qualified to buy, they will be motivated to draw up a contract immediately. If they are not serious, you need to know that now. We can exclude them from the listing agreement for one week."

Seller: "We want to try a little longer ourselves."

Salesperson: "Mr. & Mrs. Seller, how much longer will you wait? Then you do agree that if you don't sell it in that time, we would be the company that can do the job for you, correct? I'll be checking back with you in a week or two to see how things are going."

Seller: "We want to sell by ourselves."

Salesperson: "Why do you want to sell it yourself?"

Seller: "I feel I can do as the same job as a real estate salesperson."

Salesperson: "What's your specific motivation for wanting to do the work yourself?"

Seller: "I can save the commission for myself."

Salesperson: "If I could show you how I could get you as much money as you could get yourself, would you be interested?"

Salesperson: "Mr. & Mrs. Seller, if you expect to save the commission by selling at the fair market value, what do you think the buyer's attitude will be about this? Don't you think that they are also counting on saving the commission by dealing directly? Surely they are going to offer you a price less the commission, and perhaps, an even larger discount less for the property than your asking price, otherwise why would they be dealing with you? In contrast, wouldn't it be better to employ a skillful negotiator to work in your behalf, one who does this sort of thing every day and is being paid to have your interests at heart? If you will list your property for sale with us at its fair market value, we can use our skills and techniques acquired through experience to convince any buyer that he or she should pay the full fair market value."

Salesperson: "Mr. & Mrs. Seller, if you try to sell the property yourself, you will have hundreds of people in the real estate business as your competitors; but if you list your property with us, you will have these same people working on your side to try to find a buyer. We are members of the Multiple Listing Service and we are all pledged to work together."

COMMISSION

Seller: "The Acme Real Estate Company charges less commission."

Salesperson: "Mr. & Mrs. Seller, I can see how a lower fee for service might sound good to you but I don't believe it is in your best interest. Our fee at our company is based on the amount of time and the kind of marketing it will take to sell your property. I have demonstrated the marketing my company has to offer, what is Acme Real Estate Company offering?"

Seller: "I want to negotiate your commission."

Salesperson: "Fine, did you want to pay six, seven, or eight percent?"

Explain the value of offering a higher commission to the selling real estate salesperson in the form of a bonus. Explain how a fee is split between the listing and the selling real estate companies and salespeople. Include cost of marketing, etc.

Seller: "Will you list my house for less commission?"

Salesperson: "No. Any other questions?"

Seller: "If we buy our next house from you will you cut your commission on the sale of this house?"

Salesperson: "The marketing of this house should not be contingent on the purchase of your next house. My services are complete as a seller's real estate professional and as a buyer's real estate professional. You do not want to limit my ability to get your house sold."

Seller: "If my house sells in a week will you cut your commission?"

Salesperson: "Sometimes it happens like that. In those cases, what you find is that it didn't take just a week to sell the house it probably took six months. Those are buyers who've been out in the marketplace, seen the house they wanted several times, and missed it, or they may have come in too low for a house they wanted, those buyers are ready. When they see the right house, they're going to buy it. Now, if I can find those buyers in one week's time, I believe I've done my job. Wouldn't you agree?"

Seller: "Acme Real Estate Company will take my listing and sell it for a percentage less, why won't you?"

Salesperson: "Mr. & Mrs. Seller, Acme Real Estate Company knows the worth of its own efforts, my company and I will spend a great deal of time, effort, and know-how in the merchandising of your property, for which we expect to get paid. It will be worth your while to pay a little more and get the best service available than to save a little and perhaps suffer a greater loss in the long run! Believe me, Mr. & Mrs. Seller, we also know our worth and we expect to give more than value received!"

WAIT TO MAKE A DECISION

Seller: "We want to think it over."

Salesperson: "Certainly, Mr. & Mrs. Seller, may I ask if there is anything in particular that is bothering you?"

Salesperson: "I understand how you feel. Many people I work with feel the same way. In fact I've been in the same situation and felt exactly the same way. But what you are really telling me is that you have questions you still need to have answered before you go ahead. Isn't that correct?"

Salesperson: "I can understand that. Selling your home is an important decision. Please help me understand. What is it that you need to think about?" *After clarifying, respond to the actual concern.*

Salesperson: "Selling your home is an important decision. Just to clarify my own thinking, what is it that you're concerned about?" *After clarifying, respond to the actual concern.*

Seller: "We'd like to sell, but we are going to hold off for a few months until. . . . "

Salesperson: "I can see why you would want to wait, but there might be some disadvantages to putting it off until later, if you know you're going to be making a move soon. Right now interest rates and the money supply are good. Within a short time a lot of homes will be coming on the market and you will have to compete with them for a buyer. You also have to consider that it will take at least a few weeks to find a buyer for your home and secure financing. Doesn't it make sense to make the decision to sell now rather than later?"

Seller: "We want to sell but we want to wait."

Salesperson: "No problem, how long were you planning to wait?"

Seller: "Probably a couple of months."

Salesperson: "Why were you thinking of waiting?"

Seller: "We thought there would be more houses on the market in the spring."

Salesperson: "Well, that's true. Let me ask you this. If I could show you how you might be able to put an extra thousand dollars in your pocket by perhaps moving your plans up a little bit, would you consider at least talking with me about it?" *Now you have to demonstrate the drawbacks to waiting.*

Seller: "We would like to think it over first."

Salesperson: "I understand that this is a difficult decision. Are you wanting to think about the marketing of the home?"

Seller: "No, the marketing is fine."

Salesperson: "Is it our company that you want to think about?"

Seller: "No, we like your company."

Salesperson: "Is it me? Do you like and trust me?"

Seller: "Of course, we like you."

Big Pause, then slowly . . .

Salesperson: "Is it the price?" *(Generally the biggest objection from a seller is price.)*

Seller: "Well, you know, it is less than we wanted to get."

Salesperson: "I remember, let me ask you, if we could agree upon a price, would you list with me tonight?"

Seller: "Well, I appreciate what you said. It's really interesting, but I need to think about it."

Salesperson: "I can understand that. It's an awfully big decision. But just so I'm clear, will you tell me what it is that you need to think about?"

Seller: "Oh, I don't know. I'm just sort of unsure."

Salesperson: "Well, was it my marketing plan? Did you like what I had to say about how I'm going to market your house?"

Seller: "Yes, I did. That was terrific."

Salesperson: "Is the fee bothering you?"

Seller: "No. Not really."

Salesperson: "Is it the price?"

Lastly, what if they say, "We want to pray about it?" This is one I choose not to handle. I am very leery to challenge religious beliefs. Two of my friends did and here are their results:

SENARIO 1:

Seller: "We want to pray about it."

Salesperson: "Exactly, don't you think God sent me here tonight?"

Seller: "Get out!"

SENARIO 2:

> **Seller:** "We want to pray about it."
>
> **Salesperson:** "Fine, let's bow our heads."
>
> **Seller:** "Get out!"

Not what I call great results. I am not making a judgment here, I just choose not to counter this kind of objection. And that is the beauty of this business–choice.

BUY FIRST

> **Seller:** "We don't want to put our home on the market until we find another home we like."
>
> **Salesperson:** "I realize your dilemma, Mr. & Mrs. Seller, but on the other hand, can you afford to buy a new home without first selling this one? Every homeowner faces this problem, but I assure you I've never had a seller who had to move out into the street. I have to time the sale of your present home and the purchase of a new one so they coincide as closely as possible. The only way you can do that is to give your home exposure on the market while you're looking for another house. We can always arrange a possession date to insure that you have a home to move into. The opposite side of the coin is that you find a home you want, but you aren't in a position to buy it because you don't have an offer on your present home. Then, while you try to sell your home, you take the risk of someone else buying the home you want. I'm sure you wouldn't want that to happen, would you?"
>
> **Seller:** "We don't want to put our home on the market until we find a place to move."
>
> **Salesperson:** "Yes, you certainly have to have a place to live. If I could show you how you could put your house on the market now and still have time to find another place to live would you list with me tonight?"

DON'T LIKE SALESPEOPLE

> **Seller:** "We don't want anything to do with real estate people."
>
> **Salesperson:** "I understand how you feel. In years past and, unfortunately, even today to a limited degree, there are salespeople who may

not have had the benefit of thorough training and knowledge necessary to give the professional service you need to successfully sell your property. It is even true that the most common complaint about a real estate salesperson is, 'He listed my house and I never heard another thing from him.' Fortunately, we have learned from others mistakes. Our firm builds its reputation on the personal concern of well-trained salespeople who always work for your best interest. Let me give you the names and telephone numbers of some our satisfied clients who once felt the same way you do and then trusted our company to market their property."

Salesperson: "In many cases, Mr. & Mrs. Seller, that is a very valid position. Our industry has been plagued with many unscrupulous and unprofessional real estate salespeople. I am proud to say, though, that at our company we are truly your neighborhood professionals. I have shown we have some very sophisticated and highly effective methods available to help you sell your property and sell it right. That is my vow to the both of you."

Salesperson: "Mr. & Mrs. Seller, I dislike many of them, too. Unprofessional behavior is everywhere in our industry. What we have done is take the risk out of dealing with real estate people. You only have to deal with me and I will take care of the rest."

Salesperson: "Mr. & Mrs. Seller, that's understandable. But have I ever had a bad hair cut at a hair salon? Of course, but did I quit getting my hair done? Seriously, Mr. & Mrs. Seller, we are highly trained to provide you with trouble-free service. Put me to work for you and let me prove my value."

SHORT TERM LISTING

Seller: "I don't want to tie up my property. Would you take a 30-day agreement?"

Salesperson: "The average house in the area sold in 82.5 days. We like a little break on the average because we go to great expense putting a home on the market."

Salesperson: "Our normal listing period is 180 days. Mr. & Mrs. Seller, I'm sure you can understand why we need that amount of time. We are going to spend a lot of money and time to attract buyers to your home. The average length time it takes to sell a home in this area is much greater than 30 days. Now there is every possibility that your home will sell sooner than this, but we have to make sure we have an opportunity to bring you an offer once we have put forth this much effort. We want to sell your home as quickly also–make no mistake about it–because we don't get paid until we find you a buyer."

Salesperson: "Mr. & Mrs. Seller, I am really glad you brought that up. You have probably heard all kinds of claims. I'll bet someone even told you they had a buyer who was looking for a home just like yours, right? Well, Mr. & Mrs. Seller, I am going to tell you something that might surprise you. I don't have a buyer for your house right now. I don't even guarantee I can find one in 30 days; no salesperson of great integrity would do that. But if I can show you that your chances of selling your home faster with the opportunity to receive more cash rests with our company would you put faith in me and in my company?"

Salesperson: "We probably could sell your home within 30 days but we want to obtain fair market value for you, not a distress sale price. Our records indicate that it takes longer than 30 days to do this. Are you aware that most real estate activity is on weekend and a 30-day listing limits us to only four weekends or eight effective sales days?"

Salesperson: "Our normal listing period is 180 days. Mr. & Mrs. Seller, I am sure you can understand why we need this amount of time. I can also understand your concern that I might take the listing and do nothing. What I am promising is my commitment to do everything I can to find a buyer. And to prove that to you I am willing to put my commitment in writing. It lists all our special services. The commitment releases you from the listing agreement should I fail to perform as I said I would."

Seller: "I don't want to give you more than 30 days to sell our home."

Salesperson: "Mr. & Mrs. Seller, we believe so strongly in quality service that we've put our commitment in writing. The commitment provides you with maximum peace of mind, wouldn't you agree?"

Salesperson: "I would guess from what we've done tonight that you like what I've had to say, but you really don't know if I'm going to be able to deliver. How about if I put my promises in writing and give you the right to cancel the listing with ten days if I don't do what I said I'd do? Would that make you feel more comfortable about a long term agreement?"

NOT IN AREA

Seller: "You don't have an office in this area."

Salesperson: "Mr. & Mrs. Seller, do you understand how the MLS system works and how actual location of an office is not as important as it was years ago? We can plug into a network of professionals all over town who also have groups of buyers that they're working with. Through the MLS, I'm able to expose your home to the maximum number of buyers which can mean a faster sale for you."

Salesperson: "My office is centrally located, highly visible and attractive. It's easy for potential buyers to find and comfortable for them to walk into. That contributes to the flow of buyers through the office and that can mean more buyers for you."

INTERVIEW OTHERS

Seller: "We are going to have another real estate company come out to talk with us."

Salesperson: "That's totally understandable. Let me ask you, though, if I was to do all your homework for you and you were completely satisfied that I am with the best real estate company would you list with me right now?" Use the comparison chart of other real estate companies and point out where your company is always stronger.

Salesperson: "I can understand your need to talk to another sales associate. Selling your home is a big decision and it's important to select someone you can work with comfortably. Will you do me a favor, though? Will you call me after you've talked to that person? I'd like to have the opportunity talk to you again."

Salesperson: "If you're feeling confident in my ability to sell your property, I think it might be doing him or her a favor to call and cancel the appointment. In fact, I'd be happy to do it for you. I've had calls like that and frankly, I've appreciated it."

BAD EXPERIENCE

Seller: "I sold my house with your company in Alabama and had a bad experience."

Salesperson: "Please elaborate on what happened. It does sound like that was a bad experience. Mr. & Mrs. Seller, if I was to guarantee my service to you and if I fail to perform you can fire me would you list it with me tonight?"
Use a seller's service guarantee that guarantees our service if the seller puts the error in writing and gives us ten days to correct the error.

Salesperson: "Then you will appreciate the good experience you will have with me and my company. I'm only here to work for you and to get your home sold!"

SAME REAL ESTATE SALESPERSON

Seller: "I bought my home from Brittany with Acme Real Estate, I think I will list with her."

Salesperson: "Mr. & Mrs. Seller, do you understand my job here tonight and in the future is to get your house sold, not to sell it? There is a big difference between a professional marketer and someone with a buyer. I don't know Brittany, but I do know I am the best choice for getting your house sold for the most money in the least amount of time."

MORE EXPERIENCE\NEW TO THE BUSINESS

Seller: "Brittany with Acme Real Estate has a lot more experience than you."

Salesperson: "Mr. & Mrs. Seller, what does the word 'experience' mean to you? Time in the business does not mean being the best at selling your house. If I would guarantee my service to you is the best offered would you list your property with me today?"

Salesperson: "I am well trained so you can be confident that I'll have the most up-to-date information to work with in the transaction."

Salesperson: "I'm very well trained in finding buyers, assisting with financing, working with transferees, developing marketing strategies, and providing quality service. I continue to attend real estate classes. That way my clients can have access to the most up-to-date information."

Salesperson: "My office has sold many homes in this area over the past year. We've been in business for several years and are very well established in your neighborhood. You've probably noticed our yard signs. They're everywhere you look."

Salesperson: "I really love my job. I enjoy working with people throughout the selling process and helping them with their move. And I view our relationship as a joint effort. We'll work together on this project until your house is sold."

Salesperson: "You know all the power of our company locally and nationally comes to bear on the marketing of your property through me. I've chosen to specialize in your neighborhood. As a matter of fact, I walk through this neighborhood every other week. Over the past few months, we've sold several properties here."

Seller: "Are you new?"

Salesperson: "I'm new to the business, so I'm very motivated, recently trained, and knowledgeable about the most current marketing techniques. When you hire me, I'll work harder and smarter than anybody else to get your house sold. In addition, my manager's been in the business for many years and stands behind me every step of the way." *(When you're new to the business, rely on the collective strengths of your office. Include yourself as part of your office's marketing team when describing its successes.)*

DISCLOSURE

Seller: "We don't feel it is necessary to tell about the murder on the property."

Salesperson: "Why don't want to disclose that?"

Seller: "We feel it will hurt our chances of selling."

Salesperson: "I think I understand. My job here tonight is to protect you as well as get your house sold. We must disclose conditions with the house but don't worry no one can force you to sell, you will always have the veto power if an offer is not what you want."

THIRD PARTY COMPANY

Seller: "If we sell through the real estate company our relocation is offering we get a rebate."

Salesperson: "How much is the rebate?"

Seller: "$350."

Salesperson: "If I was willing to give you $350.00 would you list it with me now?"

Salesperson: "How much is your monthly payment for this house?"

Seller: "$1,450."

Salesperson: "So, if it took even one month longer to sell through the other real estate company, how much would that cost you less the rebate?"

PAYING CLOSING COSTS

Seller: "We won't pay any buyer's closing costs."

Salesperson: "You probably paid these costs when you purchased the house. If you pay closing costs for the buyers, you'll probably net about $4,000 less from the sale. But, paying them might make the difference between whether or not a buyer can afford to purchase your house."

Seller: "I'm not paying for a title policy. If the buyer wants it let them pay for it!"

Salesperson: "Mr. & Mrs. Seller, let's not concentrate on the purchase agreement. Let's look at your bottom line–what you will walk away with in your pocket." *(Review the net sheet.)*

PERSONAL PROPERTY/REAL PROPERTY

Seller: "The buyers asked that we leave our hot tub, and we want to take it with us when we move."

Salesperson: "Mr. & Mrs. Seller, how much is a used hot tub worth?"

Seller: "$1,500."

Salesperson: "Used, not what you paid for it."

Seller: "Well, maybe $800."

Salesperson: "Let's assume the buyers do not take our counteroffer if you don't give them the hot tub. Then we wait for four more months before we get another offer. During this time you must keep this house in show condition. You must be ready at any given moment to leave for a showing. The lot you want to build on just sits there and you continue to make monthly house payments on a place you no longer want. If we just take a look at your house payment of $1,385 times the four months, is it really worth the effort of moving that hot tub?"

AGENCY LISTING

Seller: "We want the right to sell the property ourselves and not pay a commission."

Salesperson: "Why would you want to compete with me to sell your house?"

Seller: "Well, maybe someone at my work might want to buy it."

Salesperson: "Oh, I think I get it, you believe the only thing you're paying me for is to bring you a buyer. Let's review my services both before and after a written offer to purchase and I think you will see I provide a great deal more than just a buyer."

PREQUALIFYING BUYERS

Seller: "We don't want any old buyer traipsing through our home."

Salesperson: "I prequalify buyers before I bring them through your property. That means less inconvenience for you and a better chance that your house is going to be affordable for the buyers that I show."

Salesperson: "Today's sellers are more educated about real estate sales and the requirements most mortgage lenders ask of a buyer. Because of this knowledge, more and more sellers are asking that the potential buyers be financially pre-qualified before accepting an offer, and they are also requesting a pre-approval letter rather than a simple prequalification. A preapproval carries a stronger, safer message that the buyers are truly qualified to purchase their home. Would you like me to get a preapproval letter from the buyer before we accept an offer to purchase?"

MANAGING ALL THE DETAILS

Seller: "Part of the reason we would consider listing our property with you is not to be hassled with all the details in selling a home."

Salesperson: "I want you to understand that I will stand in the middle of this transaction to make sure that everything gets done."

SERVICE GAURANTEE

Seller: "How will I be sure you do what you promise?"

Salesperson: "I will put my promises in writing and give you the right to cancel should I not perform. This provides you with maximum peace of mind."

OPEN LISTING

Seller: "I'll give an open listing and pay a commission to whomever brings the buyer."

Salesperson: "An open listing limits what I can do for you. It means I can only work with those buyers I happen to be working with right now. With an exclusive listing, I can actively market and promote your home to all buyers."

EXPIRED

Seller: "You didn't show the house before."

Salesperson: "Mr. & Mrs. Seller, you are paying me to be a marketing expert. That means I get houses sold. I might not actually sell it, but I will get it sold. The real estate salespeople that show houses are generally not the best marketing salespeople. We all have our specialties. My job is to find those real estate salespeople with buyers and get them to see your property. The last time your home was not personally marketed to me but we can change that. Are you ready to put me to work for you?"

SELL VA\FHA

Seller: "I don't want to sell my property VA or FHA."

Salesperson: "I understand. Would you do me a favor? At least look at all offers, and then together we can make the decision how to sell. You don't want to exclude a percent of the potential market, do you?"

Salesperson: "Our company wants you to receive the quality service you deserve. Our company does more than just promise quality service. To be sure you are completely satisfied, you will receive a survey shortly after the sale of your property is completed. This survey allows us to measure our success. It acts as our barometer and assists us in maintaining our dominance as the most preferred real estate company in the area. Does this type of confidence and follow-through convince you that my company is the right one to represent you in the sale of your home!"

HOME WARRANTY

Seller: "We are not going to pay for a home warranty for the buyer."

Salesperson: "There are several ways to market your home to eliminate, or at least reduce, the competition. One of the most effective marketing tools I've used is not only a strong incentive to buy your property but it's also a service that provides peace of mind for both you and the buyers. It's a home warranty. On average homes listed with a home warranty sell for a higher price and faster than homes without it. I think it would be prudent to protect your property with a home warranty, don't you?"

Seller: "We are not going to fix a thing after closing."

Salesperson: "If you're concerned about appliances that will break down or a furnace that quits the day you move out, let me tell you about home warranty plans. They provide you with the piece of mind you're looking for. They typically cover the items you choose and insures them against breakdown and the ensuing repairs with a low deductible fee to the buyer. Does this service sound like something you would like?"

INSPECTIONS

Seller: "We are concerned about the condition of the property. We don't want to have a lot of money in repairs."

Salesperson: "Mr. & Mrs. Seller, if you feel you may have some issues with the property that may be found at the inspection, I would suggest you have your home inspected now to determine the best course of action for anything that may come up. I can give you the names of many different inspection companies."

Salesperson: "Mr. & Mrs. Seller, because you have an older home a lead testing company can assist you in determining whether or not you have a lead paint issue. If so, the company will consult and advise you on how best to eliminate the problem in the most efficient, cost-effective way. I can recommend a number of different companies."

Salesperson: "Mr. & Mrs. Seller, I recommend that all seller clients have their properties inspected. Some problems can only be detected by a professional or by completing actual testing on such things as water and electricity. I can provide you with the names of several companies to choose from if you are interested."

SPECIAL PROPERTIES

Seller: "We want a real estate company that appreciates our unique property."

Salesperson: "Mr. & Mrs. Seller, some properties deserve special attention. Because you own a lakefront property, you can take advantage of our company's professional service and unique marketing that is designed to meet your home selling needs and draw special attention to your home."

Salesperson: "Mr. & Mrs. Seller, some properties require special attention. Because you're looking to sell a lakefront home, you can take advantage of our recreational properties program. It is designed to market this type of property and will allow me to utilize a quicker reference to find the buyer for your house."

INTERNET

Seller: "We believe the Internet is what it takes to sell property."

Salesperson: "Mr. & Mrs. Seller, we have numerous technological avenues available to help you sell this house. We have a Web site where we list our properties. We have a community location with information listed about your neighborhood. If you're an Internet user we'll have an additional means of communication by e-mail. Do these technological advantages sound like the type of service that may create a shorter, easier avenue to finding a buyer for your house?"

Salesperson: "Mr. or Mrs. Seller, we have the most comprehensive technological offering of any real estate company to market your property. We use a Web site at the number one real

estate Web site where we can advertise your house, including
a picture. We use a computer system to market your house
through the Multiple Listing Service, and you can track the
progress of your sale with e-mail. All of these technological
avenues allow us to generate leads at a greater rate than ever
before. Does this sound like the type of marketing that may
create a quicker sale of your property?"

RELOCATION

Seller: "We are concerned about where we will be moving to."

Salesperson: "Mr. & Mrs. Seller, if you need assistance in buying out of
the local area, I can refer you to one of our affiliate offices to
assist you at your next location. Would you like me to do that
for you?"

Salesperson: "Mr. or Mrs. Seller, should you need assistance moving
out of the local area, I can refer you to one of many
offices within the United States and abroad to assist you at
your next location. If you're moving locally, I can help give
your property exposure to buyers not normally familiar
with this area. Is this a benefit you would like to take
advantage of?"

FAIR HOUSING QUESTIONS FROM SELLERS

Seller: "Which buyer is the contract from?"

Salesperson: "This offer is from Mr. Jones, the computer salesman from
Dallas."

Seller: "Can I be sued if I refuse to sell to him?"

Salesperson: "If you refuse to accept Mr. Jones' offer because he is a
minority, you expose yourself to serious legal liability."

*(The Broker should document, in detail, that they have made this
recommendation).*

Seller: "What color, religion, nationality, and sex are the buyers?"

Salesperson: "I need to know why you asked that question. The listing
agreement you signed provides that this property is offered
without discrimination. If you intend to violate that
agreement, I need to know now so I can protect myself and
my firm."

Seller: "What if I refuse to accept an offer from a minority?"

Salesperson: "I presume you are interested in selling your property to a buyer capable of paying you the best price and offering the most favorable terms and conditions. Federal law requires that I present all offers and it prohibits you from not considering them on the basis of discrimination."

Seller: "What if I take my property off the market, and relist it at a later date when these people [minority] are no longer looking?"

Salesperson: "If the property on which a 'protected class' has made an offer is to be removed from the market, the circumstances prompting such removal must be carefully and completely explained and documented by the listing broker and attested to by the seller. An offer from a minority is never a basis for the removal. If you insist the minority's offer is the only reason for the withdrawal, my firm cannot agree and we will have to the terminate the listing."

Seller: "Are you aware, there is a bonus for selling my home to the 'right people'?"

Salesperson: "I appreciate the offer of a bonus, but it would be unethical and illegal for me to accept an offer when it is conditioned on the race or the religion of the person submitting the offer."

Seller: "Why must I sell my home to someone I don't like? What about my 'freedom of choice' and my 'rights'?"

Salesperson: "I cannot answer these questions for you. If you believe you have these rights, you should talk to an attorney."

Seller: "I want to list my property at $10,000 over its fair market value, but I will sell it to the 'right people' for $10,000 less."

Salesperson: "When a property is overpriced, it tends to sit on the market without drawing any interest from any buyers. That is certainly not in your best interest."

Seller: "Could you call and tell me who you are showing the property to?"

Salesperson: "Of course, although I am not sure why you want me to bother you in this way. Most of our clients hire us to screen the buyers and only show to those who are qualified. Our experience shows that clients only want to be contacted when an offer is believed to be forthcoming."

Seller: "What will you do if a minority wants to see my house?"

Salesperson: "I will show your property to anyone who is financially qualified."

Seller: "I am mad at my neighbors, and only want to sell to minorities."

Salesperson: "Limiting the sale of your property to minorities is not an effective way to get revenge on your neighbors. A sale to minorities would not necessarily reduce the property values, any limitations on my marketing efforts will mean that your property is exposed to fewer buyers and most importantly, any racial limitations on the sale of your property is illegal."

Seller: "We don't want to sell to those people [any protected group]."

Salesperson: "That's curious. I thought you wanted to sell this house."

Seller: "We do."

Salesperson: "Then why would you want to limit the market?"

Seller: "Well . . . "

Salesperson: "Doesn't it make sense to let me do my job and get your house sold to the most qualified buyer?"

Salesperson: "I am sure you are aware of the legal limitations we are under according to the Federal Fair Housing laws. This would cause way too many problems so let's sell this property to the first qualified buyer, O.K.?"

FAIR HOUSING QUESTIONS FROM BUYERS

Buyer: "What is the racial composition of the neighborhood?"

Salesperson: "Since we do not maintain racial, religious, or ethnic statistics in our office, it would not be fair for me to guess at the demographics. If you wish to research this matter you may contact the city planning department or the Census Bureau. They may have the information."

Buyer: "We only want to see homes in a [protected class] neighborhood."

Salesperson: "Let me identify a selection of homes that meet your other criteria, including size, price, schools, etc. After you have seen them and weighed everything, you can make your decision."

Buyer: "I am a [protected class]. Where would I feel most at home?"

Salesperson: "Let's consider all of the features you are looking for in a home or neighborhood. Is there any particular subdivision you would like to start looking in?"

Buyer: "Are the schools in the area integrated?"

Salesperson: "Our office does not maintain statistics regarding the racial makeup of the student body. The only school I am really familiar is the one my own children attend. They have many nationalities and religions represented there and have never had a problem."

Buyer: "Do you sell a lot of homes to minorities?"

Salesperson: "I don't separate classes of people. In the past few months I have sold six homes–all of them to wonderful people."

Buyer: "Are racially integrated neighborhoods good investments?"

Salesperson: "To the best of my knowledge, there is no correlation between property values and the race, religion, or nationality of the person who owns it."

Buyer: "Who is considered a minority?"

Salesperson: "Federal law prohibits discrimination based on race, religion, color, nationality, or sex. Thus, a large group of Hispanics could practice discrimination against a small group of Italians and this would be considered 'discriminatory' and illegal."

Suggested Web Sites

- www.realtor.org
- www.michealrusser.com
- www.cnet.com
- www.drozcorp.com
- www.forsalebyowner.com
- www.lowensign.com
- www.ntreis.immobel.com
- www.getawayweeks.com
- www.21online.com
- www.bendover.com
- www.rect.org
- www.century21.com
- www.hud.org
- www.century21judgefite.com
- www.judgefiteonline.com
- www.realtytimes.com

A Real Estate Transaction Step by Step—from Listing Through Closing Summary

STEP 1 PROSPECTING (CONTINUOUS AND ONGOING)

STEP 2 PROSPECTING FINDS SUSPECTS

STEP 3 NEED DETERMINATION AND QUALIFYING OF THE SUSPECTS

STEP 4 SUSPECTS TURN INTO PROSPECTS

STEP 5 LOAN APPLICATION (AT LEAST PREQUALIFICATION)

STEP 6 FOR SELLERS (LISTING PRESENTATION)

STEP 7 FOR BUYERS (SELECTION OF PROPERTY)

STEP 8 OFFERS

STEP 9 NEGOTIATION (COUNTEROFFERS)

STEP 10a COMPLETED CONTRACT (COMPLETELY INITIALED AND SIGNED OPTION)

STEP 10b DISTRIBUTE SIX COPIES

STEP 11 IMMEDIATE PROPERTY INSPECTION (ESP. WITH OPTION)

STEP 12 REPAIR RENEGOTIATION (AMENDMENT & OR TERMINATION)

STEP 13 APPRAISAL

STEP 14 APPRAISAL PRICE POSSIBLE RENEGOTIATION

STEP 15 AMENDMENT OF CONTRACT (IF NECESSARY)

STEP 16 LOAN APPROVAL/TITLE COMMITMENT/SURVEY

STEP 17 VERIFY HUD-1 & WALK THRU ACCEPTANCE OF PROPERTY

STEP 18 CLOSING OF PURCHASER AND CLOSING OF SELLER

STEP 19 $$$

STEP 20 HAPPY BUYERS AND SELLERS

STEP 21 FOLLOW-UP PRODUCES REFERRALS FROM PAST CLIENTS

Professionalism Checklist

The following is a professional checklist to help remind you of how you should act in the real estate business. This list is not all inclusive and may be supplemental by local custom and practice.

Always think of others first. Follow the golden rule.

Advise the clients of other brokers to direct questions to their real estate salesperson.

Communicate clearly; don't use jargon not readily understood by the general public.

Check your e-mail and messages every two hours. Always respond promptly to inquiries and requests for information.

Schedule appointments as far in advance as possible; call if you are delayed or must cancel an appointment. Be sure to get key box information and find out if the property has a security system.

Always schedule property showings in advance.

If a prospective buyer decides not to view an occupied home, promptly explain the situation to the listing broker or the owner.

Communicate with all parties in a timely fashion.

Enter listed property first to ensure that unexpected situations, such as pets, are handled appropriately.

- Leave your business card if it not prohibited by local rules.
- Never criticize property in the presence of the owner.
- Inform sellers that you are leaving after a showing.

When showing an occupied home, always ring the doorbell or knock before entering. Knock before entering any closed room.

Present a professional appearance at all times; dress appropriately and have a clean car.

Be aware of and respect cultural differences.

Show courtesy and respect to the general public.

Be aware of and meet all deadlines.

Promise only what you can deliver and keep your promises.

Be responsible for visitors to listed property; never allow buyers to enter property unaccompanied.

When the seller is absent, be sure to turn off the lights you turned on and lock doors that were locked after a showing.

Don't use the seller's telephone or bathroom. If it is an emergency, ask the seller first.

Tell buyers not to eat, drink, or smoke in the listed property.

Use sidewalks; if weather is bad, take off shoes and boots inside the property.

When a property is vacant, check that heating and cooling controls are set correctly and check the outside of the property for damage or vandalism.

Call the listing broker to report the results of any showing.

Notify the listing broker immediately if anything appears wrong with the property or a door to the exterior was left unlocked.

Notify the listing broker if there appears to be inaccurate information of the listing.

Share important information about property, including the presence of pets, security systems, and whether sellers will be present during the showing.

Show courtesy, trust, and respect to other real estate professionals.

BASIC BUDGET WORKSHEET FOR PERSONAL BUDGETS

Category	Monthly Budget Amount	Monthly Actual Amount	Difference Between Actual and Budget
INCOME:			
Wages Paid			
Bonuses/Dividend Income			
Interest Income			
Capital Gains Income			
Miscellaneous Income			
INCOME SUBTOTAL			
EXPENSES:			
Mortgage or Rent			
Utilities (gas, water, electric, trash)			
Cable TV			
Telephone			
Home Repairs/Maintenance			
Car Payments			
Gasoline/Oil			
Auto Repairs/Maintenance/Fees			
Other Transportation (tolls, bus, subway, etc.)			
Child Care			
Auto Insurance			
Home Owners/Renters Insurance			
Computer Expense			
Entertainment/Recreation			
Groceries			
Toiletries, Household Products			
Clothing			
Eating Out			

Category	Monthly Budget Amount	Monthly Actual Amount	Difference Between Actual and Budget
EXPENSES:			
Gifts/Donations			
Healthcare (medical, dental, vision, incl. insurance)			
Hobbies			
Interest Expense (mortgage, credit cards, fees)			
Magazines/Newspapers			
Federal Income Tax			
State Income Tax			
Social Security/Medicare Tax			
Personal Property Tax			
Pets			
Miscellaneous Expense			
EXPENSES SUBTOTAL			
NET INCOME (INCOME LESS EXPENSES)			

My Goal Plan

Name: _____ Date: _____

Career Goal: _____

Career Goals:

1. Short-Term Goal (less than one year)
2. Intermediate Goal (one year to five years)
3. Long-Term Goal (longer than one year)

Steps to Reaching Short-Term Goal	Timeline
1.	1.
2.	2.
3.	3.
4.	4.
5.	5.
6.	6.

Steps to Reaching Intermediate Goal	Timeline
1.	1.
2.	2.
3.	3.
4.	4.
5.	5.
6.	6.

Steps to Reaching Long-Term Goal	Timeline
1.	1.
2.	2.
3.	3.
4.	4.
5.	5.
6.	6.

Fair Housing

Self-Assessment for Real Estate Salespersons

1. Racial record keeping by a real estate company is:
   A. Lawful.
   B. Unlawful.
   C. Mandatory.
   D. Permissible, but should be prohibited.

2. Equal opportunity in housing is:
   A. The same as affirmative marketing.
   B. Provided if the real estate salesperson acts without malice.
   C. A way of guaranteeing desegregation.
   D. None of the above.

3. Equal housing opportunity laws are enforced:
   A. By the government.
   B. By private parties through law suits.
   C. By administrative procedures.
   D. All of the above.

4. Introducing the first minority family into a neighborhood:
   A. Is blockbusting and therefore a violation of the Federal Fair Housing law.
   B. Is allowed as a move to promote an increase in minority ownership.
   C. Should be avoided if the real estate salesperson feels that the minority family will be harassed or made unwelcome.
   D. Should be accomplished with assertions that the minority family will be well received by neighbors.
   E. None of the above.

5. Illegal racial steering:
   A. Is committed anytime a real estate salesperson provides racial information.
   B. Is committed when so-called fair housing organizations urge a member of a protected class to consider living in certain communities.
   C. Is committed when real estate salespeople urge buyers to consider an area on the basis of their race.

    D. Cannot be avoided, given the current interpretation of the law.

    E. Is not mentioned in federal statutory law.

6. A dual housing market is all of the following except:
   - **A.** When two different groups are given listings in different communities based on their race.
   - **B.** When buyers are warned about racial problems in a neighborhood.
   - **C.** A violation of the law.
   - **D.** Largely because of the present effects of past discrimination.

7. Illegal racial steering:
   - **A.** Is when whites charge differential fees based on race.
   - **B.** Usually occurs because a real estate salesperson has personal feelings against a protected class of people.
   - **C.** Can be avoided by prohibiting the mention of race.
   - **D.** All of the above.
   - **E.** None of the above.

8. "Equal treatment disparate (different and unequal) effect" is a concept that means:
   - **A.** A real estate salesperson can effect discrimination in some instances while treating all races and all communities alike.
   - **B.** A real estate salesperson can avoid discriminatory effects by always doing the same thing no matter what the characteristics of the community.
   - **C.** That equal opportunity advocates will protest no matter what the outcome.
   - **D.** None of the above.

9. When a member of a protected class asks to see a home in a particular area that is known for racial bias, a real estate salesperson should:
   - **A.** Tell the prospect the home is off the market.
   - **B.** Warn the prospect of the dangers of buying there and encourage him or he to look in an integrated neighborhood.
   - **C.** Show the home in the same manner as he or she would if any other prospect asked to see it.
   - **D.** Turn the prospect over to his or her broker.

10. If a member of a protected class does not ask to be shown homes located in a specific neighborhood a licensee:
    - **A.** Has no obligation to show such homes to the prospect.
    - **B.** May assume that the prospect is not interested in such homes.

    C. Need not service the prospect at all.

    D. May select homes for showing as he or she would for any other prospect.

11. All people are protected by the Federal Fair Housing Law and have a right to bring suit when:

    A. Acts of discrimination deny them the opportunity to have neighbors who are members of minority groups.

    B. They are evicted by a landlord for having minority guest in their home.

    C. They receive threatening phone calls for having sold their home to a minority family.

    D. Any of the above occurs.

12. A listing broker obtained a ready, willing, and able minority buyer who signed an offer to buy a house at the listed price. Because of the buyer's race, the seller refused the offer. The broker may:

    A. Sue the seller for his commission.

    B. Advise the minority prospect of his right to complain to HUD.

    C. Warn the seller that his refusal is a violation of the Fair Housing Act.

    D. Do any of the above.

13. Real estate salespeople who know that other salespeople are accepting listings with an understanding that showings or purchases will be limited by race should report same to appropriate authorities or else realize that they are giving tacit support to a law violation supporting the dual housing market.

    A. True.

    B. False.

14. Affirmative marketing:

    A. Is an advertising approach.

    B. Involves selling minorities on the benefits of choosing housing where minorities are underrepresented.

    C. May or may not involve a discussion of race.

    D. All of the above.

    E. None of the above.

15. When a minority prospect makes an inquiry about a home located in an area, the broker may assume that the prospect is interested only in homes located in the same type neighborhoods.

    A. True.

    B. False.

Goals

1. Financial — _____
_____

2. Career — _____
_____

3. Family — _____
_____

4. Spirit — _____
_____

5. Physical — _____
_____

6. Mental — _____
_____

7. Education — _____
_____

Glossary of Real Estate Terms

Accelerated Graphics Port (AGP)—a high-speed connection used by the graphics card to interface with the computer.

Adjustable-rate cap—a rate limit that protects the consumer from costly rate increases. Typically, the cap is two percent per year. The limit, or cap, is set by the lender.

Adjustable-Rate Mortgage (ARM)—a mortgage in which the interest rate is periodically adjusted based on the movement of a preselected index.

Amortization—the repayment of a mortgage loan by making equal, periodic payments of principal and interest over a stated period of time resulting in zero balance at the end of term.

Annual Percentage Rate (APR)—calculation disclosing total costs of financing including rate, points, and any other fees charged by the lender.

Appraisal—a report that gives an opinion of the value of the property being purchased: an estimate of value of real property.

Assumption—a situation in which a new buyer who purchases a house also takes over the responsibility for payment of an existing mortgage on that house.

Automated underwriting—a computer-based method of processing loan applications that enables the lender to process loans more quickly, objectively, and at less cost. Specific programs have been developed by Fannie Mae (Desktop Underwriter) and Freddie Mac (Loan Prospector).

Back-end ratio—the percentage of gross monthly income allowed for PITI, plus all other long-term debt.

399

Buydown—money advanced by a seller or builder to reduce the borrower's monthly payments on the mortgage; extra points to lower an interest rate.

Cable modem—Some people now use the cable-1019vision system in their homes to connect to the Internet.

Canvassing leads—part of your listing farm or someone you found by using other prospecting methods.

Capital gains tax—tax charged on profit made from sale of investments.

Central processing unit (CPU)—the microprocessor "brain" of the computer system; everything that a computer does is overseen by the CPU.

Certificate of Eligibility—a certificate issued by VA that states the amount of entitlement available to a veteran in order to qualify for no-money down VA loan.

Certificate of Reasonable Value (CRV)—estimate of value of property for a VA mortgage loan.

Closing costs—money paid by the borrower to complete the closing of a mortgage loan. This normally includes an origination fee, discount points, title insurance and closing fees, attorney's fees etc., and such prepaid items as taxes and insurance escrow payments.

Cold buyer—a buyer who has no real need to buy.

Collateral—that which protects the rights of a lender in case of default on a loan. In real estate financing, the real property serves as collateral giving lender the right to obtain title to the property in case of default by the borrower.

Community Reinvestment Act (CRA)—enacted by Congress in 1977, this act requires lenders to provide full, credit service in the communities serviced by bank.

Compensating factors—positive features which may offset negatives, increasing the possibility that the borrower's application for loan be approved.

Conditions—additional information or documentation that must be provided to the underwriter before final loan approval will be granted.

Condominium—form of ownership granting fee simple title to individual unit plus undivided interest in the common areas.

Condominium fee—fee charged by the condominium association to cover costs of operation of the condominium, maintenance of the common areas, and financial reserves.

Conforming loan—a mortgage loan meeting the Fannie Mae and Freddie Mac guidelines.

Construction loan—a loan made for the purpose of constructing houses or other buildings. Funds are generally dispersed in increments called "draws" as various stages of construction are completed.

Conventional mortgage—a nongovernment mortgage, one that is not insured by the FITA or guaranteed by the VA or Farmers Home Administration; any mortgage loan not insured or guaranteed by any government agency.

Cost of Funds Index—common index used for adjustable rate mortgages (ARM) based on the average cost of borrowed funds by depository institutions.

Credit report—a detail of information regarding an applicant's credit history.

Credit score—numerical score based on statistics showing risk of default on loan; credit score becoming important factor in qualifying for all loans.

Debt-to-income ratio—ratio used to qualify a client for a mortgage. It compares the client's total monthly housing expense (the amount being paid out) with his or her monthly gross income (the amount coming in).

Deed of Trust—financing instrument giving legal claim to the property to a trustee designated by the lender who may exercise power-of-sale in event of default by borrower.

Default—failing to observe agreed upon terms of contract or financing instrument.

Department of Housing & Urban Development (HUD)—cabinet-level federal agency housing Federal Housing Administration (FHA) and Government National Mortgage Association (Ginnie Mae); also oversees Government National Mortgage Association (Fannie Mae) and Federal Home Loan Mortgage Corporation (FHLMC or Freddie Mac).

Department of Veterans Affairs (DVA)—federal agency providing assistance to veterans, including guarantee of VA mortgage loans.

Digital Subscriber Line (DSL) modem—a high-speed Internet connection that works over a standard telephone line.

Discount point—a charge by a lender to increase yield which reduces interest rate to borrower; one discount point equates to one percent of the loan amount.

Down payment—the difference between the sales price and the loan amount paid by purchaser; amount of down payment affects other terms of the loan.

Earnest money—money given by a buyer to a title company or a seller as part of the purchase price to bind the contract.

Equity—The difference between the market value of the property and the balance owed on the mortgage. The net value of an asset.

Escrow account—an impound account that is set up and maintained by the lender. Monthly deposits are accumulated and annual payments of taxes, hazard insurance, and mortgage insurance are made from the account. Money held by third party on behalf of others; i.e., lender maintains funds in account to pay taxes and insurance on behalf of borrower.

Escrow settlement—in the western part of the U.S., settlement or closing on a loan and real property in done "in escrow."

Federal Deposit Insurance Corporation (FDIC)—insures accounts up to $100,000 for depositors in both commercial banks and savings associations.

Federal Home Loan Mortgage Corporation (FHLMC)—Nicknamed "Freddie Mac," this is term commonly used to refer to the Federal Home Loan Mortgage Corporation, a major investor of conventional mortgages. This stock-owned corporation was originally chartered to provide a secondary market for conventional mortgage packages.

Federal Housing Administration (FHA)—government agency providing insurance for FHA mortgage loans; managed by HUD.

Federal National Mortgage Association (FNMA)—Nicknamed "Fannie Mae," this is a major investor of conventional mortgages. It was originally chartered as government agency to provide a secondary market for FHA and VA mortgage loans. It is now wholly stock-owned.

Fee simple—unrestricted ownership interest in real property.

Finder's fee—payment made for procuring of purchaser for property, or borrower for mortgage loan.

First trust or first mortgage—the primary or original loan secured by real estate.

Fixed-rate mortgage—a mortgage in which the interest rate is set for the term of the loan.

Foreclosure—the legal process whereby lender receives title to real property with the right to sell the property to repay the mortgage lien.

Front-end ratio—the percentage of gross monthly income allowed for PITI.

Funding fee—percentage of loan amount charged on VA loans to provide a pool of funds for administrative costs; this fee has increased over time and is higher for subsequent use by veterans and for reservists and members of the National Guard.

Gift letter—a signed statement by a gift giver which explains that a cash gift used by the borrower to qualify for a loan need not be repaid.

Good Faith Estimate (GFE)—statement required by RESPA disclosing all costs involved in closing on loan and property; must be given to borrowers within three days of application.

Government loans—mortgages insured (FHA) or guaranteed (VA) by government; may also include state-sponsored mortgages.

Government National Mortgage Association (GNMA)—Nicknamed "Ginnie Mae," a major investor in FHA and VA loans. The government agency was created in 1968 to facilitate a secondary market by insuring mortgage-backed securities.

Graduated payment mortgage—regularly scheduled payment increases on loan.

Graphics card—a device for translating image data from a computer into a format that can be displayed by the monitor.

Gross Monthly Income (GMI)—annual income before tax and other payroll deductions divided by 12.

Hard disk—a is large-capacity permanent storage system used to hold information such as programs and documents.

Homeowners' Association (HOA) fee—fees paid monthly for maintenance and care of common facilities in a planned unit development.

Homeowner's insurance—a policy carried by the homeowner to protect the dwelling in case of fire and other hazards.

Hot buyer—a buyer who has been totally qualified and will buy within the next 30 to 60 days.

HUD-1 Settlement Statement—a statement required by RESPA to be used at settlement disclosing all costs to both buyer and seller.

Index—financial indicator used as basis to calculate ARM rate. Most commonly used are treasury securities; also cost of funds index, LIBOR.

Integrated Drive Electronics (IDE) Controller—the primary interface for the hard drive, CD-ROM, and floppy disk drive.

Interest rate cap—a cap established by lender providing protection for borrower that interest rate cannot exceed stated limits.

Judicial foreclosure—a court procedure used to obtain title to real property after default on loan; after foreclosure property may be sold to repay debt.

Jumbo loan—any mortgage loan exceeding the Fannie Mae and Freddie Mac conforming maximum loan limit.

Keyboard—the primary device for entering information into the computer.

Lender Paid Mortgage Insurance—a program whereby the lender charges a higher interest rate instead of separate mortgage insurance charge.

Lien—a financial claim against the property, i.e., a mortgage.

Lifetime cap—the maximum increase in interest rate allowed over life of loan. A ceiling and floor set by a lender to restrict interest rate fluctuations on a mortgage. The cap is indicated either as a stated percentage rate or as five to seven percentage points more than the initial rate.

Loan-to-Value Ratio (LTV)—loan amount shown as percentage of the value of the property, i.e., 80 percent LTV represents mortgage of 80 percent of value. A percentage which compares the outstanding principal balance of a mortgage loan with the value or selling price of the mortgage property.

Local area network (LAN) card—a device used by many computers, particularly those in an Ethernet office network, to connect to each other.

Lock-in rate—the interest rate to which the lender formally commits; it is typically guaranteed for a specific time period up to the closing.

London Inter-Bank Offered Rates Index (LIBOR Index)—average rate major London banks charge each other for U.S. dollar deposits.

Low/Doc or No/Doc Loan—mortgage loan requiring little or no documentation from borrower; it generally requires large down payment.

Margin—the amount added to an index to determine the note rate on ARM.

Medium buyer—a buyer who will buy within the next six months; may have a home in closing or listed or may be transferred with a specific date by which he or she must move.

Memory—storage space used to hold data. Several specific types of computer memory include:

- Random-access memory (RAM)—used to temporarily store information that the computer is currently working with.
- Read-only . . . memory (ROM)—a permanent type of memory storage for important data that does not change.
- Basic input/output system (BIOS)—a type of ROM that is used to establish basic communication when the computer is first turned on.
- Caching—the storing of frequently used data in extremely fast RAM that connects directly to the CPU.
- Virtual memory—space on a hard disk used to temporarily store data and swap it in and out of RAM as needed.

Modem—a device used for connecting to the Internet.

Monitor—the primary device for displaying information from the computer.

Mortgage—the legal instrument by which real estate is pledged as security for the repayment of the loan.

Mortgage-backed securities—income producing securities based on mortgage loan packages.

Mortgage insurance—insurance protecting lender against default by borrower.

Mortgage Insurance Premium (MIP)—mortgage insurance charged on FHA loans; includes both an upfront charge which may be financed and monthly renewal fees.

Mortgagee—the lender of money secured by real estate.

Mortgagor—the borrower of money secured by real estate.

Motherboard—the main circuit board that all of the other internal components of a computer connect to. The CPU and memory are usually on the motherboard. Other systems may be found directly on the motherboard or connected to it through a secondary connection. For example, a sound card can be built into the motherboard or connected through PCI.

Mouse—the primary device for navigating and interacting with the computer.

Negative amortization—occurs when payments may not cover the total amount of interest due resulting in increase in loan balance, a problem with some ARM programs.

Net worth—the value of a client's assets minus the total of his or her liabilities; an amount used to indicate creditworthiness or financial strength.

Nonconforming loan—a loan that does not follow Fannie Mae or Freddie Mae conforming guidelines.

Nonjudicial foreclosure—a foreclosure that does not require court action; used with deed of trust.

Note—a legal instrument or written promise specifying agreement to repay debt on certain terms.

One-stop shopping—refers to an "umbrella" company that may own a real estate company, mortgage company, title insurance, and/or other entities providing income.

Origination fee—charge by a lender for costs of a originating mortgage (usually one percent of loan amount); fee earned by a lender to process and close a loan. This is usually part of the closing costs.

Parallel port—a connection point on a computer, commonly used to connect a printer.

Partial entitlement—the amount of guarantee after a veteran has used entitlement once; may be used for subsequent VA loans.

Payment cap—limitation on increases in payment rather than an increase in interest rate on some types of ARM loans; may lead to negative amortization.

Peripheral Component Interconnect (PCI) bus—the most common way to connect additional components to the computer. PCI uses a series of slots on the motherboard that PCI cards plug into.

Personal property—all property other than real property.

Points (discount points)—a fee charged by a lender to purchase a specific interest rate; one point = one percent of the loan amount.

Portfolio lender—lender that retains a loan in its own portfolio rather than immediately selling it on the secondary market.

Power supply—an electrical transformer that regulates the electricity used by the computer.

Preapproval—an approval for a loan received prior to the borrower's selection of a home to purchase.

Prepaid—closing costs paid at the time of settlement that actually occur in the future; i.e., taxes, insurance, upfront interest.

Prepayment penalty—fee charge by the lender if a loan is paid off before end of its term.

Prequalification—a method of determining a borrower's potential qualification for a mortgage; does not guarantee commitment for a loan from the lender.

Presentation leads—people who you've talked to about selling but are not yet ready to make a move.

Principal, Interest, Taxes, and Insurance (PITI)—components of a mortgage loan including the escrow fund established to accumulate funds for payment of taxes and insurance on behalf of the borrower. This is usually referred to as the total monthly payment on a loan.

Private Mortgage Insurance (PMI)—mortgage insurance to protect the lender in case of default; required on loans with less than 20 percent down payment.

Processing—procedure from the time of the loan application through submission to an underwriter.

Rate factor—chart showing number of dollars required to pay off $1,000 of debt on a mortgage loan. Used to calculate PI mortgage payment and to determine the amount a borrower is qualified to borrow.

Ratio—see Back-end ratio; Front-end ratio.

Real Estate Mortgage Investment Conduit (REMIC)—a company formed to trade in investment pools made up of various types of mortgages.

Real Estate Settlement Procedures Act (RESPA)—federal law regulating settlement practices; requires provision of good faith estimate of all closing costs to borrower within three days of application; prohibits kickbacks for referrals of related services, and standardizes closing with use of HUD-I form.

Real property—land including its improvements plus all legal rights attached.

Regulation Z—part of the Truth-in-Lending Act requiring full disclosure of all aspects of credit financing in advertising.

Removable storage—a device that allows you to add new information to your computer very easily, as well as save information that you want to carry to a different location. Some devices include:

- Floppy disk—the most common form of removable storage, floppy disks are extremely inexpensive and easy to save information to.
- CD-ROM (compact disc, read-only memory)—a popular form of distribution of commercial software. Many systems now offer CD-R (recordable) and CD-RW (rewritable), which can also record.
- Flash memory—based on a type of ROM called electrically erasable programmable read-only memory (EEPROM), Flash memory provides fast, permanent storage.
- DVD-ROM (digital versatile disc, read-only memory)—similar to CD-ROM but capable of holding much more information.

Reverse Annuity Mortgage (RAM)—mortgage that uses equity in real property to fund payments to a borrower; especially appropriate for the elderly who need cash but don't wish to sell their homes.

Resolution Trust Corporation (RTC)—formed to sell off assets of failed savings associations.

SCSI (small computer system interface)—pronounced "scuzzy," it is used to add devices, such as hard drives or scanners, to the computer.

Second trust (mortgage)—junior or secondary trust placed on property after first trust already established.

Secondary market—a market in which mortgage loan packages can be sold providing additional funds to primary market for mortgage lending.

Serial port—a connection point on the computer used to connect an external modem.

Servicing—when a lender collects monthly mortgage payments, forwards applicable portions of payment to investor, insurance, and taxing agencies.

Settlement agent—person or entity coordinating and conducting the closing of a loan and transfer of real property.

Sound card—a type of expansion board used by the computer to record and playback audio by converting analog sound into digital information and back again.

Survey—method of measuring boundaries of parcels of land, including improvements, easements, and encroachments.

"Teaser" rate—starting rate well below note rate (index plus margin) on ARM to entice borrowers.

Temporary buydown—a lower interest rate offered for fixed period of time.

Term—designated period of time for a loan.

Thrifts—another name for savings associations; financial institution established primarily for savings and providing home mortgage loans.

Title—ownership record of property.

Title insurance—insurance policy that protects the owner or lender against loss arising from defects in the title.

Title search—study of court records to verify a seller has clear title to a property.

Truth-in-Lending Act (TILA)—federal law requiring disclosure of all costs involved in financing, including APR.

Underwriter—person responsible for evaluating the risk of default by a mortgage loan applicant; grants approval or denial of loan.

Uniform Residential Appraisal Report (URAR)—form used by appraisers to estimate the value of properties for mortgage loans.

Uniform Residential Loan Application Form—loan application form required on Fannie Mae and Freddie Mac loans; generally used on all loan applications.

Uniform Settlement Statement (HUD-1)—a standard real estate settlement form detailing all charges imposed by the buyer and the seller in connection with federally related mortgage loans; required by RESPA at closing.

Universal Serial Bus (USB)—quickly becoming the most popular external bus for connecting peripherals to a computer; USB ports offer power and versatility and are incredibly easy to use.

VA (Department of Veterans Affairs)—federal agency providing assistance to veterans, including the guarantee of VA mortgage loans.

VA funding fee—fee charged on VA loans to cover administrative costs.

Very-high bit-rate IDSL (VDSL) modem—a newer variation of the Internet digital subscriber line (IDSL), it requires that your phone line have fiber-optic cables.

Credits

Thanks to all the real estate brokers, managers, students, and sales-people for their help in this project.

Special thanks to:

Judge Fite	Jim Fite	Jan Fite Miller
Bill Steddum	Sherry Raley	Ben Yeatts
Patrick Wyatt	Chuck Edwards	Luella Blaylock
Gerald Crow	Rex Patton	John Lundquist
Pat Strong	Vicki Butcher	Chris Elwell
Randy McCracken		

Quotes by:

Lou Tice	Zig Ziglar
Tom Hopkins	Jim Rohn

Web sites:

- How PCs Work by Jeff Tyson
- How Laptops Work by Craig Freudenrich, Ph.D.
- How Personal Digital Assistants (PDAs) Work, by Craig Freudenrich, Ph.D.
- How Digital Cameras Work by Karim Nice and Gerald-Jay Gurevich.
- National Association of REALTORS® at http://www.realtor.org
- State Bar of Texas, website at http://www.texasbar.com
- Ethics Resource Center, Ethics Questions and Answers at http://www.ethics.org
- The Return of Character Education, Thomas Lickona at http://www.ascd.org
- Body Language Online at http://www.bodylanguageonline.com
- Change Dynamics at http://www.changedynamics.com

- Gil Gordon Associates at http://www.gilgordon.com
- Personal Selling at http://www.lasalle.edu
- Verbal Communication at http://www.cbpa.Louisville.edu
- Alan Chapman at http://www.businessballs.com
- About.com
- Paul Christenbury, President at http://www.MyGoalManager.com

Books:
- Jacobus, Charles, J. *Real Estate Principles*. 9th ed. Mason, OH: Thomson/South-Western, 2003.
- Nierenberg, Gerald. "The Art of Negotiating," *CRS Real Estate Business Magazine,*
- Wiedemer, John P. *Real Estate Finance*. 8th ed. Mason, OH: Thomson/South-Western, Mason, OH, 2001.
- Clauretie, Terrence M., and G. Stacy Sirmans. *Real Estate Finance Theory and Practice,* 4th ed. Mason, OH: Thomson/South-Western, 2003.
- Nance, Cheryl Peat. Modern Real Estate Practice. 10th ed. Chicago: Dearborn Financial Publishing, Inc.
- Lyons, Gail G. Real Estate Sales Handbook. 10th ed. Chicago: Dearborn Financial Publishing, Inc., 1994.
- *Real Estate Salesman's Handbook*. 6th ed. Chicago: National Association of REALTORS®, 1972.
- Peeples, Donna and Minor Peeples, III. *Real Estate Agency*. 4th ed. Chicago: Dearborn Financial Publishing, Inc., 2000.
- *American Heritage Dictionary of the English Language*, 3rd ed. Boston: Houghton Mifflin, 1992.
- Sirota, David. *Essentials of Real Estate Finance*. 6th ed. Chicago: Dearborn Financial Publishing, Inc., 1992.
- Kennedy, Danielle. *How to List & Sell Real Estate*. Mason, OH: Thomson/South-Western,
- Parks, Jerry. *Jerry Parks' Master Plan for Increase Success in Real Estate*. Englewood Cliffs, NJ: Prentice-Hall, Inc., 1976.

- Cyr, John. E. *Training and Supervising Real Estate Salesmen*. 8th ed. Englewood Cliffs, NJ: Prentice-Hall, Inc., 1980.

- Ferry, Mike. *How to Develop a Six-Figure Income in Real Estate*. Chicago: Dearborn Financial Publishing, Inc., 1993.

- Lumbleau, John J. *The Creation of a Successful Residential Real Estate Salesman*. Van Nuys, CA: Sales Training Institute, 1976.

- Griffith, Joe. *Speaker's Library of Business Stories, Anecdotes, and Humor*. Prentice-Hall, Inc., 1990.

- Nucci, Larry. *The PSI Café: Studies in Moral Development and Education,* 2003.

- Givens, David B. *Nonverbal Dictionary of Gestures, Signs, and Body Language Clues,* 2003.

- Sanow, Arnold. *Listen, Learn and Earn More*. International Listening Association.

- Dawson, Roger. *Power Negotiating Institute*. Placentia, CA.

Index

Index